'Cockie'

To Rosa

'COCKIE'

by Sam Heppner

with a foreword by Noël Coward

LESLIE FREWIN : LONDON

Contents

Foreword

by Noël Coward

WHEN I WAS appearing in my second play *The Young Idea* at the Savoy Theatre in 1923, Charles B Cochran, whom I had met only casually on one or two occasions, sent me a long and highly articulate congratulatory telegram which, not unnaturally, thrilled me very much indeed. He was then, and remained so until his tragic death, acknowledged to be one of the few great showmen in the world, and an unsolicited accolade from him meant more to me than an album full of rave notices.

This gesture of his to a young actor-dramatist at the beginning of his career might cynically be considered as no more than a wise bit of talent spotting made by a shrewd impresario who thought that I might be of value to him later on. The fact that it was, and *I* was, is beside the point. I happen to know, after years of successful theatrical association with him, that the primary impulse that caused him to send that telegram was genuine enthusiasm.

Some years later when I was rehearsing *Bitter Sweet*, Cochran allowed me four weeks' rehearsal without coming to the theatre once. When he did arrive for the first complete run-through with scenery but no dresses and Elsie April playing the score on an upright piano in the orchestra pit – he sat in the front row of the dress circle and watched the whole performance through without comment. There was a pregnant silence for a moment or two and then he said a little huskily, 'I wouldn't part with my rights in this play for a million pounds.' The Company, who incidentally had given a superb performance, cheered for several minutes. It was, I think, one of the most moving moments of my theatrical life.

I have described these two incidents in order to illustrate Cockie's quite extraordinary capacity for handing out generous uninhibited praise whenever he considered such praise to be deserved and I am sure that it was this quality in him that inspired, in later sadder years, the unswerving loyalty and affection of those who had worked for him.

Another quality that distinguished him from other theatrical impresarios was his impeccable visual taste. In the course of a long Showman's career which had embraced every form of entertainment from the sawdust and tinsel of the circus ring to *Private Lives, Bitter Sweet* and *The Miracle,* it is fascinating to reflect that he found time to acquire an expert knowledge and appreciation of the then most *avant garde* Impressionist painters. I am sure that the physical beauty of his productions was due to this innate flair.

On the other hand his musical sense was limited. He was capable of recognising a good melody but usually it took quite a time for his ear to register it.

Altogether he was a man of courage and stubborn determination. He was also immoderately generous with his own and his backer's money. In fact I don't believe that actual money meant very much to him. His ideal was to get as near to perfection in the theatre as he possibly could and, in my opinion, he very largely succeeded.

My association with him lasted for many years. There were occasional storms but on the whole the weather remained calm. In any case they were years that I look back upon with gratitude and affection and enduring pride.

NC

Overture

THERE WERE SHOWMEN in those days; and giants they certainly were – giants of the big drum, the big top and the big production.

In our own time the word 'showman' has all but disappeared.

The massive, all-round personality, the buoyant extrovert, the magic name that once electrified the theatrical scene has vanished, but this is not necessarily a cause for regret. Progress exacts its toll. The single entrepreneur presides no longer. His place has been taken, as many sadly observe, by administrators, businessmen and accountants who delegate artistic responsibility to their experts and make little or no personal contribution to the creative demands of entertainment.

Television, the disappearance of the music hall and new assumptions about the true role of the drama have changed the pattern of the playmaker's art. The Second World War, major political upheavals and different social attitudes, fashioned irresistibly by the friction of time, have imposed new responsibilities on the theatre. For good or ill? Any attempt at an answer would be a meaningless value judgment, inappropriate to this type of biographical study.

This does not prevent us, however, from admiring and cherishing the memory of the dominant figures, those great actor-managers and impresarios who exerted such powerful influences on the course of theatrical history.

We think in this context of such men as Barnum, Ziegfeld, the Shuberts, David Belasco and Billy Rose.

All American, to be sure. But we also think of one great

Englishman, Charles Blake Cochran, who was born on 25th September 1872, at 15, Prestonville Road, Brighton.

One of ten children, five boys and five girls, he was the son of James Elphinston Cochran and a young widow named Matilda Walton whose previous husband had fathered her first son, Bert, half-brother to the remaining nine.

Mrs Cochran died in 1929 at the age of ninety and, as I write, only one member of her large family survives. He is Alec, her seventh child, now aged ninety-two, rather deaf, but otherwise in good health. In some recent correspondence, he has written, in a firm and legible hand that betrays no sign of age: 'My father was a wholesale tea merchant and cigar importer, and a very good judge of both . . . I should say we were well-to-do middle class, not rich but very comfortable. We had a nurse, a cook and a general and we wanted for nothing. Our father was devoted but extravagant. He loved hunting and driving and always kept good stock. He was a *bon vivant*, a good sportsman and a member of Porter's famous club in Brighton.

'. . . we moved to Lindfield and later to Lancaster Farm, Haywards Heath.

'Charlie used to say that it was the fascination of the sideshows at Lindfield Fair that first put the idea of showmanship into his head. . . .'

Clearly, then, from these simple but fertilising contacts grew the whole man with his ensuing passion, not only for the theatre, but for the sight, sounds and smells of the broad spectrum of showmanship represented by the circus, menagerie, Wild West shows, the prize ring and the wrestling arena; all of which eventually conferred upon him lasting recognition as the greatest British showman (indeed, the only all-round British showman) of the century.

In spite of disappointments, reverses and bouts of ill fortune that would have destroyed a lesser man, his zeal for these things never foundered or diminished. It must be acknowledged, however, that he spent his early, formative years in the United

States; and he was quick to note and absorb the most useful influences from the brash, meretricious world of American show business at the turn of the century.

It is a strange, and perhaps an adventitious tribute to C B Cochran that Brighton, his birthplace, is today the home of a brilliant theatrical coterie, with a good theatre and a lively show business tradition.

Ninety-six years ago when Charles was born, Brighton seems to have had a refreshing and distinctive gaiety of its own. It was a regular haunt of actors, journalists and all manner of colourful personalities from the turf and prize-ring – Fred Archer, the great jockey who, standing on the steps of the Old Ship Hotel, was pointed out to the fascinated youngster; George Fordham, another famous jockey; Dick Dunn, a celebrated bookie; Henry Irving, Phil May, Arthur Roberts, George R Sims, Edmund Yates, Henry Labouchere, editor of *Truth*; John Corlett, editor of the *Pink 'un* and George Augustus Sala. . . .

The impulse that drove Cochran throughout his life was compounded of certain basic characteristics: unquenchable enthusiasm, ambition and a deep and abiding love of people and showmanship in all its forms.

The field in which he operated – indeed, in which he thrived so abundantly and fulfilled the innermost needs of his personality – might be raucous, noisy and elemental. Or it might represent impeccable taste and artistic quality.

For Charles B Cochran the show was the thing.

But the one overriding trait that coloured his outlook and, in all probability, explained why he allowed the world of the theatre to ravish him so utterly was his essential naivete, the innocent sense of reverence he felt in the presence of famous actresses, comedians and the great actor-managers.

Not only as a child, but throughout his life, he was as starry-eyed in this milieu as the latest of our giant radio-telescopes. This ingenuous sense of awe renewed itself daily. At the peak of Cochran's success and fame it never became tarnished by familiarity.

Those who knew him well have told me that he was basically a simple man, the perennial schoolboy, whose lack of cynicism was perhaps his most endearing trait.

'From my earliest days,' he wrote in *Showman Looks On*,[1] the last of his autobiographical books, 'I have been a hero-worshipper and I see nothing to regret in the fact. To me a genuine enthusiasm is the salt of life, and I confess to a feeling of pity for those who, from fear of themselves or of others, throw all enthusiasm to the devil. We all know them, those "knockers" – from the type who thinks it "bad form", to the type who deems it an expression of worldly wisdom and intellectual superiority to deride or belittle.

'I am not quite sure whether it has been love of achievement or hero-worship which has kept up my interest and enthusiasm in the "show business" to which I have devoted my career – possibly a blend of these ingredients in the ratio of fifty-fifty.'

On the wall of Cochran's office at 49, Old Bond Street there used to hang a playbill dated 29th December 1879. It advertised the pantomime *Sinbad the Sailor* at the Theatre Royal, Brighton, and Cochran always regarded his visit to that performance at the age of seven as one of the decisive influences that guided him towards his life in the theatre to which he remained irrevocably committed until his death in 1951.

As principal comedian in *Sinbad the Sailor*, Arthur Roberts became the boy's model and archetype of the stage funny man. The young Cochran mimicked him and repeated the bits of comedy patter he could remember, as if to conjure back and savour once more those breathless, gilded moments; and, for the rest of the Christmas holidays, he improvised bits of scenery and daubed his face with whatever colouring matter he could find.

This early, seminal experience was sustained and nurtured,

[1] *Showman Looks On*, C B Cochran, J M Dent, 1944

as his brother has told us, by occasional visits to Lindfield where the travelling fairs would strike camp and regale the local populace with country dancing and such lurid side-shows as *Maria Martin and the Murders in the Red Barn, Pepper's Ghost* and *The Old Oak Chest.*

Yet the Theatre Royal, Brighton, was the *real* theatre, the bright-lit cut-out of fantasy-life that blazed into being beyond the proscenium arch, the dash and gaiety of the pretty girls, the knockabout antics of the comics, clattering heavy-footed on the boards . . . all were part of a fateful, if unwitting, conspiracy to beckon, woo and finally ensnare him in the make-believe world of their own.

But there were other, more urgent – if, to him, slightly irrelevant – things to occupy a boy of seven. School, for instance.

His first was at Lewes, but, after a short while he was sent with a younger brother to a boarding school at Eastbourne.

To immure the boys within the school on 5th November seemed to the Cochran lads to be an act of unparalleled cruelty which they defied by climbing over the wall and walking down to the town to see the bonfires.

They returned, happy and tired, but guiltily afraid of the inevitable penalty which came in the form of summary expulsion the next morning.

Their headmaster's wrath was capped by their father's, but when Mr Cochran took his errant sons to Brighton Grammar School to see if it would admit them, Mr Marshall, the wise headmaster, said of their escapade, 'Oh, it's just high spirits. I'm sure there is nothing bad in the boys.'

A schoolmate with whom the young Cochran struck up a lasting friendship, a strange, thin, red-haired boy with a distinctly original mind, was Aubrey Beardsley, who later won international fame as the creator of highly individual expressionist sketches.

Beardsley too loved the theatre and, linked by this common interest, they talked of little else and were lucky enough to receive encouragement from a sympathetic and enlightened master who put them into productions of *Ici On Parle Français, The Spitalfield Weavers* and a Christmas play on *The Pied Piper*.

The young actors were further encouraged by reports in the *Sussex Daily News* that praised these efforts for their polish and their near-professional quality. When in 1891 Cochran returned as an Old Boy to appear in an historical comic opera, written by the masters, and called *Christopher Columbus in A-merry-key*, the *Brighton Herald* reported that '. . . in Mr C B Cochran, the Queen found an exponent capable of giving due effect to the whimsicalities of the part, his performance all through being capital'.

Among various documents of local interest, the Sussex Archaeological Society in Lewes has preserved a theatre programme and 'Book of Words' of a single performance of *The Pay of the Pied Piper* at the Concert Hall, Lewes, on 28th November 1889. 'As produced at the Dome, Brighton.' Among the characters are Herr Kirschwasser played by Mr Beardsley and Herr Seidlitz (obstructionist) played by Mr Cochran. These programmes and 'books of words' are copiously illustrated with Beardsley sketches.

During Cochran's schooldays, his father suffered a disastrous business reverse and his rocky financial position was aggravated by gambling. The boy was taken away from school and put to work in the office of J L Neale, estate agent and surveyor. This was at 2, Grenville Place, near where the Hotel Metropole stands. The premises are now a ladies' hairdressing salon, but the exterior is quite unaltered and looks the same today as it did in Mr Neale's time.

This constituted no bar, however, to Cochran's theatrical ambitions, and he spent his evenings singing comic songs at smoking concerts.

A friend of his who played the piano managed to get him a week's engagement at the Royal Clarence Music Hall, Dover.

This was in August 1890. Mr Neale released him for a week's holiday that was due to him, and he took himself to Dover. But conceit and over-confidence proved his downfall. Having managed happily enough with piano accompaniment at his smoking concerts, he arrogantly spurned the customary band-call with the result that his performance betrayed inadequate rehearsal, so much so that the audience, composed mainly of soldiers, whistled him off after his first song.

Under a leaden weight of despondency and gloom, he wrote this letter, clearly the outpouring of a lonely and deeply wounded young man.

24 Limekiln Street,
Dover
Sep 15, '91

My dear Mother,

I promised yesterday (feeling quite confident of success) to let you know how I got on last night. I do so now and must say, speaking briefly, that I was a

DISMAL FAILURE

I sang my three songs and at the end received scarcely a clap and I cannot say I deserved one. I was not to the slightest degree nervous but I seemed unable to put the 'go' that I have always prided myself on in the songs. During the evening I received the following note from the Proprietor :

'I find that you are wholly incompetent for the duties for which you were engaged and I hereby dismiss you under Rule 11 of your Contract.'

You can scarcely imagine my feelings – I felt then, if ever I did, that I would do something desperate but after a mighty conflict in my mind I turned into bed.

All that life seemed to me worth living for (FAME and popularity) had vanished and I felt that I cared for nothing – However I slept and this morning after my breakfast strolled on the Admiralty Pier (where the Calais and Ostend boats come in) and after a great battle within myself realised that one of the great questions of my life had been answered. 'Was I to be

15

a music-hall singer?' and the verdict was 'No' and so I gradually came round to the fact that I must abide by that decision, although I feel sure had I the money to look round and see all the principal song writers and wait till I got a good thing before purchasing, the result would have been different. You who know not the sweets of applause cannot imagine the blow I received after having been sought after so much in Brighton and received as though I were a genius; and also my really fine reception at Worthing.

Yesterday marks an epoch in my life and the next thing is to decide what to do now.

I must certainly better my present position at Neales' and I am determined to get riches or fame or perhaps both in some way.

The weather down here is grand and the old Town extremely picturesque. I shall start tomorrow to walk home putting up, if possible, at friends on the way. It will be a nice trip.

I do not regret in the least having tried (although it has cost me a lot and left me in debt) as I should never have settled to anything while I was under the impression that there was money and popularity awaiting me at the stage door.

I remain,

Your loving son,

Charles

Please do not show this letter 'up and dahn and rahnd the tahn' but only to the family.

Two days later he had evidently made some recovery from the shock of failure and the blow to his self-esteem, for he wrote:

24 Limekiln Street,
Dover
Sep 17, '91

My dear Mother,

When I last wrote you I was in one of my well known temporary fits of insanity. I do not know what I said but I am sure it was senseless and idiotic.

16

Of course I am very sorry that I failed but it has only given me renewed energy to go in and retrieve my lost repute which I am sure I can do.

I managed to catch a nasty cold in London, arrived at Dover late, dressed in a hurry and was a bit worried about a little matter in Town and then small wonder I failed as lots of people now in the front rank have done before me on the occasion of their debut.

However, I will wait till I see you before doing anything.

Hoping you are well,

I remain,

Your loving son,

Charles

During that winter, when he was nineteen, he said to Scotson Clark, a former schoolmate with some artistic talent, 'Let's go to America. I will earn my living on the stage. You will paint.'

And, according to *Secrets of a Showman*,[1] his first volume of autobiography, written in 1925 after his first bankruptcy, 'The next few weeks I saved every penny I could, pawned many of my belongings, and ultimately we left Newhaven for Dieppe, spent the night in Paris – we thought it might be our one and only chance of seeing Paris – and caught the boat for America at Boulogne. It was a Holland-American liner, and we went steerage.'

Although later in the same book Cochran wrote '. . . these reminiscences shall be nothing if not truthful', the above statement inclined me to scepticism. Here was a lad whose father had squandered his fortune in thriftlessness and gambling; and even though his meagre fee for an occasional smoking concert might have supplemented the wage that Brighton surveyors were in the habit of paying their office boys, it is difficult to accept the suggestion that he had very much to pawn or save, and still more difficult to believe that whatever he might have

[1] *Secrets of a Showman,* C B Cochran, Heinemann, 1926

had would have been capable of yielding his fare, even at steer-age rates, to Paris and New York.

H G Wells once said, 'The forceps of the mind is a clumsy instrument and, in taking hold of the truth, it is liable to crush it a little.' This applies equally to the expression of what purports to be the truth. I make this point in no pious spirit of censure; are we not all guilty sometimes of tailoring fact a little if only by concealment and evasion?

For the truth in this instance is that Cochran did not pawn his belongings and scrape the barrel of his modest savings.

To get to America he simply took some money from his employers, and the phrase 'I . . . was a bit worried about a little matter in Town . . .' in the second letter referred to this minor embezzlement.

Many years later, when Cochran was famous, old Mr Neale sent him a gentle rebuke for absconding with his cash. The impresario admitted the impeachment and made amends by sending his first employer opening night tickets for his shows.

Mr Neale's grandson, Mr A N S Marshall, gives as one of his earliest recollections the sight of his grandparents leaving the house, dashingly attired in evening dress, for the first night of *Cavalcade*.

CB was always very generous with guest tickets for his shows. He once noticed that Professor Denison Ross, the famous orientalist, was a frequent visitor to the circle promenade at the London Pavilion. He asked what brought him there so often. 'I come to see a certain dancer,' replied Ross. 'And if I could afford it I should be here more often.'

CB at once gave him a card admitting him to the theatre whenever he pleased.

A Case of 'Highway Robbery'

To those who know New York today, the city in the early nineties would be barely recognisable. Tramcars drawn by mules groaned and swayed along the rough streets flanked by shacks, single-storey wooden-slatted houses and neglected, seedy shops piled higgledy piggledy with cheap merchandise. Here and there were some tall buildings, anticipations of the skyscrapers to come; and at every street corner there were fruit stalls, stacked with large black melons and manned by pig-tailed Chinese, the first generation sons of emancipated negro slaves, Irish fugitives from the potato famine, refugees from the Russian and Polish pogroms, Germans, Italians, Scandinavians . . . a melting pot indeed.

Four-wheeled buggies trundled round the dusty squares. Six-shooters and large-brimmed hats, associated by future generations only with the Wild West, formed part of the standard male dress in a town where few women were to be seen.

Cochran and Scotson Clark quickly found themselves lodgings at three dollars a week and lost no time in making contact with Mrs Wade, an agent who sent them to the Star Theatre, a little way downtown from Union Square. Extras were wanted for the crowd scenes and, although the two young newcomers were accepted, Joseph Brooke, the producer, who later presented *Ben Hur* at Drury Lane, suddenly stopped the rehearsal, pointed to Cochran and said, 'I called for ladies and gentlemen, not children. What is that child doing here?'

Cochran looked younger than his nineteen years. Brooke fired him, but retained Scotson Clark at a dollar a performance. For a

time they shared Clark's not very lavish earnings and Clark
represented himself as Cochran's 'manager', recommending him
to prospective employers as a highly talented young singer of
comic songs. But no one was impressed.

A travelling champagne salesman who shared rooms in their
lodging house passed Cochran on the stairs a couple of times:
he asked the landlady who he was and invited the lad to accompany him on his calls. By this time Cochran was game for anything, but the custom of popping a cork at every visit meant
that he was drinking more champagne than he could comfort-
ably manage and it was not long before he sensibly gave up the
job.

Whether it was due to his powers of persuasion or the
impressive appearance afforded by his top hat and black cloak,
Scotson Clark did ultimately manage to find Cochran a job at
Huber's Museum opposite Tammany Hall. Its principal attraction was a freak show – the dog-faced boy, the living skeleton,
the fat lady, the tattooed man etc – but it also provided other
forms of entertainment, and Cochran was engaged to give performances of his comic songs eight times a day. He ran into
trouble almost from the start. Another artist complained that
Cochran's repertoire contained songs from his own act and, as
the man was older and more established, Cochran was obliged
to yield. He chose some other songs that didn't suit him so well.
Neither was he too familiar with them. In addition – and due,
no doubt, to the strain of doing eight turns a day in a smoky,
ill-ventilated room – his voice disappeared and, with it, his
job.

So he was once again on his beam ends. Scotson Clark got
himself a touring job and Cochran remained alone in New York.
He returned hopefully to Mrs Wade, his erstwhile benefactor,
who was casting a production of *Our Boys* for a seaside resort
town nearby. She asked him whether he had worked in this play
in England.

He hadn't, but he lied and was given a part. On the opening

night, as a famous London agent used to say, 'One of the seats was absolutely packed'! Not surprisingly, it closed a few nights later.

Back in New York, he lived in one of those theatrical digs that made a generous concession to the financial instability of the acting trade by allowing their inmates to remain there on account and settle their bills when they were in work. The liabilities that accrued were regarded as debts of professional honour and default was rare.

Out-of-work actors used then to frequent Engel's, a theatrical bar on 27th Street that displayed all the stage newspapers and magazines. One of them contained an advertisement for the entire cast of *Around the World in Eighty Days*. With Sydney Price, another hard-pressed English actor, he debated whether to apply. Auditions were being held downtown in Niblo's Garden, Lower Broadway, where the play was due to open.

Whether to apply proved a great problem because the two young men had only ten cents between them and the choice was between investing their entire fortune in the bus fare or two glasses of beer and a meal at the free-lunch counter where – in those days – you could eat as much as you liked, providing you drank, though the type of customer represented by Cochran and Price could have been no great asset to these establishments.

Despite the intense heat, they decided to walk, Cochrane losing the sole of his right boot en route.

Bill Fleming, the producer, immediately engaged Price on the grounds of his prepossessing appearance, but viewed Cochran with some hesitation. Thanks, however, to Price's persuasive intercession, Cochran was also taken on for a variety of small parts that included an Indian sailor, policeman, a waiter in London's Eccentric Club during the first scene, and a member of the Club in the last.

On the opening night Cochran gave himself a little artistic licence without the producer's knowledge. In his anxiety to mask his identity in switching from the waiter part to that of a sailor, he applied some short, black whiskers to his chin and, when he appeared on a cue from Phineas Fogg, the audience rocked with laughter at the sight of this unexpected comic entrance. Fleming, who was also in the cast and on stage at that moment, savagely muttered between scarcely parted lips, 'Get off the stage, get off, do you hear?'

The unseemly intrusion of a comedy note at that juncture had completely wrecked the delicate mood of the situation.

Cochran survived this disastrous opening and played the part straight on the ensuing nights.

The company toured and broke up in St Louis where Cochran ran into Gus Bruno, an acquaintance from New York. Bruno showed the friendliest attitude to Cochran and was not in the least discouraged by the following newspaper report:

FIGHT AT HEUCK'S

William J Fleming, manager of *Around the World in Eighty Days,* had a savage set-to with actor Cochran on the stage at Heuck's Monday night prior to the performance. Cochran lost a pint of claret. He says that the trouble was over back salary due him; also, that he refused to surrender his wardrobe.

Having seen *Around the World*, Bruno engaged him and eight of the girls to tour in a vaudeville act entitled *A Strange Family*. He called these young ladies The Eight Bowery Girls, and after a week's rehearsal in Cincinnati the backer of the show, resenting the fact that his own particular female companion was not given a preferential and more conspicuous role, bitterly withdrew his support and the whole project collapsed.

He undertook to provide the company with their fares to Chicago or home.

Home! What was 'home' to Cochran? The girls chose Chicago. So he went with them.

When Cochran boarded the train his sole capital was a watch given him by his father and twenty-five cents, but, having already managed to extricate himself from similar financial predicaments, he didn't allow this relatively minor inconvenience to disturb his faith in himself, thus giving abundant support to Oscar Wilde's dictum that 'the basis of optimism is sheer terror'.

Faced once again with the agonising choice between eating and husbanding his precious twenty-five cents, he stoically took the latter course, even though the train journey lasted all day.

Chicago looked forbidding and grey. Snow fell and the famous wind raged and whistled, penetrating his now threadbare clothes. He said goodbye to the girls and wandered off aimlessly on his own. By now he was feeling very dispirited. The buoyancy that hitherto sustained him had vanished.

He had been in the habit of leaving odd bundles of laundry in various boarding houses on the tour and was now refused admission to various theatrical lodgings because he had no luggage.

He spent ten cents on a meal and the remaining fifteen on a night's doss down in a sleazy flop house with a stove in the centre of the room and a tin chimney that went up through the ceiling.

The next morning he emerged on the streets of Chicago literally penniless. Who did he know in Chicago? He searched his memory. No one – except . . . But this was a stray thought, so remote and impossible as to be hardly worth entertaining. He remembered that when he was a child in Lindfield, a certain Mr Booth, a well-to-do American businessman, had visited the village; he came, it was said, from Chicago. The man's name had stuck in his mind so he consulted a telephone directory in a drug store and selected what he considered to be the most likely Booth of the many listed therein. Although the chance of his having made the correct choice was slender enough, his plight was such that he trudged interminably, block after block, to the businessman's office. He wrote 'From Lindfield, Sussex, England' on his card and gave it to a clerk; and when he was shown into the presence of Mr Booth he at once recognised him as the man who had indeed visited Lindfield in his boyhood.

Mr Booth was not disposed to give a job in commerce to an out-of-work actor. He even refused to take him as an office boy or messenger, and without relaxing his severe expression, his parting words were, 'I'm afraid there's nothing I can offer you, but if five dollars are of any use, here they are!'

This was a godsend. Five minutes later Cochran met two of the Bowery Girls in Madison Street. They asked him where he was staying and, on hearing that he had been refused a room because he carried no luggage, offered him a couch in the kitchen of a comfortable apartment they had managed to find in Halsey Street.

He moved in, took a bath and felt better. His confidence began to revive.

The girls found work, but he didn't. He wrote to John Hazelrigg who had toured with him in *Around the World*. Back came a telegram with the news that there was a part for him in Dayton, Ohio.

It was in a play called *Chris and Lena*. Hazelrigg was in it. The play started quite successfully, and when Hazelrigg left to take up a bigger part in New York, Cochran persuaded the manager to offer the vacant role to Sydney Price. This was arranged in a matter of days and the two young men were re-united, much to Cochran's satisfaction at being able to repay Price for his help.

But, as the tour proceeded, its fortunes dwindled and the producer said he could continue to play the agreed dates only if the cast would accept a salary cut. There being no alternative, this appeal received general, if grudging, assent and, since the proposed measure was comparable with splitting the atom, one member of the company – Marie Stuart, the leading lady – displayed such resentment that a feud developed between her and the manager.

The tour finally collapsed in Eau Clair, Wisconsin, from lack of support. The manager sold everything to raise the company's fares back to Chicago and told all the players to report at the railway station at five o'clock the next morning – all of them, that is, except Marie Stuart whom he deliberately abstained from telling either from spite or because he thought her company would be more than he could tolerate. Whatever the motive, Cochran felt so outraged by this squalid little action that he decided to warn the lady. As she was staying at another hotel, he could communicate with her only by means of a note. He intructed the night porter to deliver it but, having no money, gave him his watch. In his message he asked Marie Stuart to retrieve the watch from the porter, give him a dollar and return the watch next morning.

Everyone arrived for the train next morning. Cochran looked in all the compartments and peered anxiously at the barricr, but there was no sign of Marie Stuart when the train pulled out.

The porter had failed to deliver the message.

And Cochran never saw his watch again.

Now, back in Chicago, he was literally destitute. As he was about to doze off one hot night, he was startled into wakefulness by the sight of a hand reaching through the window of his shabby lodging.

He at once feigned sleep and, on opening his eyes, discovered that all his clothes – his only suit, in fact – had vanished from a chair by the window. A bundle of washing had also disappeared. He was marooned. Next morning he persuaded the janitor to deliver a message to the English actor E S Willard who, though unknown to Cochran, generously sent a parcel of clothes to his unfortunate compatriot.

He lived for a while on Price's charity. One morning Price announced that he was down to his last dollar and, without a word of explanation, took Cochran into a building in a side street. It was a gambling den. Men were playing roulette. Price staked his last dollar on number seven and, incredibly, the little ivory ball came to rest in the corresponding slot! Twenty-five dollars! He took ten and left fifteen on the same number which, even more incredibly, came up again, turning the twenty-five dollars into 875.

They went off in great spirits, had several cocktails and a magnificent dinner of large Porterhouse steaks. It was their first good meal for some time. Then, smoking big cigars, they took themselves off to the World's Fair.

Next day they went their separate ways in search of work, but the agencies offered nothing.

Cochran returned to their digs to find Sydney Price in a drunken stupor.

He had been back to the gambling den and lost everything.

They then decided that their situation was too desperate for them to think solely in terms of the stage, so they went in search of any kind of job – as shop assistants, porters; even barkers that some of the shops and cheap restaurants were hiring to attract custom. But they met with no success until Cochran, remembering the lively pace and frenzied atmosphere of the Chicago World's Fair, began seeking jobs at the various booths and pavilions and finally landed one selling fountain pens. He did very well at this and managed to save enough for the fare back to New York both for Sydney Price and himself.

In all these vicissitudes and adventures, the grim hardships and spasmodic reliefs, a substratum of valuable, solid experience was manifestly building up. That this experience supplied valuable nourishment to the eagerly receptive mind and personality of this restless, ambitious young man is beyond all reasonable question. The cult of American entertainment and showmanship at the end of the nineteenth century was more brash and dynamic than our own, if only because, while we were influenced no doubt by certain inbred traditions of decorum and restraint, the new, bustling, immature life of the American cities with its brash optimism and hodge-podge of national strains made no such concession to the demands of good taste. The mature Cochran, therefore, the impresario with individual, dynamic ideas and a magic touch, was clearly the product of the less inhibited American spirit, tamed and moulded by the more conventional influence of the British theatre. And, by an astute selective process, he managed to combine the vividness and panache of American showmanship with the standards of good taste that prevailed in the West End. It is agreed by all who knew and worked with him in his heyday that he was, by nature, a man of unerring taste.

And this, no doubt, was why he eventually proved to be head and shoulders above his fellow impresarios in stature and repute.

In New York the Barnum and Bailey show was preparing its summer tour and Cochran presented himself for an audition. Fifteen dollars a week. Cochran sang a scale and Lombardi, the musical director, said, 'You'll do. Go over there with the second tenors.' But when, later in the day, he sang again for Imre Kiralfy, the producer, Mr Kiralfy asked, 'How did you get in here?' and, turning to the musical director, barked, 'Mr Lombardi, why do you waste my time?'

Many years later, when Cochran was at the height of his success, Kiralfy, on a visit from America, was introduced to him at Olympia. He looked at him quizzically and said, 'Haven't we met before somewhere, Cochran?'

Once again, through an advertisement in a theatrical paper, he got himself engaged for a musical touring show called *A Breezy Time* but, having to earn his living before rehearsals began, he took a job with 'Dr' Greenberg's Medicine Show. This meant touring with a mobile booth and enacting a short playlet outside to attract a crowd. When the performance ended, Greenberg would appear and demonstrate his magic ointment after which the players would go among the crowd selling it. Cochran did this for four weeks, earning twenty-five dollars a week plus commission on the tins of ointment sold.

During rehearsals of *A Breezy Time* he got engagements at the Star Theatre, Manhattan, and another in Brooklyn and, by the time the show started, he had managed to set himself up with a little money.

A flattering report on him appeared in the *New York Musical Review*:

> One of the best stage delineators of the ludicrous side of English character that has visited America recently is Mr Charles Blake Cochran, who is now in this city as a competitor for American renown. Mr Cochran is a humorous vocalist of the funniest and most able order. He has a choice repertoire of racy comic songs, and his imitations of the London cabman, costermonger and other grotesque and outlandish types of English eccentric character, are true to nature and irresistibly laughable. His power of imitative facial expression is wonderful, he gives the English dialect 'patter' to perfection, and altogether his characterisations are inimitable.

But an uncomplimentary press notice in a Pennysylvania newspaper affected him deeply and proved largely instrumental in persuading him to give up acting.

After the Saturday night curtain in Ohio, a friend took him out to a local speakeasy where he drank some hooch and, emerging from the dingy cellar into the light, felt the full impact of the morning sun and air. Church bells were ringing and, on a drunken impulse, he seized a gaily dressed coloured churchgoer and attempted to dance with her. Taken off by the police, he spent the rest of the day and the following night in a cell and, on being hauled before the magistrate next morning, was charged with highway robbery, disturbing the Sabbath, being drunk and disorderly and assaulting a lady.

The court sentenced him to a thousand-dollar fine or jail. He had nothing. Even the seven dollars he originally carried had been confiscated by the policeman who arrested him.

The manager of the theatre was in court and, although he was thoroughly displeased with Cochran, he needed him so much for the performance that he secured his freedom by handing over, not a thousand dollars, but a mere twenty-five, which was readily accepted in full settlement by that Alice-in-Wonderland court.

As Cochran left the courthouse the local correspondent of the *New York Dramatic News* bought him breakfast and lent him five dollars for his hotel bill.

If only because it sold genuine Scotch, Kirk's, a high class grocery store at the junction of Broadway and 27th Street, became a haunt of writers and actors and a useful rendezvous for those in need of information about new shows and jobs. Maurice Barrymore, father of Lionel, John and Ethel, was a frequent visitor; and so was Ted Henley (brother of W E Henley, the poet), with whom Cochran became friendly.

Living in the same boarding house as Cochran was Tyrone Power, father of the film actor. He introduced Cochran to Mervyn Dallas, an eccentric and flamboyant character who assumed the dress and posture of an English country gentleman and who, having once played in *Richard III* with the great Richard Mansfield, said to Cochran one night, 'You ought to call on my friend Dick Mansfield and see if he can give you anything to do. Say I sent you, my boy. Say I sent you.'

Cochran accordingly presented himself at the box-office of the Garrick which was Mansfield's own theatre and headquarters. Mansfield was to the American stage what Irving was to the British; and the great reputation he enjoyed gave him the privilege of being capricious and eccentric in ways denied to lesser men. As he was reputed to be so wayward and unpredictable, Cochran was desperately nervous and tense when he asked to see the great man.

The box-office manager's response was hardly encouraging. 'He's not in,' he barked. 'I don't know when he's coming in, and if you've no appointment, you're wasting your time hanging about here.' His attitude seemed so final and uncompromising that Cochran turned to go when a voice boomed from the ante-room of the box-office: 'Isn't that someone asking for me? Why do you say I'm not here? Show the gentleman in at once. . . .' The severe demeanour of Mansfield's self-appointed protector melted at once and he sheepishly beckoned Cochran into the presence.

When the young man explained his business, Mansfield looked him up and down. 'An actor, eh? And you'd like to act in my company. . . . What have you done?'

Cochran gave him a résumé of his career and when he mentioned the Medicine Show, Mansfield chuckled. 'Good. Good,' he said. 'It's all experience. I've done that sort of thing myself. Well, young man, consider yourself engaged. Come and see me again when my season opens.' And he summoned Tommy Grahame, his stage manager, who entered a note of the engagement in his records.

Just as he was leaving, Cochran remembered to say, 'Oh, I ought to mention, sir, that it was Mervyn Dallas who sent me to see you.'

'Was it now?' replied Mansfield drily. 'Well, if you keep him away from me, I'll overlook it.'

Up to that time this was by far the most exciting thing that had happened to Cochran. A job in a Mansfield repertory! The list included such plays as *Beau Brummell* and *Jekyll and Hyde*. All the out-of-work actors at Kirk's were most envious.

He patiently awaited the start of Mansfield's season, living on his savings from *A Breezy Time*.

Then disaster, or so it seemed. He read in the newspaper one morning that Mansfield was ill, and subsequent reports stated that he was deteriorating rapidly. Mansfield's memory had gone and he would never act again.

Members of the company drifted away and looked for other work. Having eked out his savings to cover the interim period, Cochran was now penniless once again. He couldn't get a stage job so he applied to the YMCA employment bureau where he was given a job as assistant to the C of E chaplain in New York harbour. For two dollars a day he boarded the incoming liners and sought out the English passengers with offers of help and guidance in their churchgoing needs. The first man he approached with a cordial 'Excuse me, sir, are you English?' retorted in severe tones and a thick Irish brogue, 'Oi didn't com hayre to be insolted, young feller. Oi'll trow you in the sea!'

It was a depressing, boring job, and quite unpalatable to a young man of Cochran's temperament and interests, and he gave it up before the week was out.

Then he read the encouraging news that Mansfield was better and recuperating in the country; also that his forthcoming production was now in preparation. Any day, thought Cochran, the call would come. But the days passed in silence. His anxiety mounted until one morning in Kirk's he was utterly dismayed to learn that several of his actor friends had been signed up for Mansfield's company.

Clearly he had been overlooked and forgotten. Actors were all the same, he mused bitterly; unreliable, insincere, as bad as their words.

One evening, however, a messenger from Mansfield presented himself at his digs.

'We've been looking all over New York for you,' he said.

Cochran's spirits rose like a balloon suddenly deprived of its ballast. 'He *remembered*!' he cried incredulously.

'*Remembered?*' echoed the messenger. 'Finding you has saved me my job. Mansfield stopped a rehearsal, looked round at all the faces and said, "Where is the young Englishman I engaged?" Then he said to me, "Go and find him. If you fail you're fired!" '

The Quixotic Richard Mansfield

QUITE A DECISIVE event took place in Cochran's life at this period. The company toured the vast distances of the US by rail. Richard Mansfield and his wife lived in their own Pullman coach which aspired as much to the conditions of a private dwelling as a railway coach possibly could. Its contents, its books and pictures in particular, reflected the tastes and disposition of a cultivated mind.

In Pittsburgh, where the coach had been shunted into a siding, Mansfield sent for Cochran. Responding to the unexpected summons with a sense of uneasy portent, the young actor duly presented himself. It so happened that this proved to be almost the last occasion on which he genuinely merited such a description.

There was a hint of disagreeable tidings in Mansfield's gambit.

He asked, 'Do you think you will ever be an actor, Cochran – a really great actor?'

How in the world did one answer a question like this? Sensing the implied criticism, Cochran answered lamely, 'I thought I was improving.'

'Yes,' replied Mansfield gently. 'Maybe that's so. Maybe that's so. But I don't think you can hope to be as good an actor, say, as I am! In my opinion acting is not your true vocation. If it interests you, I should like you to leave the company, but stay with me, not only with the tour, but indefinitely as my private secretary. I'll pay you ten dollars a week more than you're getting as an actor.'

Cochran accepted at once, his disappointment over the sudden annihilation of his acting career being offset by the prospect of permanent employment and a larger income.

His new assignment was immediate. Ignoring all formality, Mansfield thrust a batch of letters into his hand. They were invitations to receptions and dinners and requests for jobs, newspaper interviews and advice. Each one bore a pencilled 'Yes' or 'No'. On Mansfield's behalf Cochran went away and wrote courteous replies according to these directions. Whenever they arrived in a new town, it also fell to Cochran to find a quiet siding into which the railway coach could be shunted.

While employed by Mansfield in this new capacity, he met a number of famous people including Sir Herbert Beerbohm Tree, Gerald du Maurier, Arthur Bourchier and Israel Zangwill. Visiting the theatre one night Mr Zangwill exchanged some acid words with Mansfield who peevishly instructed Cochran to escort him to the stage door.

At a supper party in Mansfield's house, Tree said to Cochran, 'If you ever come to London, come and see me; I shall be happy to have you. There is room for young men like you in London.'

Mansfield was inordinately jealous of successful British actors who pleased the American public.

Eccentricity, unpredictable behaviour and conceit are tolerable to a degree. Cochran had a benign temperament, but with the sort of autocrat who would stop a rehearsal and say, 'That man is wearing brown shoes with a navy-blue suit. Dismiss him at once!', the final clash was inevitable. Cochran quarrelled with Mansfield in Cleveland, Ohio, walked out of his private rail coach and never went back. He returned to New York where he rejoined Ted Henley, and together they opened a school of acting.

Cochran looked after the business side. Their first production was *John Gabriel Borkman* which in later life Cochran regarded as his first essay in management. It was followed by a performance of *A Midsummer Night's Dream* at Madison Square Garden. Cochran played Snug the Joiner.

This new venture did not survive for very long. Cochran next toyed with the idea of setting up an independent theatre but failed to raise the necessary backing.

He was then twenty-five, quite mature, and certainly devoid of the kind of pettiness that would have allowed his personal disagreement with Mansfield, the man, affect his abiding respect for Mansfield, the artist. Whenever his former employer was playing at the theatre, Cochran made every effort to see him on stage.

But a certain ignominy surrounded Cochran's last days in America. Mansfield returned to New York and opened at the Fifth Avenue Theatre in *The Devil's Disciple*. On his way to the first night Cochran stopped at Kirk's for a drink with Ted Henley. In the event, the simple phrase 'a drink' proved a gross understatement and Cochran went to the theatre in such poor shape that, when he presented his ticket at the entrance to the auditorium, Mansfield's manager, Joe Dillon, refused to let him in. He tried to force his way through, but Dillon and the attendants restrained him and he lunged out. A fight ensued. Members of the audience participated and the general fracas received the same amount of coverage in the press the next morning as the notices of the play.

Fearful of Mansfield's towering wrath, Cochran was surprised to find this strange, quixotic man thoroughly amused and delighted by the affair, despite his having to pay bail to secure his release from the police station.

But even this did not mitigate Cochran's feelings of shame and remorse and he decided that the time had come to return to England.

He sought out Scotson Clark with whom he had travelled to the States seven years previously and they arranged to return together.

The background to Cochran's failure to secure the backing he

needed for his independent theatre scheme is revealed in a letter
he sent his sister, Minnie.

Sturtevant House,
Henry J Bang, Proprietor,
Broadway and 29th Street,
New York.
9th October, 1897

My dear Mins,

Owing to the death of my financial 'backer' my scheme
to establish an independent theatre in New York has fallen
through. It was a pretty hard blow for me, just as I was on the
eve of doing big things here, and I'm terribly discouraged. Consequently I've made up my mind to come to London and I sail
tomorrow and shall arrive at Leith (near Edinburgh, Scotland)
in about two weeks from now. When I land, I shan't have a
penny in my pocket and I want to know if you'll lend me £50
to bring me on to London with. If so please send it to 'C B
Cochran – Poste Restante, Leith, Scotland. To be left until
called for.' Don't think I'm coming over altogether without
prospects – on the contrary, I come over with more than a fair
chance of a big London engagement, which I could have had
some time ago if I had wanted it then and also I have some
commissions to sell some American plays in London. If you give
me my first start I'll be on my feet in a week or two. Please don't
fail me as, although I may be able to borrow money by wiring
to London upon my arrival at Leith, such a course will hurt me,
as it will let the very people I wish to think that I am on easy
street – and then do some business with – know that I am broke,
and they'll want me on their own terms.

With fondest love,
Yours,
Charlie

The journey home in a tramp steamer, which was all they
could afford, took seventeen days. They docked at Leith and
proceeded to Edinburgh where Cochran wrote again to his sister.

35

The Royal Hotel,
53 Princes Street, Edinburgh.
27th October, 1897

My dear Min,

I have only just arrived here after a very rough passage and found your letter waiting for me. I can hardly thank you sufficiently for the enclosures – it was really very brickish of you to respond so readily, but I must confess that the tone of your letter surprised me.

In the first place, what do you mean when you say 'there must be something more than you tell me, for you to be in such straits'? If you think that I am in any trouble in New York, I assure you it is not so and, as for being in 'straits', I'm as well off as I ever was – I never had money when I was out of an engagement – I've never been able to save any. Then again you say 'the big position you held so long with Richard Mansfield ought alone to help you'. In what way, my dear girl, do you mean it should help me? Surely not in borrowing money to tide me over my difficulties with – I could borrow money from my friends in New York, yes, lots of it, but you must remember that I'm a very well known figure in New York life – during the last few months I have been spoken of more kindly by the press than almost any man I can remember for a long time, and this in spite of what you say about me not being able to 'afford to ride the big horse'. It would, however, never do to let my pals in NY know my true financial position as I hope to return to America before long and, in that country, when a man is 'broke' he is down – very much down. As it was, I went to a friend I could trust and borrowed my fare from NY – a matter of thirty-five dollars (£7).

If you mean my late position with Mr Mansfield should aid me in getting a new job, you are talking sensibly. I could have had lots of engagements during the summer. Directly people knew I had left Mansfield offers flocked in, for believe me, I was very popular in New York; but I believed in this Independent Theatre scheme – and if it had come off I should have been a big man – and I refused them all. When this (the Ind Thre) fell through, 'twas too late to get a first class engagement in

America, as the season opens in Oct and, as I couldn't take a second class engagement, I thought I had better come and try my luck in England. I had been offered a London engagement whilst I was with Mr Mansfield and, if I'm not mistaken, I'll not be without one very long. I didn't come over here on a fool's errand, but have something, or rather, two or three things in view. I most certainly shall never ask you for any more money as I am quite capable of making my living in London as I have done in New York for the past five years. My dear old girl, please take the preceding arguments and comments in the spirit in which they were written. I am most truly grateful to you for your financial assistance, but think that, not knowing thoroughly my American life, you are not capable of understanding my position. I may be hard up, but I'm not going to starve in London nor am I going to do anything dirty or underhand (I left New York practically out of debt – ie, when I say 'practically', I mean I did not owe any tradesmen but simply a few personal friends). I have enough professional friends to keep me from poverty in London, until I can get an engagement.

Now to the real drift of this very lengthy scrawl. Why may I not come to Brighton for a day or so and see my parents and my brothers and sisters? I had intended to get through my business in London by Saturday and run down on Sunday and stop until Monday or Tuesday. Of course I shouldn't let anybody at Brighton know that I was hard up and, as I'm pretty well dressed, I don't think for one minute that they would imagine such was the case. In spite of what you say about my making others miserable, I still have some feelings left, and what you say about Mother makes me all the more anxious to see her. However, having accepted your money, I am, as it were, on a parole d'honneur to you and shall not move without your permission. Grant it and I promise to be discreet.

I am leaving for London tonight and will let you know as soon as I secure rooms. For the present address me c/o Low's Exchange, London. Now, my dear Mins, with more thanks,

I remain,
Your loving Brother,
Chas.

PS After writing this (which I will not post until tomorrow, as I'm afraid it will not reach you in the morning) I learned that Mr Beerbohm Tree was in Edinburgh, and as I knew him very well, having met him lots of times in America, I called to pay my respects. He was most charming and promised to do all in his power for me upon his return to London next week. This assistance was volunteered – not asked for – as I chatted to him in his dressing room whilst he was making up for *Svengali*.
28th October.

I've had a busy day and not a fruitless one. I'm to see George Edwardes on Monday – I saw his representative (A Sutherland) today. Miss Mabel Beardsley is also exerting herself greatly in my behalf and she knows everybody.

With Scotson Clark he travelled to London by the night train from Edinburgh. Cochran spent the night in Bloomsbury at the Tavistock Hotel, where he had once stayed with his father, and enjoyed this comparative luxury which contrasted so sharply with the austerity of the voyage.

He found it difficult to carve his way into London theatrical circles. The fact that he had worked in New York and was well in the swim there carried little weight. He called on Mabel Beardsley, beautiful sister of Aubrey who had died meanwhile at the age of twenty-six, and went to some of her tea-time receptions where he met such distinguished personalities as Max Beerbohm, Will Rothenstein, Walter Sickert and the play-wright, Charles Brookfield.

He called, as bidden, on Herbert Beerbohm Tree, seeking to take advantage of the offer of work which the great actor-manager had made to him in America. Tree entertained him lavishly and gave him a box at the theatre, but said, alas, that, at that time, he could find no use for him.

'It would be much better,' he advised, 'for you to go back to America!'

Brookfield introduced Cochran to W S Penley who cast him in the part of an old solicitor in *A Little Ray of Sunshine* and he gave such a successful comedy performance on tour that Penley, who was the principal comedian, became intensely jealous and cut the part out when the play opened in London.

Cochran's money was dwindling. He met Henry Hess who owned a theatrical magazine called *Critic* and persuaded him to take some articles. He wrote for this and other magazines about the things he knew – America, the theatre . . .

In those days freelance journalism was a desperately uncertain and badly paid means of livelihood.

There were times when he walked the streets all night, having no room or bed.

Cold and hungry and without a fire in his cheap studio room in Carey Street – an address that was soon to have an ominous significance for him – he dashed off an article on Aubrey Beardsley, as he had known him at school, and sold it for the price of his breakfast. Realising his plight, the editor paid him generously. And he once managed to collect fifty pounds – a small fortune in those days – for an article which he knew that a magazine editor badly wanted. This was a provocative reply to an article by Ranger Gull, better known in later years as Guy Thorne, author of the controversial book *When It Was Dark*. Cochran split this unusually large fee with him.

He next went to Paris, saw *Cyrano de Bergerac* and suggested to Mansfield in a cabled message that here was a perfect part for the American actor-manager. He was frequenting Rules and the Café Royal and in one of these places he again met Mansfield who had been looking for him all over London – just as he had tried to trace him in New York.

Mansfield invited him back to America. The famous actor was then in financial difficulties and he asked Cochran to go back and list and value the contents of his great house preparatory to a sale which was calculated to restore him to solvency.

Cochran was again to be secretary and general factotum to Mansfield, and his first task was to bring to New York a great collection of costumes that Mansfield had bought from Irving.

Mansfield had accepted Cochran's advice to produce *Cyrano* and wherever it played in America, it was an enormous success.

By this time, Mansfield had such an entourage of helpers who handled the day to day duties that he retained Cochran more as a personal companion. While this gave Cochran a regular income, security and an interesting life, it was not entirely congenial to a man of his ambitions and restless nature, despite the privilege of dining in Mansfield's private coach with such people as Irving, Mrs Langtry, Sarah Bernhardt and a couple of former presidents. He was delighted, therefore, when Mansfield sent him back to England to persuade Weedon Grossmith to go to America with a new farce.

On his return, Cochran spent quite a lot of time and effort on this assignment and various other duties connected with it and was so disgruntled on receiving a cable from Mansfield to the effect that he had changed his mind about the project after all that he decided to stay in England.

Battle of the Sandwich Men

IT MAY BE suitable at this point to ponder the great variety of things Cochran had done in those early years. While to many another rolling stone such experiences might have yielded little cumulative benefit, this acutely observant young man, with a sponge-like capacity for self-education in his chosen field, applied them unconsciously to the development of his own personality.

He got a job managing an operette on tour. The stage manager was Gilbert Laye, father of Evelyn Laye.

Templer Saxe, a well known baritone, was in this production and when the tour finished he decided to try the music halls. Cochran was so successful in getting him engagements that other artists asked him to represent them and this induced him to set up as an agent with offices in Chancery Lane. Except for Houdini, all the artists he represented are forgotten today.

But at last he was settled. Cochran was running a business on his own, and doing moderately well. He was his own master, no longer subject to the capricious opinions of theatre managers and audiences, no longer at the beck and call of an eccentric and temperamental employer. He had taken another step forward.

His reputation as an agent was spreading; and his growing stature was reflected in the high calibre of the artists who later went through his hands. Yielding again to the excitement and glitter of Paris, he began operating on the Continent. One of his French clients was Odette Dulac, an enchanting *diseuse,* toast of the Rue Pigalle and second only perhaps to Yvette

Guilbert. She presently retired from the stage and took up sculpture, but Cochran's handling of her had been so successful and adroit that it consolidated his position in the Parisian entertainment world, and this resulted in his future association with Mistinguett, Alice Delysia, Yvonne Printemps and, of course, the astonishing young Russian, Hackenschmidt, whom he first saw in a world wrestling championship at the *Folies Bergères*.

Back in London, Cochran stood talking to one of the music hall managers on the steps of the old Tivoli in the Strand, when Harry Taft, an American whistling comedian, walked by with another man and joined the two of them for a brief greeting and a chat. Cochran recognised Taft's companion at once. He was Georges Hackenschmidt who had astonished the audience at the Alhambra in a most sensational manner the night before.

Jack Carkeek, a famous Cornish wrestling champion, had appeared on the Alhambra stage and thrown out a challenge to any member of the audience who would undertake to meet him. Sitting in one of the boxes, Hackenschmidt immediately divested himself of his full evening dress and made his way to the stage in nothing but the underwear that passes for the regulation wrestling kit.

Daunted by the muscles and physique of his prospective adversary, Carkeek regaled the audience with an impromptu line of patter intimating that he should not take on this challenger there and then. He was such a skilled and persuasive talker that he succeeded in inducing his audience to applaud him and boo Hackenschmidt at which the young Russian would-be contestant was naturally very disappointed and angry.

This cunning evasion on the part of the Cornish wrestler outraged Cochran's sense of fair play and, on hearing that the Russian champion was proposing to return to Paris that day, he walked back with him to his room at the Hotel Cecil, pleading with him to stay in London.

In the hotel Hackenschmidt stripped, displayed his magnificent physique, which Cochran was convinced was the finest he had ever seen, and did a few handsprings. As Cochran was leaving the hotel he met a *Daily Mail* reporter/photographer of his acquaintance and lured her back to the Cecil to interview the wrestler.

The next day a long, illustrated article appeared in the paper.

Ever an opportunist, and equipped with a natural sense of newsworthiness and the value of publicity, Cochran took a copy of the *Daily Mail* to George Adney Payne who controlled the Syndicate Halls – The Oxford, Tivoli, London Pavilion, Canterbury and the Paragon.

Adney agreed to engage Hackenschmidt for one week's trial at the Tivoli for £70. Before the opening, Cochran arranged for the wrestler to appear one night at the National Sporting Club. Here again Hackenschmidt was a sensation, and Cochran at once bombarded all the newspapers with photographs and stories of this modern Hercules, thus spreading his fame and increasing his market value. As a result the box office takings during his week at the Tivoli broke all records for that music hall. Payne wanted Hackenschmidt for another four weeks so, exploiting his strong position, Cochran gave his consent provided the fee was raised to £150 a week which Adney, after a preliminary interlude of moans and complaints, grudgingly agreed. But the crowds gradually dropped off. Though a brilliant and skilful wrestler, Hackenschmidt was no showman. He was too honest to understand the need for temporising with his opponent and spinning out the fun. He came, he saw and he conquered so swiftly that the audience felt cheated of their due meed of entertainment.

Realising that, for the time being, London was no place for Hackenschmidt, Cochran decided to present him in the provinces. Wrestling, he discovered, had an enthusiastic following in Lancashire. He went to Liverpool, saw a Mr Cleaver and agreed to hire the Prince of Wales Theatre in Claydon Square for three months. Then he invited Tom Cannon, champion of

England, who was living in retirement in Liverpool, to meet the Russian bear.

The Prince of Wales was empty – up for sale at the time – but after the contract had been signed Mr Cleaver, due no doubt to a sudden fear that exhibitions of wrestling might affect the theatre's value on the property market, tried to revoke the contract on the grounds that his licence didn't allow that kind of entertainment. Examination of the licence proved that this was not so and a Liverpool solicitor advised Cochran that he was within his rights in proceeding with the bouts as planned. Cochran insisted, moreover, that he had spent much time and money on this project, particularly on advertising and bringing other wrestlers over from the Continent.

On information mischievously supplied by Cleaver, the newspapers reported that the contest would not take place. Cochran responded by hiring hundreds of sandwichmen who paraded Liverpool bearing messages to the effect that Hackenschmidt always met his obligations and that the fight would be held as planned. Cleaver retaliated with an opposing force of sandwichmen whose wooden display panels claimed the reverse. Scuffles developed between the rival factions and there was a great wooden clatter as the sandwichmen butted one another with their boards. This bizarre engagement must have looked like some fantastic episode in one of the stories that young Mr Wells was writing at the time. News of it spread round the town and reinforced by a party of out-of-work ruffians from Liverpool's dockland, Hackenschmidt and the other wrestlers stood guard at the theatre doors to ensure that they remained open.

Newspaper stories of 'The Battle of Claydon Square' created widespread interest and the public converged on the theatre in droves. But there was further trouble when the gas company refused to restore the supply until the arrears had been paid. Cochran, who was otherwise prepared to pay in advance, refused on the grounds that this bill was Cleaver's liability, but he found himself dealing with a gas company official who, proving luckily to be a wrestling enthusiast, duly softened and turned a blind eye.

All seemed well until the evening. Soon after the gas had been restored, Cleaver hired some out-of-works who cut the supply pipe and neatly soldered up the ends. The gas company's starry-eyed official, now completely suborned by an introduction to Hackenschmidt and the other wrestling celebrities, went on an immediate quest for a gas fitter while Cochran, from the balcony outside the theatre, called for a little goodwill and patience and assured the crowd in the square that the wrestling would take place as promised.

A fitter was found. In half an hour the theatre was filled with gaslight; the crowd occupied every seat and the performance was a roaring success.

There was to be no show the following night. Cochran's plan had been to stagger the performances at intervals of two or three days to work up interest in the press and find new challengers. As agreed, he surrendered the theatre key after the first performance but Cleaver refused to let him have it back for the next.

On the morning of the second match Cochran and his companions stormed the theatre, broke a pane of glass in one of the doors and manipulated the bolt through the opening. They were in.

But not for long. Cochran reeled under a blow on the head from behind. Hired thugs seized him and threw him into the square.

There could have been no show in any case. The indomitable Cleaver had removed all the light fittings and every seat in the house!

Mammoth Fun City

ALTHOUGH HACKENSCHMIDT'S LONDON debut had been disappointing, Cochran's faith in him never waned. George Adney Payne said he wanted a top-of-the-bill to double between the Canterbury and the Paragon and Cochran begged him to try the Russian giant again.

Payne reluctantly agreed, but said he would give no more than £100 a week for both dates. After paying the other wrestlers, the cost of transport between the theatres and other expenses, there would be precious little change. But Cochran was primarily interested in proving his point.

'By the end of the week,' he assured Payne, 'you will be turning people away.'

But Payne sniffed sceptically.

'Nobody's done that for years,' he said, 'and if Hackenschmidt can he'll be worth double.'

A man of considerable integrity, Hackenschmidt refused to fake his performance, but Cochran worked on him patiently and finally persuaded him to treat these theatrical dates as pure entertainment rather than serious displays of wrestling skill.

Either Cochran was a good advocate or Hackenschmidt a quick learner for, by the Wednesday, the box office of both theatres had no more tickets to sell.

During that week, an old wrestler known as 'The Terrible Turk' who had retired and gone into sporting management confronted Hackenschmidt with a challenge from his muscular young protégé, a fellow Turk, named Madrali. This was to be the real thing, not a music hall entertainment, so Cochran

"

opened negotiations with Olympia and booked it. This marked his first promotion at the famous exhibition hall with which he was to have such spectacular associations in later years.

The press worked the public up into such a pitch of excitement over this contest that London went wrestling crazy. Small boys were to be seen everywhere rolling on the pavements in inseparable clinches. 'Holds' became dinner-table topics and led to physical demonstrations during the port when the ladies had retired.

For the first time, and for some mysterious reason, Hackenschmidt was desperately nervous. Cochran looked into his dressing room before the call and found him white-faced and very much on edge.

The hall was full. The event had attracted a large and fashionable audience, and the purse was the largest ever put up for this type of contest, and possibly for boxing as well: £1,000 for the winner and £500 for the other contender.

On the signal, the two huge men faced each other. The audience was tense and silent. Very slowly the Turk moved towards his opponent. In a twinkling Hackenschmidt seized him, lifted him shoulder high and threw him to the ground.

Madrali lay where he was. Both his arms were broken. And latecomers, who had paid a lot of money for their seats, arrived to find the match over.

Hackenschmidt became a national hero. Offers now poured into Cochran's office from all over the country.

Two years later Hackenschmidt and Madrali met again at Olympia. The match was for two falls out of three.

Hackenschmidt was once more the victor. He continued to maintain his record in this country and presently toured Australia. During his absence Cochran imported a Polish giant named Zbysco, introduced a stage hypnotist named Ahrensmeyer at the old Holborn Empire and continued to prosper with various stage acts of this somewhat borderline type. He was astute enough to recognise that, although first class music hall acts would bring audiences in, it was a safer ploy to engage acts of a more sensational kind, acts that induced the public to take sides, argue and gamble on the chances of the respective contestants and go along finally to witness the decisions; or turns like the demonstrations of hypnotism which again stimulated discussion, dividing opinion on the question of their authenticity.

He had now moved his offices to Number 60, the Strand, a good position for anyone in the music hall business, being near the Tivoli and Romano's bar.

Then came his first spell of management in the legitimate London theatre. With George Giddens, a noted comedian of the time, he took the Royalty Theatre where they produced two plays. The first was a farce called *Sporting Simpson* by an unknown author; the second a comedy by F Anstey, whose stories were appearing in the *Strand Magazine*. Anstey's play, *Lyre and Lancet,* was about 'high life below stairs'. Mostyn Pigott, a witty after-dinner speaker and writer of verse, warned Cochran that 'the rich won't want to see a play about their servants' and, whether his assumption was correct, the play failed to attract, and Cochran and George Giddens lost a large sum of money in their first venture in management.

The cost of these disastrous experiments so exceeded the capital which Cochran had accumulated assiduously in his wrestling promotions that his creditors made him bankrupt, a misfortune which was to be repeated, alas, in later years despite intervening periods of brilliant financial success.

Cochran went to see F H Payne – 'Pa' Payne, as he was known – managing director of a new company that had taken over Olympia. He offered him the idea of an annual fair and circus at Olympia on the lines of the one which was then being presented at the Agricultural Hall, Islington.

One of the backers was Bertie Rose whose father had been far-sighted enough to buy a pub near Olympia in anticipation of a colossal turnover stemming from the appearance of the

Barnum and Bailey circus in the exhibition hall. But business dropped immediately after the departure of the great American show and Bertie invested in Cochran's proposed Fair and Circus in the hope of reviving it.

Cochran filled the hall with roundabouts, coconut shies and the usual fairground attractions. Then he engaged a menagerie and a French circus troupe and called the show 'The Mammoth Fun City', a title that was presently appropriated by showmen throughout the world.

He was still a relatively young man, and in his later and maturer years he undoubtedly grew more responsible and selective in the ventures he promoted, becoming known as a man of shrewd and acute perception. All who knew and worked with him, all the people who have helped me with research material for this portrait, the stars he made, his management and production associates, his former Young Ladies, have all testified to his admirable taste.

Yet this quality was manifestly lacking in the younger man who allowed no such considerations of principle to interfere with the pursuit of gain. No stunt was too tawdry, no side-show too vulgar for him to instal it as a device for extracting the pennies from the moronic mobs with sick and simple minds.

And this trait in its turn reveals another that accords ill with the legend of the later man, though he may, of course, have changed radically. For it has been claimed that the fully-fledged Cockie persona, the man behind the great names, the creator of *Bitter Sweet* and *Cavalcade*, was not expressly interested in money *per se*. It was only useful as a means of mounting bigger and better productions. The fabulous amounts he would spend on scenery and costumes bore no relation to the get-out figure or the money-making potential of the house. Cost was immaterial. He knew what he wanted; and he got it. Idiosyncrasy and caprice took charge to such a degree that he would instruct his wardrobe mistresses to introduce tiny figures in the embroidery which, however pleasing in themselves, were invisible to the audience.

In organising his Mammoth Fun City, he first of all borrowed a hump-backed Indian bull from the menagerie and installed it in a booth designed to represent a temple. Then he proceeded to rob the pathetic little creature of its dignity by setting an Indian tapestry in red and gold on its back, gilding its hooves and surrounding it with golden vessels, incense burners and Cingalese servants. He advertised the animal as the Sacred Bull of Benares and when a sufficiently large crowd had collected, the barker would close the curtains and announce that the Bull was performing a sacred rite forbidden to Christian eyes.

He reconciled his conscience with this tasteless and inane deception on the grounds that he made no charge for this side show.

In a neighbouring booth he exhibited Sacco, the Fasting Man who had already lived for forty-eight days on nothing but water and now lay in a glass case with the intention of beating his own record.

This senseless test of endurance was attacked by *The Lancet* while the daily papers condemned it as unwholesome and degrading. One of Cochran's partners in this shoddy enterprise yielded to the remonstrations of his shocked and embarrassed wife and threatened to close it down but, on taking legal advice, Cochran discovered that, since the starving man was committing no offence, he would be entitled to stay where he was and prosecute if 'evicted' from his home. It was possible to serve him a notice to quit. But if he disregarded it, no one had a right of entry.

Always alert to the possibility and value of a good newspaper story, Cochran invited a number of newspaper men to see him press a pencilled message against the glass compartment. His note called on Sacco to abandon the experiment, adding that, if he refused, he would break into the sealed chamber. A page boy stood by with a hatchet.

Sacco scribbled his reply. There he was and there he would stay and he would invoke the law against anyone who tried to remove him from his chosen habitat.

Cochran turned to the page boy.

'Break down the door,' he ordered.

Sacco's solicitor then appeared and warned Cochran that he would apply for heavy damages if the threat were carried out. Cochran's own solicitor, who was also present, agreed that they had a strong case.

He told the page boy to disregard his previous instruction. 'We have done our best,' he grunted wearily, 'but if the man wants to kill himself, we cannot stop him.'

The press reported these proceedings so prominently that Sacco suddenly became a tremendous attraction. The entrance fee was raised from 6d to 1s, then to 2s 6d, until the public ultimately paid 5s to see him break his fast. Although some trickery was involved, he must have fasted to some extent in order to achieve the gaunt and skeletal appearance he presented on his last day. This incident cast a depressing reflection on the morbid curiosity of thousands of people and, in *Secrets of a Showman*, Cochran wrote, 'Only those who cater for the amusement of the public can have any idea how difficult it sometimes is to please them with really meritorious and interesting performances, and how easy sometimes with showman's trickery.'

This, of course, was a face-saving apologia. For, as Trinculo observed when he stumbled on Caliban, shivering with fright under his gabardine, 'Were I in England now, as once I was, and had but this fish painted, not a holiday fool there but would give a piece of silver. There would this monster make a man; any strange beast there makes a man; when they will not give a doit to relieve a lame beggar, they will lay out ten to see a dead Indian.'

Cochran was plainly conscious of the need to offer the crowd a nasty and inferior type of lollipop entertainment to gain some profit. Anything of educational interest that may have granted some concession to serious intellectual curiosity resulted in deserted booths as he discovered when he presented some Ituri Forest pygmies which an anthropologist had brought back from the Congo for research purposes.

Tom Burrows was a bigger success. Tom was an Indian club swinger who fascinated spectators with a marathon stint that lasted non-stop for forty-nine hours while Cochran and his colleagues took it in turns to observe the performance and Mrs Burrows fed her husband at intervals with a wooden spoon.

Several years earlier, in 1901 – and in recounting this episode it is necessary to break the chronological sequence and slip back a little – a seemingly trivial event exerted a profound and fundamental influence on Cochran's life.

While walking to a dinner party in West London he met Ranger Gull coming out of a pub.

Admittedly there was nothing unusual in the sight of Gull coming out of a pub. What was unusual was the fact that he was accompanied by an attractive young woman. She carried a bundle of books. Gull introduced her as Miss Evelyn Dade. To relieve her obvious embarrassment, Gull explained that Miss Dade had expressed some curiosity about public houses, wondering why men found these places so fascinating. So he asked her to visit one, and she sportingly accepted his invitation. This was a daring and unconventional thing for a respectable young woman to do in those days, and it is to be presumed that she scarcely found the experience apocalyptic.

The two men escorted her back to the house where she lived with her mother. Gull was due at the same dinner party as Cochran and when they said good night to Miss Dade, Gull promised to throw a pebble at her window by way of salutation later that night.

She had made a deep impression on Cochran. He thought of her continuously through dinner, scarcely knowing what he was eating, and contributing to the conversation mechanically, when he did so at all. And when it was time to go he saw that Gull was fast asleep in an armchair.

He decided to deputise for him. He made his way back to Miss Dade's house and hurled a few small stones at her window where she presently appeared and chatted for a while.

To her mother's displeasure, they met frequently after this. He was too much of a 'man about town', she thought, for her sixteen-year-old daughter.

As so often happens in such situations, this undercurrent of disapproval came to a head over some trifling incident. Because she imagined Cochran bore a slight resemblance to Arthur Roberts, Evelyn had been in the habit of cutting photographs of this famous comedian from the newspapers and pasting them round her bedroom walls. The treatment of pop favourites in this manner today is not therefore such a recent phenomenon!

Her mother tore the photographs down and destroyed them. This sparked off a furious row followed by a family meeting to decide what was to be done with the wayward and obstinate girl. She was sent off to stay with an uncle in Dublin, arrangements having been made for her to proceed from his house after a week or so to a convent. This happened very quickly, and her relatives had guarded her so efficiently that she was unable to let Cochran know; her sudden disappearance, so perplexingly alien to the character of the girl he knew, hurt and troubled him deeply. He eventually received a letter which had been secretly posted for her by an Irish servant. It contained a brave suggestion of a clandestine assignation at a particular confectioner's shop where they met, as arranged, and wandered round the Dublin streets planning an elopement. Her uncle would be seeing her off to the convent in the next few days and they agreed that Cochran should board the train which they would leave at the first stop, return to Dublin together and then carry on to London. But this ruse proved unnecessary because when she saw Cochran board the train a few minutes before departure time, she persuaded her uncle to go home; there was no need, she insisted, for him to wait for the train to pull out.

As soon as he moved away from her carriage door and disappeared in the crowds beyond the barrier, Cochran joined her and together they seized her belongings from the luggage van, left the station and took a cab to the harbour where they booked their passage for the journey to England.

Soon after their arrival in London they married by special licence at a register office in Henrietta Street, Covent Garden. That was in 1905. Evelyn was then twenty and Cochran thirty-two.

The Miracle

THANKS TO HACKENSCHMIDT, who guaranteed to pay
£15 a week to all the creditors until the debts were liquidated,
Cochran's discharge from bankruptcy was achieved in record
time. Furthermore, he began doing well again. So much so that
he set about helping his old friends. He wrote to his brother,
Alec:

> 7 Buckingham Gate Mansions,
> SW.
> March 29, '04

Dear Alec,

    Frank tells me you're out of a job. I can start you at once
if you like at £100 a year and I think you'll have a good chance
of getting on as my business is increasing rapidly and you can
grow with it.

    Before you take on the job, however, get it well into your
head that it means hard work and no larks – all hours with us
are business hours and no matter what arrangements for your
pleasure you may have made, they must, if anything important
crops up, be put aside to attend to business.

    If you like you can come to town and start on Tuesday when
I can put you up for a day or two.

> Yours affectionately,
> Charlie

Yet in the year following his marriage, he seems to have
been in low water again. From dealing in pretty substantial

sums of money, he now evidently had difficulty in discharging a paltry debt of forty-five pounds to a certain Mr Kent.

His promise of repayment by instalments was guaranteed by brother Alec to whom he had been offering work only two years before:

CHARLES B COCHRAN

Telegrams :

COCKAIGNE, LONDON

Tel : 4319 Central

10 Leicester Place,
London WC.
July 28th, 1906

Dear Mr Kent,

For value received I agree to pay you the sum of Forty five pounds by instalments as follows :

£7 10s	on Aug 4th
7 10s	11th
7 10s	18th
7 10s	25th
7 10s	Sept 1st
7 10s	Sept 8th

Yours faithfully,
Charles B Cochran

I guarantee the prompt repayment of instalments specified in this letter amounting in all to Forty five pounds and in the event of Mr C B Cochran failing to fulfill this agreement I hold myself liable to you for the full amount.

J A Cochran 28 7 06

And, in order to meet this obligation, he gave the following instruction to Sherek and Braff, theatrical agents :

Dear Sirs,

I hereby authorise you to deduct from my weekly drawing allowance the sum of seven pounds ten shillings (£7 10s) commencing Saturday 4th August 1906 until the sum of £45 (Forty five pounds) be paid and remit the same to my brother J A Cochran this being an amount due him by me.

C B Cochran

Anything new in the field of entertainment was bound to excite Cochran's interest.

When he was in Newcastle with Zbysco, he was greatly struck by the popularity of roller skating in the town and resolved at once to exploit the possibilities of this sport in London. In order to see the promoters he travelled to their offices in Liverpool where, he discovered, there was an even bigger and more flourishing rink.

His daring and versatility were extraordinary. Every type and variety of entertainment or recreation became his potential domain. Never once did he doubt his ability to capture new and unfamiliar territory. The public was there to be wooed and won; he had only to cast about for some new form of amusement that he believed would seize its imagination and he would switch from one activity to another with unquestioning confidence.

He would introduce – or reintroduce – roller skating to London and start a craze.

In conjunction with C P Crawford, an American showman who had introduced roller skating to the North of England, he took Olympia, advertised it as the greatest skating rink in the world, and – to use a modern expression – skating became the 'in' thing in London.

It unfortunately resulted in so many romantic escapades between young married women and their handsome instructors that this seemingly innocuous pastime gradually acquired a scandalous reputation.

The boom passed its peak and the decline was rapid.

Undismayed, however, Crawford exported the craze to Holland, Germany and France and appointed Cochran managing director of his Continental skating empire.

This required Cochran to make frequent visits to the Continent where he took good note of the world of entertainment, collecting information and absorbing impressions for possible adaptation in the weeks and months to come.

The American comic actor, Romney Brent, told me that when he wrote the stage version of *Nymph Errant* from James Laver's novel at the beginning of the 1930s, he and Cochran went to Paris on a search for artists to play the foreign parts. As their cab passed the Place Victor Hugo, Brent pointed to a large garage and said, 'That used to be a rink called St Didier, where my parents took me roller skating as a child.'

'Is that so?' replied Cochran drily. 'Well, I used to run it!'

If ever a man improved the shining hour, cast an eye on the main chance, never missed a trick – to quote some of the familiar clichés that describe the eternal opportunist – Charles B Cochran was that man. But the most ironical misfortune of his roller skating era centred on the fine rink, the best one of all, that Crawford had set up in the residential district of Berlin at the end of the Kurfurstendam. Having succeeded in encouraging the Berlin populace to take up skating, Cochran and Crawford were mortified to discover that, given the excellent German roads – yes, even then – everyone was skating freely along the highways; and, to rub salt into the wound, the best stretch of road was just beyond the rink which meant that the promoters had the bitter experience of seeing the devotees of the vogue they had created careering gaily past the windows of their comparatively deserted hall.

While, during the London boom, the main hall of Olympia was being used as a rink, Cochran pondered the question of how to make the most profitable use of the annexe. It was a credit to his fruitful imagination, if not perhaps to his sense of fitness and decorum, that he conceived the idea of a Midget City inhabited by a hundred dwarfs with their own miniature shops, theatre, circus and police and fire stations.

Is it due to our better understanding of these unfortunate sports of nature, victims of a glandular malfunction, that the idea of presenting them to a gawping public as objects of amusement is unseemly and repulsive? If so, then perhaps we judge this clever and resourceful impresario too harshly. And it may be a valid counter argument that the dwarfs participated of their own will and prized these exhibitions as a means of livelihood otherwise denied them.

Today, however, the idea suggests abominable lack of taste – particularly as the publicity arrangements went so far as to launch the enterprise with a dinner party in the Savoy restaurant with forty dwarfs disporting themselves at a great round table.

One of the midgets, an Indian named Sonaun Singh Hpoo, mysteriously disappeared from Olympia for two days. Seeking an explanation of the little man's absence, Cochran was surprised and amused to learn that he had been lured to supper by a beautiful woman who had been to see the show. Jaded, no doubt, by the commonplace forms of sexual activity and intrigued by his potentiality as a novel source of amusement – or original sin, as it might well be called – she held him captive in her Mayfair flat where they seem to have had a prolonged orgy of champagne and erotic indulgence.

What prompted Cochran to create his Midget City was the report that Barnum had made £150,000 by exhibiting the world's most famous dwarf, General Tom Thumb, in Europe. Receipts from his appearance at the old Egyptian Hall, Piccadilly, were as high as £600 a day. And when, shortly afterwards, Benjamin Robert Haydon, the painter, received £17 in a week for the exhibition of his latest picture in the same hall, he cut his throat in despair.

Cochran's flair for inventing or discovering entertainment novelties became so well-known that George Considine, an acquaintance from his New York days, wrote and asked if he could supply a new attraction for the Dreamland fair on Coney Island.

He cabled back: WOULD YOU LIKE PERFORMING FLEAS?

Considine replied: STOP KIDDING. SERIOUSLY WE WANT AN ATTRACTION.

Cochran's next communication read: I'M SERIOUS. TROUPES OF PERFORMING FLEAS WERE VERY COMMON IN MY YOUNG

DAYS. ALTHOUGH I'VE NOT SEEN THEM LATELY I'M SURE I
COULD DIG ONE UP.

Back came the message : FINE. GO AHEAD.

But where to begin? There used to be a flea show at the Old
Westminster Aquarium. He traced some people who had been
associated with the Aquarium and, through one or two further
introductions, met someone named Stewart, a successful flea
impresario, who came out of a comfortable retirement to train
a collection of these versatile parasites and take them to
America for 125 dollars a week.

It so happened that Cochran was in New York on other
business shortly before the opening of the flea circus which,
while having been a feature of country fairs in England for
many years, was quite unknown in America.

The press made much of it, the subject being irresistible to
humorous writers, while scientific journalists wrote learned
papers on the information this unusual form of entertainment
might yield on insect behaviour.

But, alas, disaster overtook the microscopic passengers.
Three were dead on arrival, the rest so lethargic that not one of
them could be coaxed into a jump. The next day all were dead.

Visitors to Dreamland sought the performing fleas in vain,
and the elaborately painted booth that Stewart had provided
stood empty.

Cochran suggested calling on some of the cheap lodging
houses and the squalid wooden shanties on Coney Island and
offering dollar bills for a dozen fleas.

It proved a fruitless and humiliating quest, for Cochran
scarcely enjoyed the reactions of suspicion and contempt which
his inquiries provoked.

Clearly there were no fleas in Coney Island or New York.
Someone at the hotel pointed out that they were plentiful in
California. Wires were sent to agents in Los Angeles and a
week later boxes of fleas began arriving.

But Stewart had lost hope. Cochran looked for him all over

New York only to learn that he had met the skipper of a tramp steamer the previous day and sailed back with him to Leith.

The spirit of showmanship – a driving compulsion to entertain the public at all levels – became such a powerful factor in C B Cochran's life that it turned him into a man who could switch from wrestling exhibitions, midgets and performing fleas to a totally different frame of mind which enabled him to experience the deepest emotional and intellectual response to the sight of Sybil Thorndyke's *Saint Joan* and Max Reinhardt's productions of *A Midsummer Night's Dream, A Winter's Tale* and *Oedipus Rex*.

His personality was kaleidoscopic, producing an infinite variety of new patterns on the gentlest impulse. Has there ever been a comparable man; a fight promoter, a Coney Island cheap-jack who, on seeing Wedekind's *Fruhlingserwarten,* could write, 'I can remember no other performance at the theatre which gripped me so painfully that I felt I could stand it no longer'?

'It remained for me to see *Sumurun,* as presented in Berlin, to become really enthusiastic about the genius of Reinhardt,' he wrote in *Secrets of a Showman.* 'It gave me supreme delight to stumble quite unexpectedly against something of extreme beauty in a theatre. Only once have I had a more vivid experience; that was the first time I saw the Russian Ballet, with its new and glorious settings by Bakst, the wonderful music of Rimsky-Korsakof, and the remarkable personnel, including Nijinsky, Karsavina, Bohm, Fokine, and Ida Rubenstein, and the then superb corps de ballet. It was in a state bordering upon intoxication that one found oneself in the street after seeing for the first time that incomparable troupe in *Scheherazade, Carnival* and *The Spectre de la Rose* in one evening.'

He walked away from the Circus Schumann Theatre in Berlin after seeing Reinhardt's production of *Oedipus* with a passion-ate longing to work with him. The idea germinated in his mind;

some kind of large-scale spectacle at Olympia, a presentation of mighty and heroic proportions.

The idea of size and lavishness began to dominate his creative thinking, much as it had with Wagner and Berlioz; I make the comparison not, of course, on the artistic plane, but merely to illustrate the inherent needs of Cochran's personality and outlook.

The fugitive from Brighton, the thrusting, ambitious young harum-scarum who struggled with unshakeable faith in rough lodgings and the seamier jungles of the American show world, was now profiting from these brittle and abrasive experiences and, at the same time, maturing into a sleek, well-groomed and recognised member of that strange world-within-a-world: the London theatre.

Personality radiated from the odd, square face, surmounted by a centre parting. Always dapper, he wore immaculate clothes, shoes with a looking-glass polish and a large diamond tie-pin, not as a vulgar advertisement of his new prosperity, but because it was a fashion of the time, particularly in the theatre world where it was regarded as a symbol of substance and a means of inspiring the confidence so essential to delicate negotiations.

He returned to London, still obsessed with the notion of some kind of mammoth production and searched his mind for a subject. After taking an option on Olympia for the beginning of 1911 he again visited Germany. He called at the Deutsches Theatre but found that Reinhardt and his associates were in Budapest. How like Cochran to make a Continental journey on the impulse, and without first ascertaining that the people he wished to see were available. He followed in their wake and suddenly in the train the idea came to him. He saw Olympia as a cathedral with a great rose window at one end, fluted columns and the lighting so controlled as to cast a gentle glow: the perfect setting for a medieval mystery play.

In Budapest Reinhardt's secretary, the Baron von Gersdorff, had warned the great German impresario that Cochran would

be joining them. A place was kept at the supper party which
Reinhardt was giving in his hotel. The party continued until
well after midnight when Reinhardt took Cochran to a café
where they discussed the project. Reinhardt was a little shaken
by the suggestion of staging a spectacular production in so large
an area as Olympia.

But, as Cochran unfolded his drawings and outlined the bare
idea, he gradually communicated his enthusiasm to Reinhardt
who, at approximately six in the morning, gave him a card of
introduction to Karl Vollmöller, a swift, imaginative and facile
writer who had already supplied the books and libretti for
several of Reinhardt's productions.

Cochran hurried back to Berlin and lost no time in presenting himself to Vollmöller who, within twenty-four hours, produced the first draft of *The Miracle,* an original treatment of
the Legend of Provence which depicted the life of a nun in the
world and was to become Cochran's most ambitious venture to
date.

Costumes and scenery were provided by the Baruch Brothers,
a big name in the heyday of the German theatre, and when the
question of the music was considered, Reinhardt was eager to
commission Richard Strauss, but Cochran talked him out of the
idea on the grounds that the acoustics of Olympia would be
inadequate to the demands of his complex and elaborately
orchestrated music. Fortunately Cochran had the support of
Madame Reinhardt in this view and they agreed instead to
approach the composer of that delightful opera, *Hansel and
Gretel,* Engelbert Humperdinck (whose name, it will be noted,
has since been appropriated by a modern pop singer).

Ernst Stern, famous scenic designer of the time, was brought
in and Cochran listened to his ideas and opinions with awe and
respect. The English producer was prepared to learn from
everyone. In dealing with problems that constantly arise in the
creation of scenery, Stern used the simplest methods and
Cochran marvelled at his skill. 'When in doubt,' he used to say,

'mask with a little black velvet.' This stuck in Cochran's mind and he used nothing but black velvet for *Odds and Ends*, his first intimate revue at the Ambassadors.

Stern completed his designs at great speed. The size of the production called for over two thousand costumes and, apart from the nuns' habits, most of them were original.

There was to be a great scene of the soldiers' homecoming with horses and dogs. Cochran took Stern to Horley where John Sanger kept his animals in winter quarters and the famous circus proprietor was glad enough to lease out twenty-five beautiful horses that would have otherwise been idle during the season of *The Miracle*.

The dogs were not so easy to find, but Cochran dutifully made a regular Sunday pilgrimage to Hungerford Market in search of specimens with 'a medieval look', as he described it. It is astonishing how, instead of delegating this kind of task to a production assistant – or even a free-lance researcher – he found the time to handle it himself.

Since, in 1911, the bill for the costumes alone was £12,000 and, in estimating £8,500 for building the cathedral scene, the Baruch Brothers lost money, it is clear that, with today's inflated pound, it would be quite impossible to mount a spectacle of this size.

Great care and judgment had to be used in casting the parts of the nun and the Madonna. First the nun: a sexy French actress who was being auditioned in the home of the Humperdincks suddenly made an electrifying appearance in a semi-transparent négligé. She wore a seductive perfume and little else, it seemed. Reinhardt said she was 'a sport' and wanted to engage her at once, but Madame Humperdinck, whose sense of propriety was thoroughly outraged, made her displeasure so obvious that the men capitulated.

Cochran next examined the problem with a famous theatrical agent one Sunday afternoon in the agent's London flat. The agent's wife interrupted the discussion at one point with, 'I've not heard you suggest me yet!' In his most gentle and conciliatory manner, the agent replied, 'But darling, this is to be an outstanding production and Mr Cochran must have somebody absolutely wonderful. . . .'

A second later he was on the floor, a twisted and semi-conscious heap. His wife, swiftly demonstrating the truth of the adage about 'a woman spurned', towered above him with nostrils distended, still holding the dinner plate that had reduced him to this condition. Cochran helped him to bed where he remained for the next two days and, in describing this incident, he used to say, 'For weeks afterwards his bald head looked like a railway map.'

While the search for artists to play these two roles continued, and Cochran, Reinhardt and Vollmöller were discussing the matter in an office in the Deutsches Theatre, Vollmöller's Italian wife, a handsome and imposing Italian woman, suddenly arrived and took her husband off to lunch.

When they had gone, Cochran said to Reinhardt, '*There* is your Madonna.'

'She looks right,' Reinhardt agreed, 'but she has never acted.'

'Then we will teach her,' Cochran replied blandly.

Reinhardt asked her whether she would like to give an audition, and when she consented, he was struck by her natural, instinctive ability. Indeed, under the name of Maria Carmi, she scored a great success.

With its chorus of five hundred, and another thousand players generally active throughout the production, an orchestra of two hundred and a weekly salary list of £5,000 which, before the First World War, was a considerable sum, this great spectacle was finally mounted and proved a tremendous success.

Yet, despite a sensational first night and good press notices, the spectre of slump hovered over the ensuing performances. Although still highly successful by normal theatrical standards, the size and cost of *The Miracle* required massive audiences to make it pay.

It attracted ten thousand people a day. But it needed twenty. While *The Miracle* became the subject of sermons in churches all over London, it provoked animosity in some quarters because of its highly-charged Catholic theme. But the public at large maintained a stolid indifference.

In collusion with W T Stead, the great journalist, who was to die not long afterwards in the *Titanic,* Cochran strove to arrest the declining fortunes of *The Miracle* with a piece of squalid and calculated knavery.

Prompted by a kindly desire to help Cochran, the scheme that Stead propounded was hardly ethical. Conscious of the great influence exerted by his opinions when they appeared in print, he undertook to write to Cochran, giving him a choice of two letters. The first was critical, but temperate and scholarly. The second, reprinted below, was bitterly hostile.

Dear Mr Cochran,

I have just witnessed *The Miracle*. But the miracle that impressed me most was the fact that in this Protestant land you were not mobbed by zealous Orangemen. Just think of what you are doing twice a day this blessed Christmas-tide!

. . . Think, sir, of the effect of this twice-a-day representation of Catholic ritual to eight thousand subjects of our Protestant King, by the hired aid of another two thousand men and women of his Protestant realm who perform the idolatrous rites of Mariolatry, and present in the most attractive fashion the aesthetic lures of the Scarlet Woman.

Has the great Protestant heart that throbs responsive to the Orange drum ceased to beat? Have you had no protests against this daring challenge thrown down to Protestants' prejudice? I fear if you present *The Miracle* at Belfast few of your performers would escape without broken heads.

How much, sir, do you receive from the secret service money of the Vatican or from the coffers of the Jesuits for this imposing and magnificent propaganda in favour of the Roman Catholic Church? . . .

It was this second letter that Cochran chose, knowing that its highly inflammatory tone would provoke widespread discussion and interest.

Because Stead had fallen out with Lord Northcliffe, the *Daily Mail* was the only national paper in which this letter did not appear.

The stunt gave a brief fillip to the box office, but the improvement was only slight.

Shortly after the opening, Lady Northcliffe had taken her mother-in-law, Mrs Harmsworth, to see it and reacted with such enthusiasm that she promised to bring her husband to a performance when he returned from abroad.

She kept her word. Northcliffe shared her zeal and said he would boost the production in his newspaper.

He thereupon instructed Hamilton Fyfe, who was then a widely read special correspondent, to write a letter expressing his astonishment that this magnificent presentation was attracting only a beggarly collection of spectators.

Cochran appreciated the motive, but feared the result. Readers were more likely to be impressed by the verdict of the general public than the opinion of one man, however famous, respectable and wise.

A reporter was sent to interview him in the hope of hearing that the box office receipts were vastly in excess of those of the previous night so that the resulting story would at once help *The Miracle* and demonstrate the influence of the *Daily Mail,* particularly in the eyes of its advertisers.

Cochran gaily confirmed the reporter's hopeful expectations. But he lied. For the box office takings had in fact slumped still further.

In good faith no doubt the *Daily Mail* and Northcliffe's other newspapers claimed next morning that Hamilton Fyfe's letter had drawn great crowds to Olympia, and this did encourage the public to go, after which the enterprise gradually prospered until it had to be withdrawn at a loss, because it needed more time to recover from its backlog of failure. It was a wry coincidence that the man who unwittingly filched this precious time from them was Lord Northcliffe who was due to go into Olympia with the *Daily Mail* Ideal Home Exhibition just when – in the maddening way that things like this happened, and still happen, in show business – *The Miracle* was playing to full houses and turning away disappointed members of the public in their thousands.

Considering the size of the cast, it was not surprising that, during Cochran's life, actors and actresses were forever telling him that they made their start in *The Miracle*, and when Gertrude Lawrence said to him, 'I was one of the children, you know,' he replied in all sincerity, 'Yes, I do know. I remember you well.'

Throughout the ensuing years, *The Miracle* was revived again and again, and the artist who played the Madonna, and who is still remembered with the most reverent affection by older playgoers, is Lady Diana Duff-Cooper, wife of Alfred Duff-Cooper, the English politician, who was MP for Oldham at the time of her appearance in this role, first in New York, in 1925.

As Lady Diana Manners, a noted figure in the contemporary social world, she was famed for her beauty and, even after her marriage in 1919, Cochran invited her to appear in one of his London Pavilion revues, but she declined on the grounds that she couldn't sing, and while it seemed likely that her appearance on the stage might attract audiences from motives of sheer curiosity, she believed this might have an adverse effect on her husband's career. It was the American impresario, Morris Gest, who had persuaded her to play in *The Miracle*.

Shortly after the first production of *The Miracle* at Olympia, Cochran was asked to take over the management of *Shakespeare's England*, an Exhibition organised by Mrs Cornwallis West (Lady Randolph Churchill) at Earl's Court.

Some huge spectacle at the Empress Hall generally brought the crowds to Earl's Court but, in setting up *Shakespeare's England*, no provision had been made for doing anything with this part of the exhibition building and, apart from its use for an occasional ball, it was empty. To Cochran, who habitually treated an unused facility in the impetuous fashion that air treats a vacuum, this glaring omission was an act of almost criminal neglect. Time was short. The Exhibition was losing money and something had to be arranged quickly to entertain the August holiday crowds. The only attraction that *could* be assembled at relatively short notice was a circus which would commit him to little more than the task of assembling a suitably balanced collection of acts from various parts of the Continent.

Although it could only be maintained on the most limp and tenuous argument that a Continental circus had any connection with Shakespeare's England, Cochran refused to allow such pedantic considerations to affect his belief that a zoo would prove a strong attraction.

And while, incongruously enough, The Big Circus and Wonder Zoo was installed as a subordinate attraction to the exhibits and booths that were calculated to whisk visitors back into the seventeenth century, the painful truth is that most people made straight for the sawdust, the clowns, the trapeze artists, the bare-back riders and the menagerie, leaving the Britain of the Bard comparatively deserted.

When faced, as he frequently was, with the problem of raising large sums of money to back his costly enterprises, Cochran often managed to do so with surprising ease; and his ability to win the confidence of backers was due either to his persuasive manner or the familiar dictum that it is easier to borrow a large sum of money than a small one.

Shortly after *Shakespeare's England* he felt a great urge to do something new at Olympia. Through his Wonder Zoo, he had had some dealings with Carl Hagenbeck, the famous Hamburg zoologist and promoter of ingenious menageries in which the animals appeared to be at liberty, as indeed many of them were, since they were separated from the spectators by a system of deep, wide trenches. In Stellingen, just outside Hamburg, Hagenbeck created a wonderful animal park, a forerunner of our own Whipsnade, where the animals lived, not in large, elaborate houses and cages, but in artificial mountain slopes, glens, valleys and plains, reproducing as far as possible their natural habitat.

To secure Olympia and Hagenbeck's participation, Cochran had deposited sums of money from his own resources, but he needed a further £20,000 which he was promised by a rich businessman who was also a great animal lover and full of enthusiasm for the venture.

While preparations were in progress, Cochran made one of his numerous trips to Hamburg with the comfortable feeling that his financial needs had now been satisfied but, owing to a mixture of trust, naivete and a curiously unbusinesslike nature, he had neglected to exchange contracts with his would-be investor who unfortunately died suddenly of a heart attack.

Plans for the great animal show were well advanced and Cochran was deeply committed.

To ordinary folk like you and me, the predicament of finding oneself suddenly deprived of the means of honouring the most heavy and manifold obligations, of finding oneself bereft of an astronomical sum of money, would represent a disaster of giant proportions. To the resilient Cochran, forever poised on the springboard of his innate optimism, a contingency of this sort ranked as one of the normal hazards and challenges of his daily life.

Walking down Bond Street and brooding over his difficulties, he thought of an idea as he passed Keith Prowse. He retraced his steps, called into the shop and asked to see Mr Prowse Jones who was then head of the firm.

He outlined his plans for the Christmas show at Olympia

and suggested that Keith Prowse might care to advance £10,000 in consideration of sole booking rights.

This proposal was immediately accepted.

Although his original expectation of £20,000 would have covered his essential needs and left a comfortable margin for contingencies, he still needed a fairly substantial sum. Cochran gave living proof of the axiom that one of the secrets of success in business, show business or any other, is to know a lot of people. It was typical of the man that, while strolling down Regent Street, he chanced to meet an ex-newspaper man of his acquaintance named Arthur Eliot who, although out of a job, was in the curious position of being able to obtain investments from monied people. And when they told each other their problems, they concluded a reciprocal agreement whereby Cochran promised Eliot a job in the Olympia show if he could find the extra capital that was needed.

Eliot thereupon went away and turned up a few days later with a guaranteed promise of £5,000.

He got the job.

Over sixty thousand people paid at the Olympia turnstiles during the first couple of days while the circus alone took £1,000 and, within a fortnight, Cochran was able to repay the advances made to him by Keith Prowse and Eliot's financier friend.

On entering the hall, visitors were electrified by the dramatic and spectacular sight of lions roaming about on mountain tops, apparently at large, and five hundred Barbary apes disporting themselves freely on the far side of a trench.

The circus included some of the finest acts in the world – a famous bareback rider from the Barnum show and a trapeze act in which one pair of artists swung pendulum-wise in the usual way while another made the transverse journey with immaculate timing to avoid collision.

Even while the Olympia show followed its successful course, Cochran was thinking ahead, looking towards his next triumph.

He was much attracted by the idea of importing the spirit of
Paris to London, of bringing to the Ambassadors Theatre the
kind of intimate revue he had enjoyed so much at The Capu-
cines. He was entering his new phase of character development
and beginning to mount productions, not now so much with a
commercial incentive as a refreshing desire to communicate his
own delight in something that pleased or moved him.

Alice Delysia

Muffled echoes of that distant era reverberate down the years from disconnected reports and impressions that it is still possible to collect from people who then drifted into his orbit.

One night in 1912 all the Gaiety girls from the cast of *The Sunshine Girl* received an invitation to a charity ball which Cochran had organised for Lord Cornwallis. I think we may safely attribute the origin of this idea to the organiser who, besides having an acute personal susceptibility to female loveliness, recognised its decorative properties at a social event.

During the evening Cochran introduced himself to Constance Luttrell, a devastatingly pretty girl of nineteen.

'I wasn't impressed,' she recently confessed to me. 'Who was this little man with a slightly red nose and an outsize cigar, I thought?' She hardly reciprocated the interest he showed in her; nevertheless his attentions became slightly tedious. With tiresome persistency, he asked to be allowed to escort her home, an offer she politely declined on the grounds that she lived with her mother who would be waiting up for her.

In the end he accepted the inevitable and, in quietly succumbing, gave her two tickets (one for her mother) for the Earl's Court Exhibition, saying that if she ever cared to call and see him at his office in Old Bond Street, she would be very welcome.

Shortly afterwards she presented herself at his office as bidden. This visit was the first of many and it became clear that Cochran was developing a more than fatherly interest in her. When she left the Gaiety to take a small part at the old Shaftesbury Theatre under Robert Courtneidge, she would arrive in her dressing room to find a posy of flowers from her new admirer every night.

The relationship deepened and grew. He sent her flowers on every occasion and none, collected her frequently at the stage door and whisked her off to the Savoy Grill for supper after curtain-fall. And sometimes they would give the Savoy a miss and repair instead to Cochran's flat in Piccadilly.

She grew to like him as a person and was happy in his company, but she deftly and firmly avoided the physical involvement he so ardently sought. These overtures and rebuffs were accompanied by the harsh little remonstrances of a spoilt and wounded ego: 'You're cold,' he would murmur bitterly. 'Cold . . . cold . . . Why are you so cold?'

But his sense of desolation was presently effaced by a new and exciting diversion. The obdurate Miss Luttrell drifted quietly out of his life, although she maintained friendly contact with him over the years – indeed, until after the death of her husband, Eric Wollheim, the impresario, in 1948. After their first brief interlude of friendship prior to the First World War, she joined Seymour Hicks, to whom Cochran had introduced her one night in Romano's; she understudied Ellaline Terris and later toured with Hicks's company.

Cochran meanwhile had become deeply affected by one of the artists he saw in Paris. 'This young woman,' he used to say, 'has a tear in the voice! It is a gift that cannot be acquired. But you can sit with your eyes shut in any theatre and know you are listening to a big artist directly the voice gives you a tremor down the spine.'

Who was this young woman? Filled with curiosity, he made enquiries and learned that she was the ex-wife of Harry Fragson, a noted British music-hall artist who, a year after their divorce, was murdered by his father. She had gone back to the stage to earn her keep.

Cochran then recalled having met her in London at a party in Harry Fragson's flat where she had delighted their guests by singing some French traditional songs. He had asked then why she didn't go on the stage. Half in jest, yet discouragingly enough, Fragson had answered the question, saying that she would drive everyone out of the theatre. 'I've tried a few times,' she whispered modestly, 'but I've never got beyond the chorus.' And it was clear that her husband's boorish observations and poor opinion of her ability undermined what little confidence she may have had.

After seeing her in Paris, Cochran asked John Tiller, 'father' of The Tiller Girls, if he could give him any information about Alice Delysia, as she called herself. Tiller assured him that she was a competent artist who was capable of deputising for all the big stars like Mistinguett but doomed, like most understudies, to obscurity.

It was not long before Cochran saw her again in Paris. This time Delysia had taken over from Irene Castle of the famous Irene and Vernon Castle dance duo and, although she was not strictly a dancer, he marvelled at her surprisingly adept performance and her natural sense of theatre.

Her contract prevented her from coming to London at once, but she promised to do so as soon as she was free. Cochran, having acquired the Ambassadors Theatre in August 1914, now resolved to devote himself solely to theatre management.

His plans for a revue were wrecked by the outbreak of war. No one knew whether the theatres would remain open. By October, however, it was 'Business as usual' in the theatre as well and Cochran mounted a little revue called *Odds and Ends* with Delysia, Leon Morton and Betty Balfour.

He introduced some novel ideas that were too unorthodox for the critics; they objected chiefly to his opening on a bare stage and showing the artists arriving through the real stage door. This, they felt, was destructive of the illusion which it was the theatre's duty to maintain.

The press notices next morning were catastrophic and, during the first few weeks, takings were poor. Yet the revue gradually began to attract some of the more discriminating playgoers who, besides recommending it to their friends, went again and again. This development was clearly giving the show a new lease of life, so Cochran introduced some new material and invited the critics again, taking the precaution this time of seating them strategically among the little knots of seasoned theatregoers who would laugh predictably in the right places, and whose enthusiasm did infect their immediate neighbours so successfully that the selfsame critics who had damned the show before now praised it to the skies.

With a brilliant company getting precious little pay – Delysia's salary was six pounds a week – *Odds and Ends* ran for nearly five hundred nights and Cochran was pocketing £500 a week as clear profit.

Under the weight of its own irreversible and deadly momentum, the war locked into place, defying the 'over-by-Christmas' optimists.

'Seeing a show' became a routine occasion for officers on leave and, after a brief period of initial uncertainty, the West End theatre settled down to a long season of robust health.

During the run of *Odds and Ends*, Alfred Butt asked Cochran if he would become his general manager at the Empire Theatre at the corner of New Oxford Street and Tottenham Court Road. This seemed a curious offer, coming at a time when Cochran was more successful than ever before and enjoying his independence. Nevertheless, he was fascinated by one or two of the ventures that Butt was then beginning to develop and agreed to accept this appointment for a large salary, a percentage of profits and the freedom, not only to retain his control of the Ambassadors, but to take major decisions on all matters affecting the Empire productions. What particularly intrigued him was the prospect of importing *Watch your Step* from New York where it was having a successful run with Irene and Vernon Castle as the main attraction.

Artists had to be recruited for the London production and

Cochran's suggestion of engaging Ethel Levey and Joe Coyne for the roles created by Mr and Mrs Castle was accepted. He also took on Lupino Lane and Phyllis Bedells for *Watch your Step* which contained a score by Irving Berlin whose tuneful and catchy songs were captivating music-lovers at all levels of taste. Indeed, Stravinsky told Cochran he believed Irving Berlin's music would outlive any other written in the early part of the twentieth century. Time has confirmed the accuracy of this interesting prediction from such an unexpected source.

With the growth of Cochran's personal stature in the theatre, his mind grew more and more sensitive to the buried nugget of talent; it took on the property of a divining twig or compass, orientating itself almost spontaneously in the direction of new and promising human material. When Phyllis Bedells left the cast of *Watch your Step*, Cochran replaced her, as *première danseuse*, with a little juvenile dancer he remembered having seen in *The Vine*, a ballet that was running at the Empire during the early part of his management there.

Within a relatively short time, she blossomed into a musical comedy star of enormous popularity and appeal. And she was known, by her Christian name only, as June.

'I gave', he wrote, 'another youngster her first chance in *Watch your Step* – someone whose life ended tragically. Ethel Levey was leaving; such a dominant personality was difficult to replace. There was nobody with a name who would not suffer by comparison, so I decided upon a contrast, and took from the chorus a young girl of flower-like beauty, delicate charm and great intelligence – Billie Carlton.

'Despite her inexperience and her tiny voice, she pleased the audience. A more beautiful creature has never fluttered upon a stage. She seemed scarcely human, so fragile was she.'

She had a nervous temperament and craved excitement and stimulation, but didn't drink, having a fear of alcohol that stemmed from a miserable childhood.

Falling under the influence of drug-takers who lured her into addiction, she tried, as we would now say, to unhook herself and succeeded for a time, going to bed early, playing golf and taking up other healthy outdoor pursuits. But she lapsed.

She looked very beautiful the last time Cochran saw her. It was at the Albert Hall.

The tragic news of her death from an overdose next morning shocked him profoundly.

'The comments which I heard made my blood boil,' he wrote in *Secrets of a Showman*. 'Billie Carlton never had a chance against heredity. That is the explanation of her downfall. . . .'

Even in those comparatively unenlightened days Cochran was generous, far-sighted and shrewd enough to regard her as a prisoner of her genes, a victim of some obscure congenital quirk that moulded and fixed her personality in an inescapable pattern.

Right or wrong, his theory was well in advance of its time.

Watch your Step was followed by several revues – *More, Pell Mell,* and a production at the Comedy by Paul Rubens entitled *Half Past Eight* which was not quite a revue, but something that Cochran called 'one of those musical things'.

This period also included a play by Brieux, *The Three Daughters of M Dupont.*

And when, in 1916, he opened the St. Martin's Theatre on a twenty-one-year lease with the musical comedy *Hoop-la,* his chorus of '. . . perhaps the prettiest collection of girls ever seen on any stage in the world' represented the first intimation of his simple but highly successful notion of enhancing the status of the show girl by promoting the idea of a top flight echelon who later became known as the Cochran Young Ladies.

'*Houp-la*', he wrote, 'created a demand for the high-priced chorus-girl and show-lady. Alfred Butt instructed his lieutenants to get the pick of my girls from the St Martin's, even if they cost double the salary of the ordinary chorus girl.'

How strangely inconsistent and tasteless it seems, therefore, that he should have tried to generate some cheap publicity by engaging Miss Ida Bernard, '. . . a handsome lady of magnificent proportions', for *Watch your Step* and announcing her as 'the champion heavyweight chorus girl of the world'.

Among those dashing and attractive show girls and bit players in *Houp-la* were Binnie Hale and Ivy Tresmand, and it was in this revue that Binnie Hale got her first chance, an event accompanied, alas, by some disquieting stresses.

She was understudying Ida Adams who displayed the curious whim of paying for her own stage dresses and stipulating that no understudy should wear them. In spite of this, Cochran had made no provision for a duplicate set of costumes and this created a major problem on the night that Ida Adams fell ill. Cochran's pleas were unavailing. Miss Adams was inveterate.

It was Delysia who saved the situation. Before each entrance, Binnie Hale walked from the St Martin's to the Ambassadors' next door where Delysia, rummaging among her own considerable wardrobe, managed to produce – and, indeed, dress – Binnie for each entrance.

Delysia's reputation was growing at a significant rate. As was his custom with so many artists, Cochran had no contract with her and when handsome offers began to arrive from other managements, including one from America for five hundred dollars a week, CB admitted his inability to compete. But he raised her salary from £6 a week to £20 and assured her that, if she stayed with him, she would be earning five times the American offer within five years.

In *Pell Mell* he paid her £50 a week; then he decided that this figure hardly did justice to her popularity and doubled it for the next show.

Watching her in the closing scene of *Carminetta,* in which Cochran flouted the accepted conventions of musical comedy by bringing down the curtain on the heroine singing a sad song, Seymour Hicks, who was standing one night at the back of the dress circle, said, 'This is the best actress I've seen for years. I'd like to see her play *Camille.'*

The Better 'ole

It was in 1918 that the famous 'Old Bill' cartoons of Bruce Bairnsfather were adapted for the stage by the artist and Arthur Eliot, Cochran's friend and erstwhile newspaperman, now Captain Arthur Eliot.

The most famous of the cartoons showed Old Bill and a comrade marooned in a dank, sodden shell-hole in No Man's Land and, to the other soldier's unquoted (and presumably unquotable) complaint, Old Bill was saying testily, 'If you know of a better 'ole, go to it!'

The stage version of Old Bill was therefore named *The Better 'ole,* and this was one of two plays that Cochran took to Brighton to read during Holy Week. The other was *The Voice from the Minaret* by Robert Hichens.

Cochran has told how he laughed uncontrollably and often while reading *The Better 'ole* and, on closing the script, decided to produce it. Frank Collins, his stage director, then read the two plays, without knowing which one the impresario had chosen; he not only took it for granted that Cochran had selected the Robert Hichens play, but was dumbfounded to learn the truth since *The Better 'ole* seemed to him to be clumsy, banal and puerile to a degree.

Cochran's child-like delight in it, however, is not surprising in view of his sense of humour which, according to many who worked with him, was – if it existed at all – of a distinctly naive and primitive kind.

Cochran's sense of publicity and public taste, however, were another matter. When he put on *The Better 'ole* at the old

Oxford Music Hall, which later gave way to the Oxford Street Corner House in St Giles's Circus, he converted the box office into a dug-out and transformed the foyer into a battle trench with sandbags everywhere so that patrons were immersed in the atmosphere of the front even before they had taken their seats. He also conceived the idea of throwing slides of the Bairnsfather cartoons on to the screen during the overture. In the confusion of the first night they were projected upside down, which proved to be a fortunate mistake. The audience yelled with joy.

Despite its rudimentary humour, *The Better 'ole* epitomised the laudable resilience of the Cockney spirit in adversity; it gently brought out the indescribable conditions of filth and discomfort under which the troops were then living, and it deeply stirred the patriotic emotions of the audience.

In the hands of C B Cochran, who had developed such an astute insight into the psychology of the theatregoing public, *The Better 'ole* got away as a smash hit with over eight hundred performances to its credit. Other companies played it throughout the British Isles. It was a riot in Manchester though, mysteriously, a flop in Oldham, Wigan, Bolton and Blackburn. It went well in Australia and five companies toured the United States where, unaccountably perhaps, hick town audiences responded agreeably to the Cockney sentiment with its homespun nuances, its delicate combination of rough humour and pathos.

The French had their own Bairnsfather in an artist named Poulbot whose evocative drawings of children in wartime were dramatised under the title of *Les Gosses dans les Ruines* at the Theatre des Arts in Paris.

Cochran acquired the British rights of this production and, at the point in *The Better 'ole* where Bill, Bert and Alf sadly contemplated the terrible destruction around them, and Bill said, 'Thank God our 'omes are still standing,' the lights were lowered and there followed a shortened version of the French play.

It was in this interpolated sequence that Sybil Thorndyke,

who was already leading the company at the Old Vic, played her first West End part.

Until Cochran took it over in 1918, the London Pavilion was a music hall, and not a very successful one. The first thing he did was to close it for a month, remove the mirrors, the gold angels and all the other meretricious trappings and redecorate the interior in a smart and fashionable style.

He opened it with a revue by Arthur Wimperis called *As You Were* in which Delysia scored a great hit with Herman Darewski's memorable song *If You Could Care for Me*.

Several American managers wanted the show, but only with Delysia. One of them offered 2,500 dollars a week for her, plus fifteen per cent of the profits to Cochran, and what made this offer particularly attractive to them both was the fact that this mammoth salary represented five times the sum she had turned down while playing in *Odds and Ends,* and she had done so on Cochran's assurance that her earnings would reach that figure within five years if she stayed with him.

Tempted though he was, Cochran finally resolved a desperate inner struggle by refusing the offer, as he had already planned to put Delysia into *Afgar*. His decision represented a colossal gamble and, indeed, a fantastic sign of confidence. But he gave the American bidder first option on *Afgar,* starring Delysia, after its London run.

It played for two years in America. And it was then that Delysia vindicated Cochran's prophecy by earning five times five hundred dollars a week within five years.

Then came the inevitable flops, a salutary corrective to incipient delusions of infallibility.

Written partly by Seymour Hicks, *Jolly Jack Tar* failed at the Princes Theatre to do for the senior service what *The Better 'ole* had done for the army.

There followed another war play, *In the Night Watch,* with a cast that included Madge Titheradge and C V France. The action was set in a French battleship, but this particular venture met with no great success for which Cochran blamed Madge Titheradge and her wilful misunderstanding of her role.

Cochran was indefatigable. New ideas, new projects and experiments germinated, as if by cell division, within his mind. He never banished or deferred a good idea on the grounds that he was too busy to tackle it. The suppression of an idea was, to him, a kind of infanticide and he cheerfully allowed the stream of opportunity and challenge to carry him wherever it might lead. While other managements showed caution, believed that enough was enough and had their hands too full to embark on additional ventures, Cochran lived under a restless compulsion to implement every notion he considered remotely viable. And, as a rule, he was certainly attracted more by the personal appeal it made to him, and only secondarily by its commercial possibilities. The large proportion of successful productions he mounted made him therefore a kind of natural barometer of public taste.

In the first postwar year, he had productions at the Garrick, St Martin's, the Pavilion and the Oxford. He also took over the Aldwych Theatre and was promoting boxing at the now defunct Holborn Stadium.

Ever since the Mansfield production of *Cyrano de Bergerac*, he had a hankering to stage Rostand's masterpiece in England and, with Robert Loraine in the leading part, presented it at the Garrick Theatre after trial runs in Edinburgh and Glasgow.

But his handling of this production gave early signs of a disastrous, if endearing, character trait that was to bring him so much trouble; an inherent weakness that allowed his unbridled enthusiasm to damage business efficiency and clarity of thought.

He spent so much money on the production of *Cyrano* that he was bound to suffer a loss in so small a theatre as the Garrick, even when playing to capacity business. Indeed, the play was a success. It filled the theatre every night. But the loss increased with each performance.

There was only one possible solution: to transfer to a larger theatre. After four weeks at the Garrick, he managed to secure

Drury Lane. The imponderable dangers associated with a transfer, a heat wave, Loraine's withdrawal from the cast after a dispute over the financial provisions of his contract, all militated against the fortunes of the *Cyrano* revival from which Cochran emerged with an £8,000 loss.

Towards the end of 1919 he presented a musical comedy called *Maggie* at the Oxford and *The Eclipse,* a farce by Fred Thompson and E Phillips Oppenheim, at the Garrick. Neither play made much of a stir.

Several more productions followed, but both their titles and fortunes were so undistinguished that there would be little point in cataloguing them. These failures, however, did have the effect of making Cochran see the truth about himself. For, after *The Dancing Man* at the Garrick Theatre, he wrote, 'I blame myself entirely for its complete failure. It was badly cast, badly adapted and badly produced. I am afraid that even then I was undertaking too much, and that my productions were not getting the personal attention I had given to my earlier successes.'

Battles in the Ring

IT WAS, as we have seen, the fixated schoolboy in Cochran that gave his approach to life its abiding zest, a refreshing keenness that familiarity failed to blunt.

Stage-struck and star-struck as a boy, he remained so throughout his life. He was helplessly fascinated and beglamoured by those rare beings who were selected not only by some inherent quality of personality and talent but also the opinion of press and public to tower above the nameless crowd. For all their essential humanity, their larger-than-life-size appearances gave them – in Cochran's eyes, at any rate – the vestments of a magical aura. Even his declining years betrayed no hint of disenchantment.

It was an engaging quality that must have contributed greatly to the sporadic successes and continuing fame of this bluff, simple, uncomplicated man.

He loved the theatre and he loved the stars, and this was a passion that consumed him from the moment he saw *Sinbad the Sailor* in Brighton at the age of five.

It was also on the promenade at Brighton or the steps of one or two of the seafront hotels that he used to see the English boxing champion Jem Smith. To young Cochran, he was a demigod of a man who deserved boundless admiration and hero-worship.

Such relatively insignificant experiences as these helped to give Cochran his love for the stage and the ring, and he diligently studied the news of professional boxing every week in the *Licensed Victuallers' Gazette*.

Thus it was that, in 1919, despite his numerous theatrical ventures, he launched a series of matches at the Holborn Stadium, although this was by no means his debut as a boxing promoter. In the July before the outbreak of the First World War, when his plans for producing a revue at the Ambassadors Theatre were held up, he staged a fight at Olympia between our own lightweight champion, Freddie Welsh, and lightweight champion of the world, Willie Ritchie.

In spite of the fact that this match was negotiated before the era of the inflated purse, Ritchie demanded $25,000, win, lose or draw. Cochran agreed to this fantastic sum. Apart from events at the National Sporting Club, there was little boxing in London at the time and the announcement of this match at Olympia aroused considerable interest. It was preceded by a good deal of publicity but, owing to the size of Olympia, a number of seats were empty which meant that Cochran just about broke even on his costly and speculative investment.

The fight lasted the statutory twenty rounds, and Welsh, winning on points, was proclaimed lightweight champion of the world, which title he presently yielded to Benny Lennard.

Cochran opened at the Holborn Stadium five years later with a contest between Bombardier Billy Wells and Joe Beckett. The Bombardier had not at that time acquitted himself too brilliantly and Cochran put him up against Joe Beckett largely as a delaying exercise to control Beckett's premature eagerness to meet Carpentier.

Beckett had an arrangement with Cochran that, should he defeat Wells, he would next encounter Frank Goddard and, if triumphant, would then meet the great Carpentier himself. He knocked Wells out in the fifth round.

The following month Cochran presented an unknown young soldier named Corporal J Blumenfeld who later became famous as Jack Bloomfield.

During this period all sporting eyes were on Jimmy Wilde. Cochran wanted to sign him up, but had difficulty in finding a suitable opponent. He eventually ranged Wilde against 'Pal' Moore, the American bantamweight champion. Wilde had never fought in London before and said he would like to have the experience of doing so before the big encounter. Cochran accommodated his wishes by arranging an interim match for him with Alf Mansfield, another American, and during this bout, Eugene Corri, the referee, stopped the fight when Mansfield had taken as much punishment as was deemed proper.

After Joe Beckett's victory over Bombardier Wells, Cochran matched him against Goddard, whereupon the National Sporting Club adopted the surprising and distinctly unsporting manoeuvre of getting Goddard in the ring with Jack Curphy for the Lonsdale Heavyweight Belt.

To Cochran's great good fortune, Goddard won, thus preserving the status quo and leaving him still in a position to challenge Beckett, with the winner going on finally to meet Carpentier. This cardinal fact raised the market value of the two contestants who, in normal circumstances, could have reasonably counted on a purse of £500, but, with the prize attraction of Carpentier in the offing, other promoters made competitive bids for the boxers which forced Cochran to pay Beckett £2,500 and Goddard £2,000.

The Beckett-Goddard fight was an ugly affair. In the first round, both men took vicious punishment and bled copiously from the mouth.

As the second began, Goddard drove a steam-hammer punch into Beckett's ribs, but a few moments later Beckett landed a right hook on his opponent's jaw and, while Goddard staggered about the ring as a result of this attack, Beckett concentrated on this vulnerable and sensitive target, raining blows on it until Goddard went down and remained motionless, trying to rise on the count of nine and then collapsing helplessly.

The way was now clear for the famous Beckett-Carpentier fight. But this major event was not without its snags for Cochran.

The match was fixed at Olympia for 2nd September 1919. During the preceding weeks, public interest was gently worked up and became very intense as the day approached. Then Cochran received the shattering news that Carpentier, who had not been well during a recent fight, was still no better and that his release from the army, which had been confidently anticipated, had been delayed. Cochran had paid a substantial deposit for Olympia and, having skilfully manipulated public expectation to a feverish pitch, knew that any change of programme would prove anti-climactic – to say nothing of the fact that a good substitute attraction would not be easy to find.

Even postponement was out of the question because Olympia was not free for nearly twelve months.

When the cancellation of the fight was announced, boxing enthusiasts took the news to mean that Carpentier was inventing excuses to cover his fear of Beckett. So, while visiting Paris, Cochran reached an agreement with Carpentier's manager that the French boxer would be prepared to meet Beckett any time after 1st November. Also that if he defeated Beckett he would meet the redoubtable Jack Dempsey.

While offering to refund the seat money, Cochran set about arranging a spectacular triple bill: Joe Beckett *v* Eddie M'Goorty; Fred Fulton *v* Arthur Townley; and Walter Ross bantamweight champion of Great Britain *v* Charles Ledoux, bantamweight champion of Europe.

Boxing journalists maintained that Cochran was being very foolhardy, that he had forfeited his judgment or simply gone mad.

These speculations as to his sanity provoked such widespread talk and interest that their publicity value proved immense. He sold seats for the fight at specially reduced prices through the box offices of his theatres and also at the Holborn Stadium. Most people, declining a refund of the money they had paid to see Carpentier, seemed happy enough with the alternative programme.

Sir Charles and Lady Cochran at the first night in June 1948 of a show given by Carmen Amaya and her troupe of gypsy dancers. Less than a week before, Cochran had been knighted. *(Keystone)*

(Right) The future impresario at the age of seven. C B Cochran (above) with the 'equestrian director' of a mammoth circus Cochran staged at Earls Court before World War One. Cochran was by now in his thirties. (Below) In 1924, Cochran brought Rodeo to Wembley, and he is seen here signing the contract with cowboy impresario Tex Austin. (Radio Times Hulton Picture Library)

(Left) Cochran admires the costume of Phyllis Stanley during rehearsals for the 1938 show, *Happy Returns*, at London's Adelphi Theatre. *(Keystone)*.
(Below) Cochran (extreme right) at a dress-parade audition for the 1929 show, *Wake Up and Dream*. *(Radio Times Hulton Picture Library)*

(*Above*) Cochran returns from New York in 1928 with Noël Coward and four of the Cochran Young Ladies aboard the SS *Berengaria. (Radio Times Hulton Picture Library)*. Six years later, in more sober mood, he is pictured *(below)* with his wife and party at London's Waterloo Station at the start of another trip to America, this time to produce the show, *Conversation Piece. (UPI)*

But more troubles followed. Ledoux hurt his hand and his match with Ross was cancelled. Luckily two other good boxers who were under contract to Cochran for the Holborn Stadium were able to step in. The next misfortune, however, was M'Goorty's conviction on a drink charge at Bow Street fifteen days before the match. The newspaper reports of this incident inevitably reflected on the sale of tickets but did not prevent the takings reaching a record figure of nearly £19,000.

The quality of the boxing was good that night and the audience certainly got their money's worth. Beckett knocked M'Goorty out in the seventeenth round, thus clearing the way for himself to greater achievements and, one night towards the end of the month, Cochran entered the ring at the Holborn Stadium and announced that the long-awaited match between Beckett and Carpentier for the heavy-weight championship of Europe would take place in that arena on 4th December.

Even though it meant presenting the fight in a hall that held only three thousand people, when he could have sold ten times the number of seats, he was determined to arrange the event as soon as he could in case one or other of the boxers, or possibly both of them, suffered defeat during the intervening period.

To compensate for the small capacity of the Holborn Stadium and justify the event financially, Cochran made fantastic adjustments to the price structure.

Few believed he would succeed in disposing of ring-side seats at twenty-five guineas and standing accommodation for five. Nevertheless, he did. And the box office turned away hundreds of applicants for tickets even at those prices.

London received Carpentier with tremendous enthusiasm and acclaim. Spotted in a box by the London Pavilion audience, he was cajoled into mounting the stage and addressing the audience in French while Delysia translated the message.

Gifts arrived for him by every post, but M Deschamps, his astute manager, saw to it that presents of food or confectionery remained uneaten!

There were further moments of anxiety on the eve of the fight because Carpentier developed a painful inflammation in his right arm. Doctors gave him poultices and he had treatment from a masseur. To prevent suspicion, greasepaint was applied to the discoloured area.

Notwithstanding Carpentier's popularity, the crowd naturally hoped for a British victory and gave Beckett the moral benefit of their support. But Beckett went down in the first round. The fight lasted seventy-three seconds. Everyone in the Stadium was thunderstruck. Carpentier's supporters rushed into the ring and carried him shoulder high. Women threw flowers and the Prince of Wales congratulated him.

They all celebrated at Delysia's Knightsbridge flat – Carpentier, George Graves, Seymour Hicks, Herman Darewski, Charles Cuvillier, composer of *The Lilac Domino* and *Afgar* in which Delysia was then appearing, and other celebrities from the Cochran shows.

The next day Carpentier signed his contract for the Dempsey fight at a fee of £20,000. Cochran was confident that it would draw a minimum gate of £100,000.

He went to America to negotiate for Dempsey. But other promoters were after the same prize, among them William Fox, the film producer. Cochran's most formidable rival, however, was Tex Rickard who seemed to have a private arrangement with Jack Kearns, Dempsey's manager.

Cochran's financial position was good. He even had $200,000 in a New York bank and confidence in him was greatly fortified by laudatory reports in the American papers.

His probity went before him, and one New York press man who knew him wrote, 'The great London promoter will be good for any sum he names. He has backed many ventures which were failures financially, because of conditions over which he had no control, and has paid the deficits without a murmur.' Another commented, 'Charles B Cochran is quiet and unostentatious, with a well-modulated gentle voice, and a most approachable manner.' 'He is about the best listener,' wrote a third writer, 'while at the same time astonishingly convincing in his talk, that I have met in years.' And finally: 'It is hard to probe Cochran to the bottom; but he stands up well under a fire of questions, and impresses with his ability even to handle a heavy-weight fight situation.'

And, in the light of these plaudits, he himself wrote, 'My enterprises have oft-times brought me into the limelight of publicity, but this was the first time, I think, that my appearance and manner were considered worthy of description to the extent of columns in hundreds of papers all over the United States. The famous writer, Thomas S Rice of the *Brooklyn Daily Eagle,* described me as having "the shoulders of a light heavy-weight, and the springy step of a highly trained athlete in perfect condition". My eyes, he said, were "a sort of cross – in colour – between brown and blue. It must be an excellent combination, for there has never been a time when he could not see a good thing." '

All this was honey and balm to Cochran who, being human, received compliments with relish and was perhaps a little more susceptible to flattery than most. Inclined also to be more egotistical than the average person, he loved public adulation and purred in the radiant glow of publicity.

But there were complications over this new project. Rickard wanted the fight to take place in the United States, but not at that time because of a certain amount of lingering prejudice against Dempsey, due to his avoidance of military service during the war. Cochran, however, aimed at staging the fight in London where this objection didn't apply.

His discussions with Rickard were friendly enough, but he left New York with nothing settled, and when he heard that Carpentier was receiving more attractive offers and was powerless to implement his own without the assurance that Dempsey was available to him, he flew to Paris, doubled his price and added £20,000 for good measure – but on condition that

Carpentier would meet Dempsey only under his promotion.

In the midst of these tricky negotiations involving vast sums of money, Cochran received a crippling blow. He had been getting bad headaches in New York. Doctors said he was over-tired.

The headaches persisted in London when he was putting his new revue, *League of Notions,* into rehearsal. Following an examination, he was ordered to bed and told that he must take a complete rest for several months and put all thoughts of business from his mind. He was forbidden to see a single letter, cable or newspaper and, although trustworthy representatives acted for him in London and New York, this complete isolation from the outside world was a form of slow torture, particularly at that time when such large and costly projects were in course of negotiation.

Owing to political events in the US, the possibility of the fight taking place in New York was now ruled out. William A Brady, who acted there for Cochran, wrote, 'I know that Mr Miller, Governor of New York State, will not permit the Carpentier-Dempsey fight to take place in this State. There is a rabid lobby of ministers and religious fanatics working in Albany to pass all kinds of laws against baseball, the movies and boxing, and their principal argument is the Carpentier-Dempsey match and the purse that is being offered.' Cochran never saw this letter. But Evelyn felt she should be guided by Brady and sanctioned his decision against trying to stage the fight in New York. In addition, new financial snags arose, due largely to restrictions imposed by the French government on the export of currency. This, to Brady, spelled final defeat and he took it upon himself to withdraw Cochran's deposit and drop the venture on his principal's behalf.

The fight ultimately took place in Jersey City where Dempsey was the victor. And it was not until he was convalescing in Spain that Cochran read all the correspondence, firmly insisting that, had he been well and fully aware of the daily changing situation, he would never have abandoned his determination to mount the contest in London; and from our knowledge of the man, his single-mindedness and tenacity, it is reasonable to assume that, if illness had not rendered him powerless and ignorant of all that was happening, he would have had his way.

It is quite possible that his illness was aggravated, if not actually caused, by the ugly, grasping and deceitful attitudes that bedevilled the boxing game. Cochran was a man of integrity. Never in his career as a showman had he broken faith with the public; and it is axiomatic that the honest and trusting man who expects to find his own standards reflected in others is no match for those habitually engaged in sharp practice.

After Beckett beat Bombardier Billy Wells in a return match at Olympia a year after their first encounter, Cochran signed him up to meet the American Frank Moran. Beckett complained of an injury to his hand and asked for a postponement which Cochran granted. As the weeks passed and no new date had been fixed, Moran returned to America, after which Beckett immediately arranged to fight Tommy Burns through another promoter.

Time and time again, negotiations in this strange half-world were wrecked by argument and misunderstanding, genuine or otherwise.

Finally when Cochran booked the American, Pete Harman, to meet Jimmy Wilde for the World Bantam Championship, Harman cabled him on the eve of his sailing date to say that he couldn't leave America. In fact the projected engagement had so increased his market value in the ring that he stayed in the States to exploit it, leaving Cochran with £12,000 worth of empty seats and every penny of the spectators' money to be refunded.

This was the final blow, the last act of treachery. The passionate enthusiast, eager and bright-eyed, who loved the ring so much that he eventually became involved in it as a great boxing impresario, left it – temporarily, at least – a saddened and disenchanted man.

The First Rage

Incapacitated by illness, his lack of personal control had led to grievous delays in the preparation of *League of Notions* which was to open at the elaborately rebuilt New Oxford Theatre, 'the finest in London', as he claimed, and the postponement of the first night was costing him £400 a day in rent and salaries.

The Dolly Sisters, who had arrived from America to star in the show, persuaded Mrs Cochran to overrule the veto on information imposed by the doctors, and when Cochran learned the position, he insisted that *League of Notions* should open on 17th January 1921, come what may.

Before leaving New York, he had contracted for John Murray Anderson to produce and for the famous Trix Sisters to make their London debut in this show under his management.

Earle Leslie, who later became Mistinguett's partner, danced for him on a bare, darkened stage on the eve of his departure, and he too was recruited to the existing cast.

Using no outside money, Cochran financed the show entirely from his own pocket. But he was present at none of the rehearsals and couldn't attend the first night which, to a man of his disposition and temperament, was a tragic deprivation.

The Dolly Sisters displayed magnificent devotion, taking it in turns to nurse him and give a measure of relief to his wife. His feeling of helplessness and impending disaster was heightened by the size and number of his responsibilities which, despite his many able and faithful lieutenants, demanded his personal attention. At the London Pavilion, *London, Paris and New*

York needed a drastic overhaul, and the problem of finding new attractions for the Garrick, the Princes, the Aldwych and the Apollo was now urgent. There were endless troubles at the New Oxford. And, just before his illness, he had subscribed £12,000 for shares in the new Palace Theatre company.

League of Notions opened to such a wildly enthusiastic audience that Ellaline Terriss went on stage at the end, explaining that she was there in place of her husband, Seymour Hicks, who was in a play out of town and who, as one of Mr Cochran's oldest friends, had intended to take the curtain on his behalf.

Set on a fair course with the help of a glowing press, *League of Notions* enjoyed such continuous and unfailing prosperity that a long and triumphant run seemed beyond all question. Yet such are the vagaries of this unpredictable trade that a combination of wayward events may suddenly conspire against the most firmly based and thorough-going success.

Almost overnight *League of Notions* fell victim to a transport strike, an electricians' strike and the hottest summer that London had known for years. All places of entertainment suffered, and the New Oxford was not exempt.

Cochran had meanwhile engaged Arthur Wimperis to do the book and Herman Darewski the lyrics of *London, Paris and New York.*

This was his first London Pavilion revue without Delysia, who was then in America, but the new star attraction was Nelson Keys.

Hugh Wakefield, sleek and debonair, compered the show; and it was in this production that June had her first singing part. When Maurice and Leonora Hughes, a husband-and-wife dancing act, left the show, Cochran replaced them with Dorothy Dickson and Carl Hyson. This was their first appearance in London and, when George Grossmith was casting *Sally* and Dorothy Dickson made a bid for the name role and got it, Cochran was delighted to release her for this big opportunity. And it was in *Sally,* of course, that she made her name.

Cochran greatly admired Keys as an artist, but found him perverse, autocratic and difficult, traits which led to endless squabbles and arguments. During Cochran's absence in Spain, Keys ignored the authority of those he left in charge. He told all the chorus girls to walk out during rehearsal; on another occasion he ordered a number of shirts from one of the most expensive shirtmakers, saying that Charles Thorburn, the front-of-house manager, would sign for them. Thorburn rightly protested that, if the shirts were needed for the show, they should have been ordered through the office. So Keys applied a little moral blackmail, threatening to walk out of the show if the shirts were not accepted on behalf of the Cochran management. Poor Thorburn had no alternative but to pay and keep the temperamental artist happy.

Reports of these incidents reached Cochran's ears on his return. But Keys made no allusion to them and when he broached the subject of the next show Cochran said, 'But I just daren't take you, Bunch; you're too expensive for me. You cost too much to dress. I used to think Delysia's dressmaker's bills were ruinous. And she has to *look* gorgeous. But your bills are twice as big as hers. Do you know what you've spent since *London, Paris and New York* opened? Over seven hundred pounds. Look, here's one item. Forty-two pounds for your fake teeth for the Japanese scene. And here's another. Shoes. Four guineas. And another pair. Four guineas.'

Keys reacted with great indignation to these criticisms.

'You don't expect me to go on stage looking like a tramp, do you? I only wear the best – on and off.'

Cochran peered down at Keys's feet.

'Those,' he said, 'look like Mansfield's ready made.'

'And why not?' Keys retorted, obstinately illogical. 'They're very comfortable!'

Cochran once said to Douglas Byng, 'I'll never have Bunch Keys in any of my shows again.'

But he did.

It was during this period that Cochran was beginning to slip into major financial difficulties. He had reserved a budget of £25,000 for his great plan of reconstructing the New Oxford Theatre. But the initial work revealed grave and totally unsuspected structural faults. One which developed in the proscenium arch was so serious that it looked as if the whole building might have to come down.

There were strikes. Contractors refused to give estimates and the final cost rocketed to something in the region of £80,000.

In Spain, where Cochran went to recuperate, he at once fell in love with the country, the colourful scenes, the green shuttered windows on yellow, sun-blistered walls, the pictures of Goya, Murillo and Velasquez in the Prado, the traditional singing and dancing with their vibrant undercurrent of barbaric and elemental passions that transfigured the hot Seville nights . . .

Because of his large and expanding circle of acquaintances, he was the sort of man who met someone he knew wherever he went and, being of a friendly and sociable disposition, naturally attracted others, making new friends everywhere. Inevitably, therefore, in Spain too, he gravitated into the orbit of a select and brilliant coterie whose members included such international artists as Serge Diaghileff, Stravinsky and Don Pedro Morales.

Owing to some confusion over the time of the performance, Cochran arrived at the Salon Imperial, the principal music hall in Seville, just as the show finished. He spotted Diaghileff among the audience streaming out into the street; and that chance meeting had fateful consequences.

'I don't think you'd like this show,' said Diaghileff. 'But if you go to the Kursaal you'll see the most beautiful girl in the world.'

Cochran acted on his advice the next night. Although Diaghileff had not identified his mysterious beauty by name, one of the girls in the show was so incredibly beautiful and unquestionably better looking than any of the others that

Cochran had no difficulty in picking her out. He at once sought an introduction to her, and this was arranged through Carlito, the young son of a restaurateur at whose premises Cochran was a frequent visitor.

The girl's name was Trini Ramos and Cochrane at once conceived the notion of presenting 'the most beautiful girl in the world' on the London stage. Suspecting his true intentions – all the more perhaps because he was alone, his wife having returned to London to stay with her mother who was ill – his proposition was predictably misunderstood by Trini's parents, her mother in particular, who gratuitously vouchsafed the information that, although Trini had been offered diamond rings, she never went out without her. Carlito, as translator, explained that Señor Cochran was a big London impresario and that his interest in the girl was purely professional.

These explanations must have sounded familiar enough to the case-hardened mother of a lovely girl. Cochran was so taken with this magnificent Spanish beauty that, in his impetuous way, he offered her a three-year contract and a promise to have her taught English, singing and dancing. Here his essential nature showed itself again; this madcap proposition was utterly in character, typical of this impulsive romantic, trapped irrevocably by enthusiasms uncontrollable even then by long experience.

His buoyant faith, his unquenchable zeal, his naive and quixotic responses and lack of cynicism were such a likeable side of his nature.

Trini's ultimate decision to accept his offer was precipitated by a family row about money. This took place just before she was about to accompany Cochran to a bullfight – on the understanding that she would be duly chaperoned and travel with him in an open carriage and pair – and, in an irrational fit of pique and rage, her father seized her festive gown and hid it. It is a matter of elementary psychology that the girl would react in precisely the way she did and Cochran's wishes were correspondingly granted.

In London he announced the imminent presentation of 'the most beautiful girl in the world' at the Pavilion and, served as abundantly as ever by his brilliant flair for publicity, he kept her incommunicado and – when they were in public together – heavily veiled, resisting the earnest pleas of the press photographers on the grounds that 'no camera would do justice to her smile'. The truth was that, in trying to get the stage photographers to take pictures of her, she proved such a wayward, intractable little gamin that they had to abandon the attempt, but it was typical again of Cochran to convert failure into success and contrive to extract some advantage from trouble.

While Trini was in London, Cochran arranged for her to have the training he had promised her and eventually gave her a little song in English in *Fun of the Fayre*. Audiences delighted in her quaint accent and mispronunciations. Her private life in this country, however, was troubled and stormy because her mother, who had insisted on accompanying her to London, scarcely left her side for a moment and interfered incessantly with her most innocent associations, her friendship first with a young actor in the show and next with a commercial traveller at the boarding house where she lived. These attentions became so irksome and suffocating that, to the rage and sorrow of her over-anxious mother, Trini disappeared one day with all her belongings and moved to another boarding house without revealing her whereabouts. The mother enlisted the aid of a large proportion of the Spanish colony in London in trying to intercept her nightly at the theatre, but Cochran arranged for Trini to arrive and leave at different doors, and never by the Stage Door.

A little while later her brother arrived from Spain, then her father, both joining in this curious exercise from the most laudable if wrong-headed motives, and the Spanish Consul declared that never during his long residence in London had his peace been so disturbed.

But some kind of *modus vivendi* was ultimately reached. The family went home and Trini's personality flowered. She did a single act in a variety bill that followed *Fun of the Fayre* at the Pavilion, sang and danced in the *Midnight Follies* at the Trocadero and also appeared in cabaret at the Kensington Palace Hotel. If not quite the toast of London; if she didn't manage to create the sensational effect that Cochran had expected her to, she was highly popular and became more so in New York where Shubert gave her the leading role in a musical play at the Winter Garden Theatre.

Cochran discovered that the popularity of *Fun of the Fayre* was drawing support from his *League of Notions* so, recognising the depressing truth that the simultaneous promotion of roundabouts *and* swings could be a self-defeating policy, he withdrew the *League of Notions* in spite of its partial recovery from earlier misfortunes, and at Christmas 1921 produced his first pantomime, *Babes in the Wood*, with Rosie and Jennie Dolly as the children.

With the help of a good press, the box office figures were excellent in the first weeks, but immediately the school holidays finished the takings slumped ruinously and Cochran closed the show as soon as possible to cut his losses.

He next put Seymour Hicks into a translation of a French comedy which he mounted under the title, *The Man in Dress Clothes*. Possibly because the critics didn't like the play, the initial returns were poor, and Cochran was on the point of taking it off when, remembering that Lord Northcliffe admired Seymour Hicks as an artist and liked him as a person, he persuaded him to see the play from a box. Northcliffe, who had already received a glowing account of the play from Max Pemberton, went to a matinee and watched the last act from the wings.

He liked it. So much in fact that he told Seymour Hicks he

would instruct the editors of all his newspapers to publicise it. Hicks at once adopted a risky stratagem. 'I appreciate it very much,' he said, 'but, you know, Cochran doesn't believe in the press.' Everything now depended on the caprice of Northcliffe's reaction. Notoriously unpredictable, he might easily have replied, 'Then be damned to him!' Instead, however, he retorted, 'Oh, doesn't he? Then I'll show him!'

In the days that followed, the *Daily Mail* and the other Northcliffe newspapers were full of *The Man in Dress Clothes*. The box office prospered, but only for a limited time and, after the effect of these editorial blandishments had worn off, takings fell once again and *The Man in Dress Clothes* ended its comparatively short run.

Tireless and invulnerable, Cochran looked ahead – to another production, and yet another. In the history of the theatre it is doubtful whether any one man has launched so many productions, not only in rapid succession, but simultaneously, like some marathon juggler keeping a set of Indian clubs in the air without respite.

His next venture was not merely 'another show', but the most elaborate and costly spectacle he had so far staged. This was a revue called *Mayfair and Montmartre,* which title in itself contained the promise of magic.

London was agog with the promise of the new revue because it heralded the return of Delysia whose long absence in the United States had starved London theatregoers of her electric and delicious presence.

Unfortunately – and this underlines the hazards and imponderables of investing huge sums in human material, and the appalling risks incurred by unforeseen events – Delysia contracted a throat infection shortly before the opening and the doctor ordered her to spend a week by the sea.

Cochran had no alternative but to postpone the opening, never a very happy or propitious course to take, and one resolutely avoided by theatre managers except in a case of acute emergency which this certainly was.

When they opened, Delysia's voice was still hoarse, but she surmounted this handicap with captivating bravura. She sparkled and gave . . . She was her old self.

It was not the only time that Delysia's health had induced Cochran to consider postponing an opening.

Several years later in the early thirties she was seen to be not quite her ebullient self during the dress rehearsal of *Mother of Pearl*.

In her dressing room after the curtain, a worried Cochran said, 'I'll gladly postpone the opening. It's no good going on unless you're absolutely radiant and sizzling with your famous sex-appeal.'

'My dear Cockie,' she twinkled, 'you needn't worry. When I make my entrance ze front stalls will be looking like a bed of asparagus!'

As the opening of *Mayfair and Montmartre* approached, so many people applied for first night tickets that Cochran returned over £1,100 in cheques, and the glitter and opulence of the theatregoers who took their seats, the electric first night atmosphere and the number of famous personalities whose presence was to become such a characteristic of a Cochran opening, inspired a great feeling of promise, enjoyment and success. The audience included Prince Obolensky, Lady Diana Duff-Cooper, Sir Philip Sassoon, Sir Thomas Beecham, Ellaline Terris, Robert Loraine and many great names of the time.

But the criticisms in the morning papers were hostile, chiefly because Cochran had shown an incredible lack of tact and vision in the scene that opened the second part of the show. He conceived the idea of portraying a group of dramatic critics discussing the first half and making them overplay, to the point of caricature and burlesque, all the clichés, the stock expressions and familiar banalities of dramatic criticism. He failed to recognise that this sketch was loaded with danger and was surprisingly ingenuous enough to think that, because it identified no specific personalities, it would give no offence.

Here was another example of his judgment, normally so meticulous and shrewd (except perhaps in the sphere of comedy), slipping strangely and unaccountably out of gear.

Displaying to a man the natural reaction of protest under the weight of a common attack, the critics resented this slight on their professional craft and literary pretensions and took no pains to conceal their wrath next morning.

How naive could Cochran have been? The most elementary knowledge of human psychology should have warned him that the mere avoidance of personalities grants no immunity from the collective anger of the group, be it ethnic, national, commercial or professional.

The newspapers were solidly against the show and their bitter strictures inflicted such crippling damage on the box office that a few days after the opening Cochran considered himself a ruined man.

He felt lost, saddened and deserted. He saw it as an inexplicable betrayal – *et tu Brute?* – when even his good friend Sidney Dark complained that there was 'nothing pretty in a row of female backs'. What could be more beautiful than beautiful women? And had he not chosen those backs with the greatest care?

Why, the people who did come to see it – either because they had booked in advance, didn't read the critics, or paid no heed to them if they did – enjoyed every moment of the show, laughed in all the right places and left the theatre happily. As he brooded on the injustice he had suffered, his feelings of resentment, injury and obsessive self-justification so distorted his normally rational outlook that he wrote long letters to the press threatening to bar the critics from his next revue; he argued and shouted and reduced his household, Evelyn and the servants, to startled, cringing shadows who went about talking nervously in whispers. The master was having one of his bad turns.

In the ensuing years these uncontrollable rages and bouts of temper became more frequent. They contradicted his public image. Although an autocrat in the theatre, a man given to stern admonitions and directives while a show was in preparation, he never raised his voice or behaved without dignity, no matter how grave the provocation. At home, however, he was different. These outbursts were caused either by business reverses, financial problems, the failure of productions he personally admired and, above all perhaps, Evelyn's complaints of his indefatigable sexual adventures.

He worked ceaselessly on the show, making endless alterations, and gradually restored some interest in it. People liked it in its revised form; and they told their friends. Publicity by grape-vine revitalised the box office and the eventual recovery of *Mayfair and Montmartre* reached a point where Cochran began to recover his production costs at the rate of £1,200 a week – until a new disaster quickly ended this more hopeful development. Delysia had gone to Paris one Sunday to see her own personal throat specialist and wired Cochran, 'Am terribly sorry. By doctor's orders I am absolutely forbidden to use my voice or it will be lost for life. Am absolutely heartbroken. Will be back Wednesday. Explain to all.'

When the news broke, box office takings dwindled to a trickle. Mabel Green, taking over from Delysia, did as best she could, but an individual talent like Delysia's was irreplaceable.

Losses assumed a runaway character and when they reached £20,000 Cochran withdrew the show.

His nostrum for recovering his position was not to sit back and brood on his losses, to hesitate and await the propitious moment for attempting a come-back, but, like the gambler at the roulette table, irresistibly fascinated by the possibility of a change of luck, to embark at once on another venture.

As the New Oxford Theatre was now empty he quickly opened

negotiations to bring *Chuckles of 1922* over from America. He imported the whole show, paying the artists' fares and guaranteeing salaries and running expenses. A new comedian named Bobby Clark was to be the big draw.

Cochran gave two performances a day and charged seven and sixpence for the stalls.

The success of the rehabilitated *Mayfair and Montmartre* had depended solely on the continuing appearance of one artist, Delysia. And despite the disastrous consequences of this policy, we find Cochran adopting it yet again – and immediately afterwards! – in regard to Bobby Clark.

From the great bursts of laughter that greeted his entrance, in one scene as a woman acrobat or perhaps as a lion tamer in another, it was abundantly clear that the show without Bobby Clark would be no show at all. A discovery from the 'sticks', he had never played the big cities, let alone New York, but he was a riot in London where the Guitrys were full of praise and Leslie Henson saw him six times.

Yet Cochran bought the show *knowing* that Irving Berlin had contracted to star Bobby Clark on Broadway a few months later, and that, since this represented a major opportunity for the new comedian, it set a definite limit on the length of his appearance in London.

Strange, strange man. . . .

Cochran Makes a Vow

COCHRAN LIKED *Phi Phi,* its music particularly, when he saw it in Paris. But he first of all decided not to do it in London because of the difficulties of adaptation. The owners of the property took him to see it again – after a good dinner – and changed his mind for him. He was in a euphoric mood and no doubt feeling the delightful sensation that comes when the melodic lines of a score, already faintly etched in the mind from a first hearing, are confirmed and retraced.

Like invisible writing brought out by chemical reaction, how jauntily those evanescent little figures reintroduce themselves to memory. For an impresario a subjective experience of this type can be dangerous and deceptive, tending to reconcile him to a work of indifferent quality, and overlooking the fact that audiences usually base their judgment on a single hearing only.

As he had originally feared when his feelings and reactions were perhaps a little more realistic, the process of adaptation presented difficulties. Hastings Turner and Arthur Wimperis wouldn't take it on, so Cochran hired Fred Thompson and Clifford Gray, but their attempts to render the subtle French couplets in English lyric terms produced immense creative and artistic problems.

In time – and however unsatisfactorily – they were overcome, as they simply had to be, but Cochran had a gnawing suspicion that he had made a mistake by the time he came to stage *Phi Phi* at the Pavilion. In his perfectionist eyes 'make-do' was never good enough.

This theatre had become associated with so much of his work

in which he took justifiable pride. But, despite his admiration for the music, he was slightly ashamed of *Phi Phi,* considering it now to be rather vulgar and unworthy of the tradition he was gently nurturing. He was by this time enjoying considerable repute as a showman of taste, vision and sensibility. And he was loth to disturb this impression.

He carried out his threat of barring the critics on the first night of *Phi Phi.* Notwithstanding his personal opinion, it played to good houses for five months, and Cochran was convinced that, had he invited the critics, it would scarcely have lasted as many weeks.

Yet it seemed to be the rule that almost every show at the London Pavilion was, in varying degrees, successful.

'If only I had confined myself to this theatre . . .' he once sighed ruefully.

Few of us learn from our mistakes. In this respect Cochran was perhaps less educable than most. Only a few years after his health was severely affected by overwork and a weight of responsibility that almost dwarfed the burden proverbially carried by Atlas, he was again incurring massive and frightening commitments.

His financial position was now very bad. Instead of trying to rehabilitate it gradually by relatively modest projects and a careful avoidance of anything too ambitious, he did exactly the opposite, striking out with a reckless disregard for the possible consequences. In the autumn of 1922, he went to America and, on his return, announced that, during the following year, he would present *Partners Again,* the comedy introducing the two Jewish characters, Potash and Perlmutter, *Anna Christie, So This is London!, Dover Street to Dixie, Little Nelly Kelly* and the *Music Box Revue. . . .* But wait! There was more! A Sacha Guitry season at the New Oxford and a series of matinee performances by the great Eleanora Duse.

These plans, which by the summer of 1923 were fully implemented, were costing this financially exhausted theatrical tycoon

£17,500 a week which he aspired to recoup – with a substantial profit, of course – from cumulative receipts in all the theatres.

Not unexpectedly, the roundabouts slumped when the swings boomed and vice versa, but in the final reckoning their capricious gyrations and pendulum movements presented a dismal picture.

Once again it was a hot summer, and it kept the public away.

Theatrical ventures are threatened by so many exasperating uncertainties. Cochran used to make his nightly tour of the box offices, taking barometer readings of the receipts with the baffled incomprehension of an investor studying the unaccountable fluctuations of his share prices. Why was it, for example, that *Partners Again* should play to a packed house one night and a half empty one the next?

'If a show fails to pull the public in from the start,' he used to say, 'you know where you stand. You take it off and cut your losses. But when the takings go up and down, you're in a quandary; you don't know whether to kill it or let it run a little longer. And the trouble is that that "little longer" tends to be protracted indefinitely and you come out in the end thousands of pounds down.'

This happened in the case of *Partners Again*.

It was with great pride that Cochran introduced *Anna Christie* to a London unfamiliar with the works of Eugene O'Neill. He discovered to his surprise that even members of the cognoscenti like A B Walkley, the famous drama critic of *The Times*, knew little or nothing of this important new playwright whose emergence in the American theatre had created such a stir among the intellectual fringe.

The script of *Anna Christie* came into his hands while he was in New York, but he did not read it at once. He read it some time afterwards in the train to Paris and, during his next trip to New York a year later, he went to see a performance of it in Erie, Pennsylvania. The production by Arthur Hopkins moved him deeply, as did Pauline Lord's brilliant acting.

In the flush of satisfaction and excitement as the curtain fell, he was seized by an acute desire to share this illuminating experience with London theatre goers. Knowing that as it was likely to appeal to a limited audience only, he could not expect to make any money with it and was more likely, indeed, to lose some. And if his immediate resolve to bring it to London showed laudable artistic integrity, it also illustrated how his great enthusiasms and deep love of the theatre could override practical and financial considerations. In view of his personal financial position, this was certainly no time for Cochran to be thinking of appeasing the cultural needs of the London theatre. But that was the way he ticked.

On 10th April 1923, he received a telegram from Duse saying that she would like to play six matinees in London under his management. This meant the fulfilment of an ambition he had nursed for many years during which this great tragedienne, living in retirement since 1913, had persistently refused his invitations. Now apparently, she had decided the time was right, but her appearance under the Cochran aegis proved to be her swan song, for she died in the same year.

Auspiciously, or so it seemed, her capitulation arrived on the day that *Anna Christie* opened.

Eugene O'Neill's play positively enraptured that strange, unrepresentative and cruelly misleading corporate animal, the 'first-night audience'. By this time Cochran had made his peace with the critics who were there in force and, true to tradition, sat impassive and enigmatic in the sea of acclamation around them.

But the next morning they showed their hands. '. . . an historic night in the theatre . . .'; '. . . an exquisite performance,' wrote James Agate of Pauline Lord.

This unanimous praise was unmistakably reflected in the box office. But only for a while. And the reason soon became apparent, illustrating the gulf between the sensations registered in the seasoned, analytical eye of the professional critic and the shallow demands of the socialites, the philistine businessmen and members of 'the smart set' who were to be seen nightly in the best stalls all over town, and to whom 'the theatre' was merely the icing on the cake, a tinsel toy of make-believe and mummery. It was a place they visited 'to relax' and, as Shaw said, 'leave their brains in the cloak room with their hat, coat and stick'. Because of the praise it earned from critics, *Anna Christie* unfortunately became known as – to quote a sadly revealing expression – 'the best show in town', and one can plainly visualise tall, grinning, tail-coated numbskulls with immature tastes converging on the Strand Theatre, full of good food and wine, and bent on a gay night out. Their disappointment must have been so shattering that their denigration of *Anna Christie* in their offices and clubs next day set up those widening ripples of word-of-mouth comment that ultimately make or break a play.

Takings during the first week were over £2,000 and they dropped week by week until they hovered round £700 in the twelfth. With the get-out figure at £1,300 the financial picture gave no cause for jubilation. The figure shot up for one week following an article about the play by J L Garvin in *The Observer,* but slumped again thereafter.

During the 1923 season the Cochran legend grew. His name appeared on so many playbills that the public conceived him to be not only the most powerful, enterprising and active theatre manager but also the richest, when in fact he was losing money at an alarming rate, sometimes as much as £2,000 a week.

In next presenting *Dover Street to Dixie* at the London Pavilion his main object was to introduce the brilliant and vivacious Florence Mills and the dazzling, spirited team of coloured artists who had so captivated New York. Having made an unsuccessful bid for this coloured troupe, Sir Alfred Butt acquired another negro show called *Plantation Days* which had been playing in Indianapolis where Cochran had already seen it with scant enthusiasm.

Butt put this show on in London before *Dover Street to Dixie* and, as it was tepidly received, Cochran feared that it would affect his own production through association and prejudice, although, leaving aside the fact that both shows contained a coloured element, there was no real similarity between them.

The *Dover Street* half of the show consisted of a white company while the *Dixie* part was coloured.

When the curtain rose the first-night audience was tense and restrained; there was even a faint suggestion of hostility in the atmosphere.

Stanley Lupino cavorted and capered about the stage, getting few laughs, and giving a progressively dull and jaded performance in consequence.

A poor enough beginning. But in the second half the coloured artists, with their uninhibited zest and vitality and the magic of Florence Mills herself, roused the audience to a pitch of near-hysterical enthusiasm.

Here surely was a big winner. It was indeed. While a heatwave damaged the other theatres, *Dover Street to Dixie* played to £3,200 a week.

But the impresario was clearly having a run of bad luck. Troubles arose with the Ministry of Labour over work permits for the American players and Cochran, normally such a determined and resolute fighter, now felt too weary and dispirited to challenge this new obstacle which, being of a bureaucratic nature, was perhaps more frustrating and intractable than most.

When, therefore, the curtain came down for the last time on *Dover Street to Dixie* and the week's takings had stood at the exasperatingly healthy figure of £2,400, Charles B Cochran made a vow: that he would bring Florence Mills back to London.

And he kept it.

Trouble from the Animal World

NO ONE CAN say how *Little Nelly Kelly* would have fared but for George M Cohan's personal direction, and the fact that this great producer arrived from America to help Cochran stage the show without making any charge whatsoever for his services represented a large and welcome saving to Cochran whose financial position was, by this time, really acute.

It was quite a slight musical comedy, conventional enough, and with some moderately attractive round melodies, its accent being more on the music than the comedy, a fact of which George M Cohan was all too painfully aware as he sat in the stalls during rehearsals, murmuring, 'There are only half a dozen laughs in this opera and if you cheat the audience of one, we're sunk!'

One thing this show did was to give June a further step forward.

But with *Little Nelly Kelly* too Cochran made a grave miscalculation. As the early receipts did not look very promising, he agreed to let the New Oxford Theatre a few months hence, and by the time the show left London to renew its career in Manchester, it was beginning to draw big crowds. It flourished in Manchester too, but the profit availed little against the burdensome and cumulative losses which Cochran was incurring from his other unsuccessful ventures, misfortunes, errors of judgment and sheer bad luck. Full of gathering and overwhelming menace, his separate financial problems suddenly conjoined to trap him inexorably. Bankruptcy now seemed almost unavoidable.

Such was the quality of his charm and personality that he retained the friendship and sympathetic understanding of some of his biggest creditors. One of them was James Willing, founder of Willing's Press Service, the advertising agency that handled his productions. Willing called a meeting of the other creditors in his office where Cochran explained his position and appealed for a year's grace. He had made money before and would make it again. All he needed was twelve months and a demonstration of faith on the part of everyone present.

They agreed that he had been singularly unlucky; and they gave him his moratorium.

He had by this time lost most of his theatres and, having been so consistently ill-starred in this sphere of entertainment, he decided to present no more stage productions for a time, but realise an ambition he had long cherished in a much more broad and rumbustious area of showmanship.

In the silent cinema at the time, Westerns were extremely popular, as indeed they still are, and Cochran conceived the idea of presenting a Rodeo or Cowboy Championship at the Wembley Stadium during the British Empire Exhibition. He secured the necessary finances and left for Canada and the United States in search of cowboys, horses and steers.

When he finally assembled his great company of rope spinners and trick riders he returned to London having arranged for them to follow later.

As this took place in the days of Prohibition, the ship that carried the cowboys and girls was 'dry', and when she anchored at Tilbury for the night, great quantities of beer were smuggled aboard and these crude, noisy, unpolished hicks from remote farms in the semi-developed areas of the American continent gave themselves a rip-roaring party.

No such bizarre miscellany of living cargo had ever descended on London. Two shiploads of Wild Westerners, judges, veterinary staff, four hundred head of cattle and four hundred horses represented an unprecedented feat of organisation in transport.

Pedestrians stood and gazed wide-eyed as twenty coaches filled with handsome, broad-hatted, whooping young folk in the picturesque attire of the Mid-West ranchlands roared along from the docks to Wembley.

During the Rodeo, the cowboys created a great stir by exercising their skill in the London streets, lassoing top hats from the heads of City businessmen and gratuitously uniting startled men and women within their lariats' gentle thongs. Everyone was too amazed and delighted to object; and there were no complaints even when two policemen were found roped to lamp-posts at daybreak in Regent Street.

Cochran was determined to outshine Barnum and Bailey's *Greatest Show on Earth* which had come to this country at the beginning of the century. And he did.

He decided that, in order to excite world interest, he should present not only a spectacular demonstration of horsemanship and skill, but introduce an international competitive element. Great sums of money were spent on pens, chutes and corrals designed to protect the public from the wild Braemar steers imported from the cattle ranges of Texas and New Mexico.

Once again Cochran's keen sense of publicity asserted itself when he instructed his advertising agents to announce the event with posters giving the phonetic pronunciation of the word: Ro-DAY-o. This prompted everyone to say it, which was precisely his intention.

Not realising, perhaps, how rough and primitive they were, Gordon Selfridge received the visitors with an elegant, sophisticated luncheon party at Lansdowne House where anyone counting the cutlery and silver ashtrays after the event would have had something of a shock. They raided the cellar and made off with his champagne. Fortunately they didn't drink it, but their idea of playing skittles with the bottles all over Lansdowne House was hardly calculated to improve their precious contents.

The first performance of the Rodeo drew fantastic crowds and Cochran was greatly encouraged, believing that it would put him back on the road to financial recovery.

But it was a costly venture. When Cochran had first discussed it several years before in New York with Tex Austin, who organised the competitions, he was persuaded that a Rodeo in London would be far too expensive a project. In spite of this, however, he now believed that the outlay would be justified if he seized the opportunity presented by the Wembley Stadium during the great Exhibition.

Eager to prove the superiority of English stock, the Marquis of Hamilton laid a ten-pound bet that no cowboy could bulldog one of his Highland steers. ('Bulldogging' is the art of seizing a steer's right horn with the left hand, throwing the animal and simultaneously tying its front legs to a back one.) Mike Hastings, the tough, wiry young cowboy who was selected to meet this challenge, looked sadly into the animal's eyes and said, 'It's a shame. I'm afraid of hurting such a purdy li'l creature.' Allowed one minute only, he threw the steer single-handed in just over sixteen seconds.

Big troubles, however, threatened.

The Rodeo opened on a Saturday afternoon in mid-June. Eighty thousand people were there. £10,000 changed hands at the entrances, and Cochran felt so happy and encouraged by the atmosphere of success as the spectators filed out of the Stadium at the end of the show that he told a friend he wouldn't have sold his interest for £50,000.

But the evening show was attended by a number of unforeseen hazards. The light was bad and, owing to the surface of the Stadium not being properly finished, a steer tumbled, broke its leg and had to be shot, a rare enough event in this type of display, though capable of happening, of course, at any time. And the fact that it did happen on this opening Saturday night gave the RSPCA valuable ammunition for the campaign of protest it had already organised.

As a result of this unfortunate incident, Cochran at once stopped the steer-roping and allowed the men to use only their 'chicken ropes' which broke under strain. Nor were they permitted to tie their lariats directly to their saddles; the lariats were now connected by pieces of string that would inevitably snap under a steer's full weight.

These adjustments did not satisfy the RSPCA. They sent a telegram to the Prime Minister, asking him to do what he could – by introducing special legislation if possible – to prohibit the Rodeo.

And they prosecuted Cochran and Tex Austin. The atmosphere at Wealdstone Police Court, where the two men were not allowed to sit among the law officers but put in the dock, was distinctly hostile. Acting for the Society, Sir Henry Curtis Bennett made an extremely moving and heartrending speech, stigmatising the defendants as the blackest scoundrels who sought only to exploit the base emotions of those witnessing these cruel and revolting exhibitions.

Cochran briefed his friend, the great King's Counsellor, Sir Edward Marshall Hall, for his own defence.

But most unfortunately the case was adjourned after the first day's hearing and the ill will created by the action, even though no verdict had as yet been given, discouraged animal lovers – and who in Britain is *not* an animal lover? – from attending the Rodeo. Receipts slumped calamitously.

Cochran was paying substantial legal fees for his defence and it was reasonably certain that, if the verdict went against him, he would spend several months in prison. Besides inflicting incalculable damage on his business interests, therefore, the postponement of the trial scarcely contributed to his peace of mind. Or Evelyn's.

One of the devices which Marshall Hall employed to influence opinion was to make the startling revelation that certain officers and veterinary surgeons of the RSPCA collected financial rewards for laying evidence that led to convictions, and when it was realised that these particular employees of the Society had a pecuniary as well as a humane motive for reporting alleged transgressions, public sympathy swung round to the men in the dock. It cannot be emphasised too strongly that this practice is no longer employed.

When the case was dismissed and Cochran and Austin acquitted, the delighted yells and whoops of the cowboys outside the police court could be heard half a mile off. But it was too late.

Due to the adverse publicity created by the case, the popularity of the Rodeo plummeted to the depths.

For Cochran it had become a kind of desperate gambler's throw. Depending on the whims of fortune, it should have made or lost £50,000. It did neither. There was no loss and no profit. It took £130,000 and cost roughly the same amount. His investment of time, money, effort and profound mental discomfort did nothing to redeem him from the financial anxieties that lay like a stone on his mind and heart. Moreover, he had squandered a precious chunk of his twelve months' reprieve.

Some of the creditors who, at the meeting in James Willings's office, had agreed to withhold their pressure on him, now became alarmed.

They petitioned him for bankruptcy to save what little they could from what little there was.

But if ever a man succumbed to this painful and humiliating process with the sympathy and goodwill, not only of his friends and the press and public, but even the victims of his runaway misfortunes, that man was certainly Charles B Cochran.

The Harkers, the great firm of scenic designers, waived their claim against him.

And was there ever another bankruptcy meeting which the creditors closed by lustily singing *For he's a jolly good fellow* – and promising the central figure funds for new ventures?

With the irrepressible buoyancy of a cork, Cochran popped

back. Among the many friends and well-wishers who threw him a monetary lifeline were Archie Selwyn, Sam Harris, Al Woods, Irving Berlin and David Belasco.

A E Abrahams, the London theatre owner, showed the utmost generosity in writing off certain liabilities and Major Montague Gluckstein of the J Lyons company gave him a new lease of professional life with the offer of a nightly show in the Trocadero Grill Room.

His business association with Major Gluckstein went back to the immediate postwar period when he opened the London Pavilion with *As You Were*. Delysia's performance in this revue had created such excitement that the Major sought his permission to offer her an engagement to sing two songs in the Trocadero after the curtain.

Cochran was generally rather opposed to his artists endangering their voices and stamina in smoky, crowded restaurants and cabarets, but the geographical situation in this case could not have been more advantageous – Delysia would have had to walk a mere few steps from the Pavilion stage door to the Trocadero opposite. Knowing, moreover, that her excessive generosity had made serious inroads into her financial position, Cochran said, 'Right, you can have her at twenty-five pounds a song – that is, fifty pounds a show.'

·Major Gluckstein readily seized his hand in agreement, and Delysia fulfilled a two weeks' engagement which proved so successful that Major Gluckstein renewed the contract. She could have played at the Trocadero indefinitely, but gave up after a short while under the strain.

To ensure a modicum of livelihood in the shape of a publisher's advance and a reasonably good prospect of further income from royalties, Cochran wrote his first book of reminiscences, *Secrets of a Showman,* which Heinemann published in 1925. Three further volumes of autobiography, which tend to duplicate and repeat each other in places, survive as milestones of disaster in the life of Charles B Cochran. His standard remedy, on reaching the end of his financial and creative resources, was to apply himself to the gentle task of setting down some reminiscences of his colourful life with a shrewd eye to their cash value, although despite the urgency of his need, he certainly committed these recollections to paper at a more leisurely pace than Samuel Johnson who wrote *Rasselas* in a few days to pay for his mother's funeral.

In the meantime, and as the result of some exploratory meetings with Major Gluckstein, it was agreed that Cochran should proceed with some type of lavish nightly entertainment in the Trocadero Grill Room.

The site occupied by this famous restaurant has seen many changes since the end of the latter part of the nineteenth century when it was the Argyll Rooms, a famous night resort which lost its licence and next became the Trocadero Music Hall.

Cochran was present at its reopening as the Trocadero Restaurant in 1896.

But it was in 1924 that Major Gluckstein, who was responsible to the J Lyons company for entertainment, announced to his board that he was proposing to ask C B Cochran to stage a nightly cabaret at the Troc. 'It has a reputation,' he said, 'for serving the finest food. We must see that it gives the finest entertainment...'

Save for Sundays, Good Friday and Christmas Day, Cochran's Trocadero entertainments ran without interruption for fifteen years.

He lavished as much care on them as he gave to his revues at the London Pavilion next door. He signed no contract with Lyons and continued on the same verbal understanding and the same fee – which at £400 a week erred on the distinctly generous side – until the shows came to an end with the outbreak of war in 1939.

The first production was a shortened version of *Coppelia*. Attractive and picturesque though it was, Cochran and the Lyons management agreed that ballet, even of this light and popular kind, was not an ideal choice for supper table audiences and they effected a change of policy by introducing something more on the lines of revue, but without dialogue. It was perhaps the forerunner of the type of musical spectacle to be seen today in London's *Talk of the Town*, the Paris Lido and the Casino in Beirut.

The ensuing productions were staged under such titles as *Piccadilly Circus, Bon-Ton, Supper Time, Merry Go Round, Champagne Time, Revels in Rhythm, Round and Round.* . . . Cochran's loyal, creative entourage was duly roped into service. Elsie April handled the music, Cissie Sewell the dance. Doris Zinkeisen designed the sets and choreography was directed by Frederick Ashton, who had appeared in the early shows as a nameless member of the corps de ballet, and Massine. Maurice Edmonds, the stage director, who died in 1967, was last employed as stage-door keeper of the Queen's Theatre, London.

Just before *Bon-Ton,* the third production in which Massine devised a ballet called *The Pic-Nic,* based on a picture by Goya with the music of Albeniz, Cochran was taken ill and rushed to a nursing home for an operation. But, as soon as he was well enough, he summoned all the artists – principals, the corps de ballet, Doris Zinkeisen, Massine, Edmonds and others – to his room where they paraded in costume, showed him the designs and supplied him with a full report of progress.

Among his Young Ladies in those early Trocadero shows were Anna Neagle and Florence Desmond. He gave Florence Desmond away in 1935 when, famous by that time for her brilliant impersonations, she married the ill-fated Tom Campbell Black.

A 'Dreary' Coward Song

THE FAMOUS AND eminently fruitful Cochran-Coward association had begun in 1923 when Cochran saw *The Young Idea* at the Savoy Theatre and noted with a thrill of delight that the author, then unknown to him as a playwright, was the young actor whose performance in *The Knight of the Burning Pestle* he remembered having enjoyed at the Kingsway Theatre three years earlier.

He admired *The Young Idea* so much that, after the fall of the curtain, he went next door to the Savoy Hotel and wrote the author a congratulatory note suggesting an early meeting.

'A few days later,' Coward wrote in *Present Indicative*,[1] 'I lunched with him at the Berkeley, and flushed with perfectly chosen wine and still more perfectly chosen words of encouragement. I don't remember any premonition sitting behind my chair and nudging me into realisation that this was the first of an endless procession of similar lunches that dotted through future years, that hundreds of restaurant tables, bottles of hock and *entrecôtes minutes* were waiting for us. It only seemed an extremely pleasant hour, significant because I hoped that he might be persuaded to produce a play of mine one day.'

Cochran was at that time preparing a revue and had commissioned Ronald Jeans to write much of the material. And when he asked Coward for some sketches, Cochran didn't realise that this promising newcomer had already written a few lyrics and sketches for other revues and that he was, at that time, engaged in writing *London Calling* for André Charlot – despite the fact that, only a year or two previously, Charlot had listened to

[1] *Present Indicative*, Noël Coward, Heinemann, 1937

several of Coward's songs with mounting aversion and ill-temper, afterwards remonstrating with Beatrice Lillie and telling her that she must never again waste his time by sending him young nonentities with no originality or talent.

He formed this opinion after hearing Coward play and sing his songs rather indifferently in the key of E flat with the result that they all sounded very much alike.

Encouraged by Cochran's invitation to contribute to his next revue, Noël Coward asked to be allowed to write some of the music. After discovering that Coward was not only an actor but a dramatist, Cochran was now even more startled to find this astonishing young man purporting to be a songwriter as well and he treated the claim with sceptical disdain.

'Don't try to do too much,' he advised. 'Your dialogue is good and you write excellent sketches. Stick to what you know.'

In that legendary office in 49 Old Bond Street where Cochran was now installed, the fledgling Noël Coward pleaded, argued and importuned his new patron to let him write music for the revue, but Cochran was adamant. Philip Braham was to be the principal composer and that was that. Finally worn down by this protracted and fruitless exchange, Cochran felt impelled, in fairness, to make one concession: if Coward chose to submit a batch of songs, he would hear them with a view to taking one or two that might please him. Coward went away and started writing his sketches and lyrics. Ideas came easily; the dialogue and rhyming couplets flowed. But, governed either by his subconscious will or a deliberately opportunist motive, he contrived his sketches in such a way that they evolved quite naturally towards a musical finish. And while Philip Braham and the other songwriters from whom Cochran had commissioned music were still procrastinating or wooing their muses, this resolute and confident young *soi-disant* composer arrived at an early production meeting with half a dozen musical sketches.

When Cochran read the sketches and heard the closing song

relevant to each one, his disbelief softened and intermittent smiles of pleasure lit his face.

The show was *On with the Dance*. Being very conscious of having written and directed the major part of the show, Coward was dismayed to find his name missing from the posters that went up in the rehearsal period and felt that the flamboyant announcement, 'Charles B Cochran's Revue', was something of an exaggeration.

Grievances about billing are a familiar enough bugbear of theatrical life, though perhaps less common today when such delicate matters are settled in advance by artists' representatives.

Coward hurried to the Midland Hotel, Manchester, and stormed into Cochran's room in so indignant a mood that he did not even wait for him to emerge from the bathroom, but lodged his ill-timed complaint to the dissonant *obbligato* of the tap water chasing itself down the plug-hole.

He delivered his tirade with a pathetic lack of dignity. But Cochran remained magnificently calm and finally mollified the angry young writer with a glass of sherry.

Some days after this little storm had subsided, Coward raised the question of his contract which was based on his sketches and lyrics alone and took no account of the music for *On with the Dance* which was now predominantly his.

In dealing with this request, Cochran showed infinite and disarming charm, but turned it down on the grounds that he could not seek any more money from his backers; he suggested that, instead of revising the contract, they should have a gentleman's agreement whereby, if the revue was a success, he would not be forgotten.

A costly and elaborate production, *On with the Dance* contained a great number of scenes and opened in Manchester after a paralysing final rehearsal that started at six o'clock on the Monday afternoon and continued almost non-stop until lunch time the following day. The most shattering incident during this marathon rehearsal was a full-scale, stand-up row between

Cochran and his magnificent and greatly cherished Delysia who sat frigidly resplendent in a beautiful Hungarian gown and refused to go on until he had agreed to some imperious and petulant demand.

'Again!' he thought, wearily recalling a previous act of mutiny when he had beaten his stick on her dressing room door after she had angrily locked herself in because the musical director wanted her to sing *Remember* in strict three-four, barrel-organ style, and she wanted to do it *her* way. On that occasion too she had won.

Leonide Massine, the *maître de ballet,* rehearsed Cochran's weary chorus girls to the point of exhaustion while Imre Magyari and his Hungarian musicians, who were not needed until the finale, slept and dozed in their dazzling gypsy blouses all over the theatre, in the corridors and halfway up the stairs.

At eight o'clock on the Tuesday morning Cochran ordered coffee and ham and eggs for all the artists and production staff. Then he telephoned the theatre manager at his home and told him the rehearsal had been disastrous and that the opening would have to be postponed. This, said the manager, was impossible as the first night was sold out and the rest of the Manchester run solidly booked.

Clearly there was no hope of a reprieve. At 1 pm Cochran dismissed the cast who took to their beds as quickly as they could and snatched a few hours' sleep. Cochran and his stage director, Frank Collins, then spent what was left of the afternoon checking over and settling the running order. Miraculously that brief respite restored the players and gave them a new reserve of energy.

And they opened that night in top form. The audience raved.

At the celebration supper party Charles B Cochran fell asleep and was carried to his room – still asleep.

On with the Dance proved equally pleasing to London audiences who saw it at the Pavilion, and the most popular number in the show was *Poor Little Rich Girl* which was played in clubs and restaurants all over town. Its survival was due solely to Coward's filibustering obstinacy in a further tussle with Cochran who liked the song least of all and wanted to take it out of the show because it was so 'dreary'.

Until they adjusted to one another, the early days of Cochran's association with Coward were distinctly stormy, more so perhaps than at any other time, and the cause of their friction was undoubtedly the matching strength of their wills and personalities.

Despite the success of *On with the Dance*, Cochran's promise to review the percentage arrangement in consideration of Coward's music was forgotten. And it was never mentioned again by either of them.

'Stick to the Theatre'

IT WAS AT the London Pavilion in the late twenties, the era of *One Dam Thing After Another, This Year of Grace* and *Wake Up and Dream*, that Cochran demonstrated the power of the Word. By the simple device of calling his chorus girls Young Ladies he created a legend. The semantic change was accompanied by a very positive physical one that vested the proverbial stereotype of the showgirl, shallow and meretricious, with a new image of poise and sophistication.

In terms of the prevailing social definitions, however, one of his Young Ladies scarcely merited the description. She was a Cockney with no education or background. Her name was Lily Sheil and she was the daughter of an East End washerwoman who was frequently ill and so abysmally poor that she settled her daughter at the age of six in the East London Home for Orphans. Lily stayed there until she was fourteen. She quarrelled with her mother and left home, going into service as an under-housemaid in Brighton. From her meagre wages she dutifully sent her mother a few shillings a week. Then, in response to a newspaper advertisement for girls with 'good teeth', she got a job at Gamages demonstrating a new tooth brush.

One of her customers, an ex-officer, gave her a job in his business and, although he was twice her age, he eventually married her.

She was a strange, thoughtful, ambitious girl, and extremely beautiful. Her husband realised – and so did she – that her unfortunate accent would impede her progress in whatever she chose to do. He deplored such expressions as 'lumme' and 'ooer' and cringed when she said things like, 'Blimey, wot an 'at!' but, being no Professor Higgins, he sent her to RADA where Nancy Price took her in hand and wrought such magic that she acquired sufficient confidence to begin looking for stage jobs.

Maybe her speech was better. But her name was still Lily Sheil. She added 'ah' to Sheil and, taking her husband's second name, began calling herself Sheilah Graham.

It took her quite a while to break in. Archie de Bear saw her. Although his *Punchbowl* revue had only another three weeks to run, he urgently needed a replacement for one of his chorus girls who had fallen ill.

After checking that she could do the high kick, he engaged her at three pounds a week.

Her husband, who was once connected with the Birmingham Rep, had a slight acquaintance with John Drinkwater. He wrote to the playwright-poet and asked if he could possibly arrange an interview with Cochran for her.

Drinkwater obliged, and when *Punchbowl* closed Sheilah Graham received a note from the Cochran office summoning her to an audition.

She sang the title song of *Rose Marie*, while Cochran sat impassively in the stalls, flanked on either side by a production assistant. When the audition was over she heard him cry, 'Get the name of that last girl!' And he engaged her for the chorus of *One Dam Thing After Another* — at four pounds a week.

She understudied Mimi Crawford and, going on for her one night, found herself hailed as a discovery by every paper next morning.

Cochran sent his congratulations and a ten-pound bonus. He said he would make her a star and gave her a three-year contract which took her next into *This Year of Grace* with a small speaking part. She was earning ten pounds a week. At nineteen, this was good money.

Sheilah Graham next tried to do a little writing. She sold a piece to the *Daily Express* on 'The Stage Door Johnny – by a chorus girl' and, in 1933, went to America.

Predictably, and in a civilised and painless fashion, her marriage ended. She began working on the New York press and, two years later, moved to Hollywood where she broke into highly-paid journalism. Her by-line became a legend throughout the United States; and she formed a long association with Scott Fitzgerald who called her his *Beloved Infidel*.

Tracing this amazing career in his book *More Escapers*,[1] Eric Williams writes, 'By writing her story, long after Scott Fitzgerald's death, Lily Sheil/Sheilah Graham finally made good her escape, not from her lowly class into the upper classes, but out of the class system altogether.'

One Dam Thing After Another was a phenomenal success and a very big money-spinner yet, through his extraordinary, blundering and characteristic mismanagement of the financial arrangements, Cochran derived no profit from it whatsoever.

In spite of having made the most solemn resolution to give up all business connection with the ring, he now became attracted by the idea of presenting the fight between Micky Walker of the US and Scotland's Tommy Milligan for the middleweight championship of the world. The last event of this kind to be held in England had been promoted by Cochran. That was when Freddy Welsh wrested the lightweight championship from Willie Ritchie. And Cochran was now anxious to stage this equally spectacular contest.

He needed backing and duly acquired it from an investor who stipulated that the agreement should include a half share in the profits from *One Dam Thing After Another*.

Different interpretations of this deal led to an unfortunate misunderstanding. While Cochran's backer maintained that his investment granted him an interest in both enterprises jointly, Cochran harboured the mistaken belief that the fight and the revue were to be treated as independent projects.

[1] *More Escapers*, Eric Williams, Collins, 1968

On anybody's estimate, the revue – like any theatrical enterprise – was a highly speculative venture while the money-
making potentiality of a world championship seemed to be a
foregone conclusion.

But events contradicted these all too facile assumptions.

Cochran put up the biggest purse that had ever been offered
in this country. Although Walker's New York manager, 'Doc'
Kearns, had accepted Cochran's original offer of £10,000, other
promoters raised the bidding so dramatically that, in his anxiety
not to be squeezed out, Cochran entered the Dutch auction and
finally secured Walker for the astronomical price of £22,000.

His idea was to hold the fight in the open. Blackpool seemed
the perfect venue and he began making arrangements for building a stadium to take a hundred thousand people. The Mayor
and the Corporation gave their support to this proposal and
Cochran was offered an excellent site on the South Shore. But one
of the aldermen who had an interest in the Blackpool Pleasure
Park raised some opposition and Cochran had to back down
under the threat of an injunction.

The Corporation offered alternative sites that were free from
such objections, but Cochran was now beginning to fret about
the delays. Milligan and Walker were pressing him for a firm
date, so he abandoned the notion of holding the event in the
open air and booked Olympia for the night of 30th June 1927.

As soon as he arrived in this country, Kearns objected to
referees that Cochran recommended and demanded that the
fight should be refereed by no one less than the Prince of Wales.
Cochran settled this difficulty by inviting a number of famous
sportswriters to a special reception at the boxers' training base,
Fred Karno's houseboat off Taggs Island. To guarantee a fair
decision, he put forward several eminent and highly respected
referees and collected votes on their names from the assembled
pressmen. The majority vote went to Eugene Corri and Kearns
was obliged to accept this decision.

The week of the fight was a busy one for Cochran. He was in

the middle of rehearsals for *One Dam Thing;* he was presenting Suzanne Lenglen in a series of lawn tennis matches at Henley during the Regatta; and he had to direct some of his attention to a new musical comedy at the Shaftesbury Theatre.

The box office situation at Olympia reflected the traditional pattern. It had been Cochran's experience that an early bid for the expensive seats was always made by the hard core of real boxing enthusiasts. This was followed by a period in which the general public gradually took up the cheaper ones, leaving about one third of the house unsold – until the day of the fight itself when, thanks to a great surge of public interest and a crescendo of newspaper comment, photographs and speculation, the box office was obliged to turn people away in their hundreds.

Then it happened. The Nemesis of ill-fortune that pursued Cochran so relentlessly throughout his life was poised to strike again.

While driving back to London with Suzanne Lenglen, he saw on the contents bills of the newspapers, not the anticipated references to the fight, but a report of immense and shattering significance: Jimmy White, the financier, had committed suicide.

In the hours that followed it was clear that this event had rocked the Stock Exchange and ruined countless investors. It had wiped the fight off the front pages and thrown the City into such disarray that great numbers of people who would certainly have been at Olympia were now side-tracked by more urgent problems.

Interest in the fight collapsed overnight. Hundreds of people who had booked seats by telephone did not claim them. Gaping rows of empty seats spelt catastrophe.

And, on the day of the fight, the box office sold a mere trickle of tickets, probably less than a hundred in all.

The fight was, in fact, an interesting one. And, although it went for ten rounds, victory for Walker was plainly established in the early stages. The Scots boy showed great speed and agility, but could not deliver the punches. He was game enough but, as the tenth round began, he was clearly in no state to receive any more punishment.

A left hook from Walker sent him reeling. He brought himself shakily to his feet only to be dealt the *coup de grâce* by a further left hook on the jaw and a simultaneous blow on the body.

In his personal handling of the press arrangements Cochran revealed his ever-fresh, masterly touch. He invited a dozen ace press photographers to take pictures of the contest from a cradle slung high above the ring. A corps of motor cyclists waited below to collect the plates which the cameramen flung down after each exposure. They conveyed them to other motor cyclists who were waiting at strategic points along the route from Olympia to Fleet Street, beating the traffic jams at top speed. As a result, the papers were able to bring out illustrated editions while the fight was still in progress.

In conformity with his policy of giving the public value for money, Cochran had booked several other supporting fight attractions and spent a great deal of money on advertising, extra seating and other incidentals.

The failure of this event, which was to have restored his fortunes, cost him £15,000, and he lost a further £5,000 on his lawn tennis venture.

But the success of *One Dam Thing After Another* yielded little financial benefit because, under the terms of his contract, all the profits were absorbed by his partner in compensation for his own losses on the fight.

In order to meet his liabilities without crippling himself too severely, Cochran was forced to give his fight backer a 'piece' of his next revue, Noël Coward's *This Year of Grace.*

It was fortunate for them both, and certainly for the backer who enjoyed substantial rewards from these hideously inequitable arrangements, that Cochran's productions were now in an extremely healthy and flourishing state.

While everyone lauded and toasted and congratulated him on his spectacular successes in the theatre, while he was fêted and lionised, he privately endured the bitter and ironic knowledge that, in the financial sense, his triumphs were empty.

The outwardly successful major impresario of the late twenties, the man whose name spelt magic was, in fact, a forlorn and chastened figure.

His bank manager gave him a simple bit of advice, a four-word counsel that remained emblazoned indelibly on his heart and mind.

'Stick to the theatre,' he said. 'Stick to the theatre.'

The Long-Suffering Evelyn

Cochran was now convinced that, in Noël Coward, he had struck a rich source of potential revue material that sensitively caught the spirit of the times. It satirised contemporary manners, *mores* and conventions. It pilloried the decadence and boredom of spoilt youth and it appealed, what is more, to the sophisticated and monied classes who, in a more rigidly stratified society than our own, represented the financial mainstay of the theatre. And this, despite the fact that these audiences were often themselves the target of the author's barbed and corrosive wit.

It is a curious fact that my earlier observations on the sensitivity of national, ethnic and professional groups, and the closing of their ranks in the face of criticism, did not then apply – and do not apply today – to class groupings. They accept destructive identification in burlesque. The satirical treatment of their own vanities and foibles has a cathartic effect, helping them to come to terms with their inner feelings of guilt.

It was this timely recognition of Coward's several gifts that prompted Cochran to commission a complete revue, book, lyrics and music, from him.

The result was *This Year of Grace* which again had its try-out in Manchester before settling down for a good run at the London Pavilion.

And it was in this revue that Cochran introduced Tilly Losch. His unusual card-index mind had stored a pleasing memory of her dancing one night for him in Salzburg where, having arranged the choreography for Reinhardt's production of *A Midsummer Night's Dream*, she also took part in the ballet.

She had already made a considerable stir in Austria when, as a child prodigy, she had danced in a ballet, *The Snow Man*, composed by Erich Wolfgang Korngold when he was no more than thirteen. In later years Korngold wrote several operas that were widely performed on the Continent before Hitler cast his lunatic shadow on Jewish composers; his 'modern' harmonies stimulated much controversy in the musical world.

Cochran's habit of treating the whole world of entertainment, here and abroad, as a kind of huge tapestry from which he could draw some obscure little stitch, a coy, insignificant thread, overlooked by the less perceptive, and apply it to his current needs, showed itself four years later when he engaged Korngold to arrange Offenbach's music for his Adelphi production of *La Belle Hélène*.

It was quite clear at the Manchester opening that *Dance, Dance, Little Lady,* sung by Sonnie Hale and Lauri Devine in a scene imaginatively designed by Oliver Messel, was to be the hit of the show. Cochran himself particularly admired it. His first night companion was Arnold Bennett who was asked next morning by a local reporter whether he thought it was a good song.

'Good?' he replied. 'It's more than that. It's magnificent.'

The other number from the show that survives to this day as a Noël Coward 'evergreen' was *A Room With A View* sung by Sonnie Hale and a young – indeed, very young – lady, named Jessie Matthews. Not that this was her first Cochran show. A few years earlier, when she was fifteen, Cochran had picked her for a small part in the *Music Box Revue* at the Palace Theatre. It was during a catastrophic period when he had seven resounding flops and this was one of them.

Two or three hundred girls were waiting to be auditioned for the *Music Box Revue* when Cochran finally gave his attention to '. . . an interesting-looking child with big eyes, a funny little nose, clothes which seemed a little too large for her and a huge umbrella.'

After she had stepped forward and danced and sung, Cochran said to her, 'All right, my girl, you're engaged.' She replied, 'Oh, I don't know so much about that. I'll have to go home and ask my father first.'

He called her down to the stalls where he was sitting and told her what she would be doing in the show. Having already played 'girl' in pantomime, she exclaimed, 'But that's only chorus work!' which startled and dumbfounded him so much that he quickly promised, 'Don't worry, you shall have a few small parts as well.'

That first meeting took place shortly before his bankruptcy, and when *Music Box* folded after pitifully few performances, Jessie was snapped up by Charlot who put her into one of his revues at the Prince of Wales. It was such an unqualified success that Charlot transferred it to New York and took Jessie Matthews with him for the American production.

It went badly. Meanwhile Cochran was preparing yet another revue. This was *One Dam Thing After Another* which might indeed have been an ironical comment on his consistent run of disastrous enterprises.

While this was in preparation Jessie received a cable: DON'T DO ANYTHING UNTIL YOU HEAR FROM ME. COCHRAN. The Charlot revue was nearing its end, so it was not long before Jessie presented herself at Cochran's office. To be plunged from success to failure at the age of eighteen is an acutely dispiriting experience, and Jessie returned to London in a distinctly glum mood which was scarcely relieved by Cochran's surprisingly inept and tactless greeting.

'Hallo,' he said, 'what a hell of a flop you've been!'

Where was the familiar warmth and charm? In recounting this interview to me, Jessie Matthews said, 'I was only a kid. I was terribly depressed by what had happened in New York.

If he'd commiserated with me I'd have eaten out of his hand. He was the great Cochran, but I didn't care.'

'Look here,' she said to him sharply, 'it wasn't me personally. Don't pick on me. They just didn't like the show.'

Her spiky riposte disarmed him. He wasn't used to it. He mellowed a little and chattered guiltily of this and that to bridge the conversational hiatus. Then he asked, 'How much did Charlot pay you?'

'Thirty pounds a week.'

'I understood you only got twenty.'

'Well, I don't know where you heard that, but your information is quite wrong. I got thirty.'

Cochran looked puzzled. He pondered. Then, sticking to his guns, he persisted, 'I heard it was twenty . . . I'm quite sure.'

This was really most exasperating to the young girl.

'Well, I don't know who told you that. I'm telling you I got thirty. Are you calling me a liar?'

Very well; he was the greatest impresario in the English theatre, but this eighteen-year-old slip of a thing stood up and walked out of his office.

His secretary stopped her halfway down the stairs, seized her hand and propelled her back into the office.

For someone who was little more than a child to treat him with such disdain was a new experience for Cochran. Far from angering him, it evoked his admiration.

'You can't walk out of my office like that,' he said. Now his eyes were twinkling. 'There's something I want to talk to you about.'

Still petulant, she retorted, 'If you insult me, I *will* walk out. Anyway, you are wasting your time. I've got some shopping to do . . .'

'You can't afford to go shopping,' he said.

'That's where you're wrong,' Jessie countered. 'I saved two hundred pounds, and that will keep me till my next job. Goodbye!'

She got up and walked out again. Once more Cochran's secretary chased her down the stairs and brought her back. The exercise was becoming a routine – like one of his own rehearsals.

'Look,' said Cochran, a little testily this time, 'don't keep shooting off like that. I want to talk to you. I'm offering you a contract.'

Still cross, Jessie retorted icily, 'I don't know that I'm interested.'

'Three years,' he said blandly. 'Eighty pounds a week for the first year, a hundred and fifty the second and two hundred and fifty the third.'

It became a familiar ploy of Cochran's that artists grew to recognise – a preliminary affectation of Scrooge-like penny-pinching, leading gently to an offer of flabbergasting and quixotic generosity.

This cat-and-mouse tactic evidently gave him considerable private amusement. It was flattering to his ego, moreover, to release a chrysalid Santa Claus figure from the outer shell of the hard-headed businessman.

Jessie's magnificent contract secured her financial position and enabled her to build her reputation, first in *One Dam Thing After Another*, then in *Wake Up and Dream* and *This Year of Grace*. *One Dam Thing After Another* introduced the slick and refreshing airs of those two eminently gifted young writers, Richard Rodgers and Lorenz Hart. Besides Jessie Matthews, the cast included Sonnie Hale, Morris Harvey, Richard Dolman, Mimi Crawford, Max Wall, Greta Fayne, Douglas Byng, Joan Clarkson and the delectable and soigné Edythe Baker who played *My Heart Stood Still* on her spectacular white grand piano. This took place a year or so before Herbert Clayton and Jack Waller, who had ravished London with *No, No, Nanette*, acquired the rights of an early Rodgers and Hart show called *Kitty's Kisses* which they adapted for the London stage as *The Girl Friend*, the prototype of Sandy Wilson's burlesque pastiche, *The Boy Friend*, still playing as a successful revival at the

Comedy Theatre as I write. This show introduced *Blue Room* and *Mountain Greenery.*

Importing the music of that splendid pair of American writers to West End audiences represented yet another feather in the cap of C B Cochran, outsize showman, impresario extraordinary, quick-witted, far-sighted doyen of the musical comedy stage who gave it a new dimension of taste, style and quality and who, by this time, was gradually acquiring the simple, affectionate nickname of Cockie.

Such was the reverence in which he was held that only his confrères, the biggest stars, his intimate friends and those fledgling careerists who strove painfully to advance their own status by impertinent *bonhomie,* allowed to themselves the privilege of using it. Even a comedian like Duggie Byng, a Cochran artist of many years' standing, showed fitting respect by a strict adherence to 'Mr Cochran', while Cochran, of course, called him 'Duggie'.

On being introduced to his fluffy young protégées, Mrs Cochran, as much a mistress of the witty aphorism as some of these ladies were to her gently philandering spouse, would sometimes greet them with, 'I know you haven't slept with my husband because you don't call him "Cockie"!'

In his dealings with the attractive young women who peopled his world, he acted out the conventional stereotype. His behaviour in this sphere gave support to the popular legend that his power to give or withhold employment to attractive young women – and, indeed, his daily association with them in the course of his working life – meant that, while he was no more nor less human than other men, he would naturally succumb to the rich and plentiful opportunities for sexual diversion that presented themselves.

Yet he was utterly devoted to his wife and, save for these jarring infidelities, the marriage was in most ways an excellent one. Ever mindful of her, he would telephone Evelyn two or three times a day, no matter how occupied he might be. Knowing something of his temperament, it is even arguable that his helpless capitulation to feminine allure may have nourished and sustained the marriage more successfully than the most resolute attempts to suppress the temptations that beckoned on all sides.

He plied her with flowers, gifts and endless little attentions. He satisfied every little whim and desire she expressed, sometimes to excess.

She was very fond of a certain type of chocolate cake, obtainable only at a West End patisserie. And when he began bringing them home, she received them with good grace and manifest relish. But she at length became so surfeited with them that, being in a rather bad mood one evening, she flung his little offering out of the window and it fell on a lady's hat.

Society grants at least one abiding weakness to its especially gifted or outstanding members. Except in his own chosen field of the theatre, speculative by its very nature, Cochran showed no interest in gambling – that is, in cards or the turf. And his drinking was purely social and moderate; never compulsive.

'So far as I know,' Romney Brent told me, 'Cockie had only one weakness: beautiful women.'

'He was a fine listener,' Jessie Matthews recalls, 'until . . . ! You would be discussing a bit of stage business with him or an artistic problem in a darkened theatre during rehearsals. He would listen intently and keep his eyes fixed on yours. Then they would suddenly swivel away because some lovely girl had strolled into the house and you knew you had lost him for good.'

Except in so far as one may reasonably deplore the bad social consequences of irresponsible sexual behaviour as a possible cause of illegitimacy, disease and marriage breakdown, contemporary ideas of sexual morality are so fluid that it ill becomes anyone, least of all a man's biographer, to pass moral judgment on this highly controversial subject which today divides the most respectable opinion. What psychologists have called the Casanova complex, the eternal pursuit of the ideal woman and the perfect sexual experience, may be a sad indication of arrested maturity, the fixation of the sexual component of personality at the adolescent stage; but it is certainly no crime. And it is perhaps reprehensible only in cases where it inflicts misery on innocent parties.

Cochran's promiscuities were light and ephemeral. He did not complicate his private life, as did many of his fellow impresarios, by installing fancy women in expensive flats. But it must be admitted that his meandering attachments did cause Evelyn much bitterness and pain.

She was outwardly casual about them. She feigned indifference and shrugged them off with the pretence that she felt no jealousy. This attitude probably had a dual motive: it was partly a face-saving panache, a device for presenting a gay, 'don't care' front to the world; and it was also designed, perhaps not even consciously, to avoid giving Cochran the perverse satisfaction of *knowing* that she cared. For she did care. And she suffered deeply.

Although many wives resign themselves, however uneasily, to the inherently predatory natures of their husbands, it was not, in Evelyn's case, his extra-marital escapades in themselves that distressed her so much as the squalid discoveries and nasty little repercussions, the flagrant indignities that would shatter her so suddenly and unexpectedly.

A friend arriving at the flat one day found her in tears. She had just returned from her milliner, who had been cruel and mischievous enough to drop a hint about a certain actress.

'It's not that I mind the affair itself,' Evelyn sobbed. 'She's very lovely and I can understand it. But to be told about it by *her*! That's what hurts so much.'

After one of their dinner parties in the flat they decided to play roulette. He was at that time having an affair with a continental dancer. As he unfolded the green baize cloth, he murmured, 'It's awfully dirty!'

'Yes, Cockie darling,' replied Evelyn sweetly, 'just like your little friend's drawers!'

Shocked to learn that Evelyn knew his secret, it is said that he went the colour of the cloth.

She often created a mild sensation by throwing off some caustic remark designed to reveal her knowledge of such an association. It might, for example, have been in the Midland Hotel, Manchester, that she greeted an attractive little creature at Cochran's breakfast table with, '. . . and how is our husband this morning, my dear?'

She spoke with an odd lisp and would twist her mouth expressively when delivering herself of these explosive little witticisms.

Cochran once made an abortive overture to Patricia Burke which she gently resisted. The incident was thereafter 'forgotten' by both parties; and it did not in any way affect his subsequent attitude to her, either socially or in business.

To escape from the unhappiness caused by Cochran's endless pursuit of women, Evelyn began drinking and used to say she would 'get comfy with nips of brandy' in the evening. This habit alarmed her doctor who suggested that she should substitute the nips of brandy with apples.

'But, doctor,' she protested, 'I can't eat fifteen apples every night!'

On one occasion the tables were turned on Cochran and the experience reduced him to near panic. During one of his Continental tours in quest of talent, he engaged a famous Polish singer for a London revue. As she was a single act and brought her own wardrobe and music, there was no need for her to arrive in London until the dress rehearsal which went perfectly smoothly. Shortly before curtain-up time for the opening on the following night, Cochran, resplendent in tails, *boutonnière* and monocle, gaily went the rounds of the dressing rooms to wish his artists luck and cheer them along. This was his habitual practice. When he gently tapped at the door and admitted himself to the Polish singer's room, she immediately locked it behind him, flung the key out of the window, and threw open her négligée revealing nothing but her dainty self. Despite her limited English, she imperiously commanded him to ravish her, using an Anglo-Saxon word that was, in our own day, to earn Kenneth Tynan wider fame – or infamy – than all his work for the National Theatre.

For once Cochran was unhinged. He hammered at the door and called wildly for the stage manager who eventually arrived with a pass key and released the trembling impresario from his erotic prison.

The Artistic Temperament

THERE IS A tendency to regard what used to be called 'temperament' as a myth of the thirties and that anyone exhibiting it today would merely be guilty of intolerable conceit and bad manners. The word in fact was a euphemism that has simply gone out of fashion. In our own more forthright times any actress who is wayward, obstructive and autocratic is simply called a bitch.

But it is true, as Cochran was shrewd enough to recognise, that any artist is liable to be in an acute state of nerves on a first night when his or her entire career might hang on a bad or indifferent performance or the agonising mental block that causes a 'dry'.

And he made due allowances for the fact. But this did not relieve his natural exasperation over some displays of tantrum, particularly when they took the form of holding management and public to ransom with the dreaded words, 'I won't go on!'

The price of making an appearance would be the concession of some outrageous demand. Cochran was himself inclined to be adamant and unyielding, and this battle of wills that hardened into a stalemate within hours of a first night opening created an ugly situation, infecting everyone at the back of the house with anxiety and depression at the worst possible time.

Cochran never forgot one such incident concerning Spinelly who came over from Paris to appear in his 1926 Revue. During the last rehearsal on the day of the Manchester opening, she demanded some change in her finale entrance which Cochran refused. She thereupon stated quite categorically that she would not take the curtain call. The argument continued beyond the time scheduled for the opening of the show while the public clamoured to be admitted and Jesse Hewitt, the distraught theatre manager, pleaded that he couldn't hold them at bay any longer.

'Will you go on?' Cochran yelled to Spinelly in a last effort to break the deadlock.

She shook her head.

Her performance in the show was splendid and the audience were so entranced that they repeatedly called 'Spinelly! Spinelly!' when the other artists were taking their curtain calls and she failed to appear. Cochran then went on stage and the shouts for Spinelly mingled with cries of 'Speech!'

He took Hermione Baddeley and an American comedienne named Elizabeth Hines by the hand, propelled them to the wings, seized Spinelly, who was standing there in a fluffy dressing gown, and escorted all three down stage. It was fitting that they should take their curtain call together.

A gasp went up from the audience when they saw their much favoured French artist in such unexpected attire.

'Ladies and gentlemen,' said Cochran, 'I am sorry that Mademoiselle Spinelly's dress for the finale has not arrived from London. I beg you to accept her apology. And mine. But I am sure you would rather see her in her négligé than not at all!'

In a stage whisper, loud enough for Cochran to hear, Ernest Thesiger, who was standing behind him, said, 'Now I know why they call you a showman!'

Following its success in Manchester, *Cochran's 1926 Revue* opened at the London Pavilion where Spinelly worked herself up into another fit of temperament that set off shocks of alarm in everyone connected with the show. Despite the confidence he inspired and the universal belief that 'Cockie can handle it', Spinelly's tantrums proved extremely unnerving.

She had a particular admirer who was always hovering about

the stage door and calling to collect her from the theatre during rehearsal breaks. While the dress rehearsal was in progress, he accosted Cochran in the auditorium and blandly informed him that, unless Spinelly's name was put up in lights immediately, she would not appear on the following night.

'If that is so,' Cochran replied, 'she had better not appear for the rest of the evening.'

This retort was evidently conveyed to Spinelly at great speed because when the time came for her next scene, she was nowhere to be found and her understudy had to go on at two minutes' notice.

Within a very short time all the newspapers were on the telephone, asking Cochran where she was and whether it was true that she would skip the opening.

To both questions he could only reply truthfully that he did not know.

This mystery prompted the suspicion that, in view of his flair for publicity, Cochran had engineered the actress's disappearance. But on this occasion he was entirely innocent; it was Spinelly's friend who had telephoned the rumour to Fleet Street.

Cochran called a further dress rehearsal on the afternoon prior to the opening, made no attempt to get in touch with Spinelly and was prepared, if necessary, to open with her understudy. He steered clear of the stage, left the rehearsal in the hands of Frank Collins and watched everything from a darkened dress circle.

On her first entrance, Spinelly appeared and stayed with the show for the full rehearsal. But she was evidently very piqued and cross, and this black mood remained with her from curtain rise to curtain fall. It broke through so blatantly in her performance that the whole show suffered and its reception was very lukewarm. It bore no comparison to its Manchester opening and, as a result, was only moderately successful.

She knew herself, having once said to Cochran, 'Yes, I can be a devil in the theatre.'

When, as co-manager with the American impresario Archie Selwyn, Cochran took *This Year of Grace* to New York he became involved in another tussle of temperament when Beatrice Lillie complained about the quality of her material in spite of the fact that Maisie Gay had handled it with considerable success in London. She wanted to play other parts in the revue which, besides being reserved for specific artists, were not, in Cochran's opinion, suitable for her.

Relations became distinctly strained. They reached a point where Bee refused to talk to Cochran at all. As if this were not enough, frightful last minute difficulties cropped up with the scenery and lighting and, able to stand no more of it, Noël Coward took the day off when everybody was poised for the final rehearsal, and Cochran managed it himself.

The dress rehearsal was a disaster. Cochran went round to Bee's dressing room immediately afterwards. He cut one of her scenes right out and gave her firm orders as to what she would play and how she would play it.

They both lost their tempers – this was unusual for him – and shrieked at each other, Bee saying that she would not appear.

Cochran threatened to invoke the power of American Equity to force her to carry out the provisions of her contract. This had the desired effect. She went on.

Next morning Cochran received a telephone call from Sir Robert Peel, Bee's husband, who had arrived in New York for the opening.

He said, 'I have passed a dreadful night with your leading lady.'

'Then I'm glad you had to sleep with her,' Cochran replied, 'and not I.'

The show was due to open at eight-thirty, and Cochran left the theatre at seven to go back to his hotel and dress.

He was in a glum, pessimistic mood. After all the troubles
and misadventures, he didn't believe anything could go right.
How Bee would behave was an unknown factor, and a worry-
ing one. He hadn't exchanged a word with her that day.

But her first entrance reassured him. The audience went into
paroxysms of delight. And she played all the lines prescribed
for her – or perhaps I should say 'under-played', which is the
essence of her art – with the originality and skill that make her
the superb comedienne she is.

The curtain fell to a tumult of applause and Bee rushed into
Cochran's arms and redeemed herself with the words, 'Cockie,
dear, you were right – and I am so sorry!'

During the New York production, one of the girls fell ill
through drinking hooch in a speakeasy. Cochran called the whole
company together – everyone, including Noël Coward and
Beatrice Lillie – and lectured them on the subject of bootleg
liquor. Anyone who went to a speakeasy, he said, would be
instantly dismissed.

'Every one of us,' he continued, 'is an ambassador for Britain.
We have a duty to uphold our country's reputation, for our
country will be judged by the way we behave.'

Then Noël Coward punctured the solemnity of this little
address with a stage-whispered, 'Rule Britannia!'

Bitter Sweet

IT WAS DURING the early summer of 1928 when *This Year of Grace* was playing to capacity at the London Pavilion that Cochran and Noël Coward went to New York for a couple of weeks with no specific object other than to study the contemporary theatrical scene and see such shows as *Funny Face* with Fred and Adele Astaire and the Theatre Guild production of *Porgy,* the dramatic version of du Bose Hayward's novel which later formed the basis of George Gershwin's brilliant negro opera, *Porgy and Bess.*

Two things happened as a result of this visit. One was that Cochran immediately secured the British rights of *Porgy.* The other was that Archie Selwyn persuaded them to produce the New York version of *This Year of Grace* described in the previous chapter. Bee Lillie was to play Maisie Gay's part and, to suit his own style, Coward would have to rewrite some of the material he had devised for Sonnie Hale.

When all the details had been agreed Cochran and Coward returned to England in the *Berengaria,* reluctantly sharing a cabin because of accommodation difficulties; and it was during the voyage that Coward drafted the first act of *Bitter Sweet.* He read it to Cochran and described the story line of the unwritten acts.

Cochran saw the whole thing in his mind's eye and definitely agreed to do it. Providing Coward could finish it in time, Cochran planned to present it in the spring of the following year, 1929.

I am uncertain of the wisdom of telling the story of the origin of *Bitter Sweet* which must already be familiar to many, but, for the benefit of those to whom it is not, I shall let Coward tell it himself as he did in *Present Indicative*:

> The idea of *Bitter Sweet* was born in the early summer of that year, 1928. It appeared quite unexpectedly and with no other motivation beyond the fact that I had vaguely discussed with Gladys (Calthrop) the possibilities of writing a romantic Operetta. She and I were staying with Ronald Peake, her family solicitor, in Surrey, and an hour or so before we were due to leave, Mrs Peake happened to play to us on the gramophone a new German orchestral record of *Die Fledermaus*. Immediately a confused picture of uniforms, bustles, chandeliers and gas-lit cafés formed in my mind, and later, when we were driving over Wimbledon Common, we drew the car to a standstill by the roadside, and in the shade of a giant horse-chestnut tree mapped out roughly the story of Sari Linden.
>
> The uniforms, bustles, chandeliers and gas-lit cafés all fell into place eagerly, as though they had been waiting in the limbo for just this cue to enter.

The entire work was by Coward. Book, lyrics and music. Except for one thing: the title. This was suggested by Alfred Lunt.

'Noël and I found great difficulty in choosing the cast,' wrote Cochran. 'Evelyn Laye seemed to be the logical heroine, but we could not secure her services for the London opening.'

While this was true enough, it implied that Evelyn Laye was committed to some other production, but this was not so. His brief dismissal of the facts concealed a highly charged emotional situation which he no doubt glossed over in deference to her feelings.

When Coward began writing *Bitter Sweet* he had Gertrude Lawrence in mind for the leading part. But, as the writing progressed and the melodic line of the score embraced a range manifestly beyond her capacity, he and Cochran decided that Evelyn Laye was unquestionably the most suitable artist for the part. So far as they knew there was no obstacle to her accepting it; indeed they fully expected her to seize such a golden opportunity with fervour and rejoicing.

But she surprised them by declining.

Somebody suggested Peggy Wood to Cochran. He had remembered her delightful performance in *Buddies*. So he cabled Coward who was then in America. Coward sought her out and she danced and sang for him. He was so sure she was right for the part that he at once sent a cable to Cochran who left it to his judgment, flashing his assent back across the Atlantic.

Casting the part of Carl, the hero, presented a further problem and Cochran and Coward embarked on a wild-goose chase in all the big towns of Germany and Austria in search of someone with good looks, a fine tenor voice and a genuine Continental personality. On the strength of the odd hint, word or promise dropped casually here and there they would hopefully resume the chase even though one disappointment followed another with grim monotony.

Finally they returned from a fruitless journey and gave the part to George Metaxa who was already in a Cochran revue in London and, as it happened, filled the role eminently well.

But with La Crevette they had no problem at all. Coward had written the part with Ivy St Helier in mind. She slipped right into it and was sheer perfection.

When Noël Coward finished writing the operette, he read and sang it to Cochran. Elsie April played for him. Besides being a near-genius, it is difficult to say exactly what Elsie April was. She was, I suppose, Cochran's chorus mistress, musical adviser and controller of the musical arrangements that he commissioned from people like Orellana who orchestrated *Bitter Sweet*. A small, blue-eyed, bird-like little thing in hats – 'those *hats*!' as show folk still say when her name comes up – she had exceptional musical knowledge which was governed by the most refined perception and taste. The long intervals, and winsome harmonic sequences; the unusual key changes and poignant angularities of phrase to be found in much of Coward's music owe a great deal to Elsie April, and her influence on his composition has clearly survived her death. Trust Cochran to find – and keep with him for many long years – this irreplaceable helpmeet whose quaint, unprepossessing appearance gave small enough indication of her tremendous calibre.

When Coward ended his halting, rough and ready version of the operette, singing all the parts in clipped, reedy accents, Cochran said, 'If we can put this on the stage as I visualise it, it cannot fail.'

Then he bade Elsie April and Coward goodbye, put on his trilby hat, seized his walking stick and sauntered along Piccadilly in the afternoon sun to the London Pavilion. He was oblivious of shops, pedestrians and the general bustle around him. His mind was creating the scenes for the show. What scope it offered for charming decor and costumes.

When he reached the Pavilion, his general manager, Hal Lewis, said to him, 'You look pretty happy this morning.'

He beamed in response.

'I am,' he said. 'I've got an old age pension. Coward's operette is a gem, with a great title.'

After a rapturous two weeks in Manchester, *Bitter Sweet* opened at His Majesty's Theatre on 18th July 1929 to a not-very-smart and faintly hostile audience. They had not expected such undiluted sentiment and demure posturings in crinolines and bustles from the smart young iconoclast who had so bitingly satirised the contemporary world. He had written it, they said, with tongue in cheek. This was not 'real Coward'. Some, like W J Turner, the eminent musicologist and critic, wrote, 'Inept as the incidents of old-fashioned musical comedy were, it would not be possible to find in the annals of Daly's Theatre anything more preposterously unreal than this.' *Bitter Sweet* had 'finally smashed my hopes of Mr Coward, for a more inane and witless composition never left the pen of a distinguished author'. And he continued to attack the play with phrases like, 'The plot or libretto . . . is really so contemptible that one must dismiss it as complete nonsense.'

At the climax of the duel scene, three dramatic critics who were standing at the back of the stalls suddenly confronted one another with umbrellas poised and swung into a mock imitation of the sword-play.

They were Hannen Swaffer, Gordon Beckles and Ewart Hodgson, all members of the Express newspapers group.

Not unnaturally, Cochran was furious about this unseemly frolic and wrote a stinging letter of complaint to Lord Beaverbrook.

In spite of adverse criticism *Bitter Sweet* ran at His Majesty's for six hundred and seventy-three performances, continued to play for two sensational weeks at Golders Green and Streatham Hill and reopened for a further run at the Lyceum where it ended only because the Melville Brothers who controlled the theatre had booked Chaliapine in for a season of Russian opera there.

Evelyn Laye attended a matinee and immediately regretted having rejected Cochran's offer of the leading part. She asked him to forgive the pique and obstinacy she had shown and asked if he would give her the part in the New York production which she knew was in preparation. A large-minded, generous man, Cochran bore no grudges. He might – and often did – say, 'I'll never employ that man again!' But his acerbity evaporated in a short while. If ever a man forgave and forgot it was C B Cochran. An apology from a woman, and an extremely beautiful woman at that, proved quite irresistible.

Cochran melted at once. And Evelyn Laye opened in *Bitter Sweet* at the Ziegfeld Theatre, New York, in the following November.

This is how Noël Coward described her performance.

'She played as though she were enchanted. Early on in the

ballroom scene she conquered the audience completely by singing the quick waltz song, *Tell Me, What is Love?* so brilliantly, and with such a quality of excitement, that the next few minutes of the play were entirely lost in one of the most prolonged outbursts of cheering I have heard in a theatre.'

Evelyn Laye's association with Cochran had begun when she was a young beginner.

She had toured and played a few small parts at the Gaiety and secured an introduction to him through a friend. Living a sheltered life with her mother and father, she was an unworldly little thing who powdered her face with prepared chalk.

Receiving her in his office, Cochran said, 'You're very pretty. Would you like to come under my wing?'

Before she could recover from her astonishment and answer his question, he went on :

'It's your twenty-first birthday tomorrow, isn't it?'

'Yes, Mr Cochran, it is.'

'Well, I am going to give you a three-year contract as a birthday present!'

This was a typical Cochran reaction. In the presence of a pretty woman he was bereft of all resistance and completely vulnerable. In all likelihood his *alter ego* incredulously heard him giving this quixotic, extravagant promise. The child had disarmed him with her fresh, English beauty. But what could she do on the stage? Of this he had no knowledge whatsoever beyond his own intuitive flair for assessing personality and ability on sight.

She was flabbergasted. Hardly knowing what to do or say, she thanked him in a dream-like, mechanical fashion, ran down the stairs and out into Bond Street where she continued to run. She just couldn't stop running.

At first she was given no spectacular parts. But she was working for Cochran, the master, taskmaster, and father figure of the contemporary theatre. During this period she took over from one of the Dolly Sisters in revue when they went back to America.

But Cochran could also be generous and forgiving to men. During the London run of *Bitter Sweet* he had twice dismissed Robert Newton, an unknown newcomer at the time, for being drunk on the stage. The next day, after another bout of drinking, Newton said to Billy Milton in their joint dressing room, 'Give me some money, Billy. I'm flat broke, but I must have a large whisky before I see Cochran.'

'Sit down,' Billy commanded peremptorily. 'Don't be absurd, Bobby. You've had far too much already. Look at you, you're in a disgraceful state.'

Bobby persisted so doggedly that Billy yielded and gave him a shilling or two. Off he went to the private bar upstairs, knocked back a double and presently confronted an amazed and startled Cochran with, 'Mr Cochran, I wish to speak to you.'

'Mr Newton,' Cochran replied – how they maintained the correct, old world frigidity! – 'Mr Newton, I have nothing whatever to say to you!'

'You must hear my side of the story, Mr Cochran,' said Newton.

'Well,' Cochran parried, 'what is it?'

'The reason I am intoxicated tonight is that you have given me such a piffling part when I am so very talented. Give me something in which I can show my ability – and I will remain sober.'

So Cochran reinstated him yet again and he went to America as Noël Coward's understudy in *Private Lives*.

It was clear that, when they read of Evelyn Laye's great triumph in New York, many of our own theatregoers wished they could have seen her in the London production. Two things happened to make this possible. The New York run had finished, because Ziegfeld had other plans for his theatre; Evelyn Laye stayed in America to make a film, however, and there was talk of her going into a new Ziegfeld production.

Meanwhile Peggy Wood yielded to the strain of her nightly performance in London and was under doctor's orders to rest.

In his eagerness to speak to Evelyn Laye, Cochran telephoned her without considering the five-hour difference between the two countries, and when she sleepily answered the phone, he said, 'I'd like you to come home and take Peggy Wood's place for a month.'

That early morning hour was no time, and bed no place, to have to make such an important snap decision.

'When do you want me to leave?' she asked.

'There's a boat sailing today,' Cochran urged.

'I could probably just catch it, but I don't know how I stand with Ziegfeld. I'm supposed to be doing a play for him. Let me talk to him and I'll cable you to say whether I'm sailing.'

Just as she was about to hang up, she said, 'Oh, I forgot to ask . . . what's the money?'

Cochran was taken aback. 'That's a funny question,' he said, 'from you to me! I haven't thought about it. But you know we never fall out over that. I'll tell you on the first Saturday night.'

'Of course,' she replied, 'of course,' suddenly realising that she was speaking, not to any hard-headed theatre manager, but to Cochran, the incurable sentimentalist, generous to a fault. And she calmly went back to sleep.

Extricating herself from her negotiations with Ziegfeld she left for Britain two days later.

And she scored a tremendous hit in the London production of *Bitter Sweet*.

It was turn and turn about. Peggy Wood came back to the show that Christmas and saw it through to the end of its sub-urban run. Evelyn Laye took a holiday in the South of France where Cochran telephoned her to say that he had secured the Lyceum for an extension of *Bitter Sweet*. She raised objections.

'First of all,' she said, 'I'm down here for a rest which I badly need. And secondly people will think I can't play anything but Sari Linden.'

But once again, she was giving this negative response to the irresistible Cochran whose masterly gift of persuasion completely demolished everything she said – and back she went to the Lyceum.

Casting the mind back to this scintillating Cochran era, one tends to associate the year 1929 with *Bitter Sweet,* and it must be admitted that the memory of this show has eclipsed other contemporary productions that were staged under the Cochran aegis.

It is scarcely remembered that *Bitter Sweet* was preceded at His Majesty's Theatre by *Porgy* which proved such a sad failure in spite of its direction by Rouben Mamoulian.

Wake Up and Dream was on at the London Pavilion and Cochran also had Lynn Fontanne and Alfred Lunt playing in *Caprice* at the St James's Theatre. It was in 1929 that Cochran presented a straight play which probably gave him more artistic satisfaction than anything he had done before. This was *The Silver Tassie* by Sean O'Casey, a dramatist whom Cochran held in the utmost reverence. Because of its deeply moving and in-flammatory anti-war theme, the timorous W B Yeats at the Abbey Theatre, Dublin, had turned it down.

This was a devastating blow to O'Casey for whom *The Silver Tassie* represented a personal achievement of the greatest intel-lectual and artistic significance. And the very fact that Cochran said he wanted to read it gave a tremendous fillip to his shat-tered hopes. The matter arose in the first place when Cochran was talking about the play to Eileen O'Casey, the playwright's young wife, who had just returned from a period of acting in America. Together, they examined the possibility of her going into one of his late cabaret shows, but he discouraged her. Sean was so much older than Eileen. 'You'd be out very late every night,' said Cochran, 'and your husband is too nice a man for you to leave all that time. You sing very well; why don't you audition for *Bitter Sweet*?'

She took his advice and appeared in *Bitter Sweet* as one of the bridesmaids.

Cochran engaged Raymond Massey to produce *The Silver*

Tassie and, consistent with his policy of recruiting the most celebrated and gifted artists to supply the essential components of a fine production – Massine for ballet, Bakst and Messel for decor – he commissioned the liturgical chant from Martin Shaw and wondered if he dare approach Augustus John for the big second act.

Instead of making the overture himself, he said to Eileen O'Casey, 'You go and ask him. He is more likely to say yes to you than to me.'

'I'd be terrified,' she replied.

'No, no; please go. I'm sure you can persuade him!'

She went as bidden to John's house in Chelsea where, typically, the great, leonine personality demurred, protesting that he didn't understand the technical requirements of the theatre. 'My goodness,' he said, 'I've never done sets before. I really don't think this is what I could do. I've read the play. A marvellous play. . . . I loved it. . . . Oh, well. All right, you've persuaded me. But I don't believe it's in my field at all.'

For all John's self-deprecating attitude to the task, Cochran afterwards declared that '. . . he brought in many more fresh ideas than lesser artists claiming greater technical knowledge – indeed, I consider that his scene was a masterpiece of theatrical design'.

The Silver Tassie provoked so much controversy that 'some,' said Cochran, 'thought I ought to be canonised for it, while others thought I ought to be burned at the stake'. He himself regarded it as the finest work yet accomplished by one of the greatest living playwrights.

He took great pride in his friendship with the Irish dramatist and quietly rejoiced in the fact that Eileen had played in *Bitter Sweet* and later in his Adelphi production of Offenbach's *Helen*.

And it was an exciting moment when he received the following letter from Shaw:

Ayot St Lawrence,   4 Whitehall Court,
Welwyn, Herts.   London SW1
23rd Nov 1929

My dear Cochran,

I really must congratulate you on *The Tassie* before it passes into the classical repertory. It is a magnificent play; and it was a magnificent gesture of yours to produce it. The High-brows *should* have produced it: you, the Unpretentious Show-man, DID, as you have done so many other noble and rash things on your Sundays. This, I think, will rank as the best of them.

I hope you have not lost too much by it, especially as I am quite sure you have done your best in that direction by doing the thing as extravagantly as possible. That is the worst of operating on your colossal scale: you haven't time to economise; and you lost the habit of thinking it worth while.

No matter! a famous achievement. There is a new drama rising from unplumbed depths to sweep the nice little bourgeois efforts of myself and my contemporaries into the dustbin; and your name will live as that of the man who didn't run away.

If only someone would build you a huge Woolworth theatre (all seats sixpence) to start with O'Casey and O'Neill, and no plays by men who had ever seen a five-pound note before they were thirty or been inside a school after they were thirteen, you would be buried in Westminster Abbey.

Bravo!

George Bernard Shaw

One other production of the year 1929 was an American comedy, *Paris Bound* which, strange to say, Cochran acquired almost involuntarily! He had seen it in New York the previous year. While finding it quite witty and enjoyable, he believed that the plot, which centred on a divorce, would be offensive to squeamish British tastes.

It was presented by Arthur Hopkins with whom Cochran had been associated in the London production of *Anna Christie*.

The following year Cochran received a cable from Hopkins

saying that Herbert Marshall and Edna Best wanted to take a financial interest and appear themselves in a London production of the play. This put a different complexion on the matter. Cochran believed that London audiences would be glad to see this popular British couple again since they had more or less settled in America.

Accepting this proposition in principle, the next thing a very surprised Cochran knew was that, without so much as any further negotiations or an exchange of contracts, the play, the leading players (who were entirely innocent of 'this curious way of doing business', as Cochran described it) and the miscellaneous impedimenta connected with the production arrived suddenly in this country like an unsolicited package.

Paris Bound did quite well at Golders Green, although what profit it made there was quickly lost when it played at the Lyric Theatre, notwithstanding the excellent quality of the cast which included Laurence Olivier 'who', wrote Cochran in 1932, 'has since made a reputation as a film actor'.

He was once again dissipating time and money on unprofitable ventures and if *Bitter Sweet* had not redeemed his fortunes, the outlook for him at the end of the decade would have been bleak indeed.

The Cochran Magnanimity

WITH *Bitter Sweet* successfully launched, Noël Coward went on a world trip. During the farewell party given for him in New York by Gertrude Lawrence, she exacted a promise from him: that he would write a play for them both.

He began to regret that promise which repeatedly invaded a mind otherwise disposed to occupy itself with nothing save the pleasures of idleness and travel. Vainly he sought the idea that wouldn't come; his creative mechanism distilled nothing from his torpid imagination or the glum, bored faces of his fellow passengers.

In the *Tenyo Maru* he did some work on an abortive novel which he eventually discarded.

Then, going to bed early one night in the Imperial Hotel, Tokyo, he conceived not only the idea for *Private Lives*, but the title as well, the moment he put the light out. He lay awake working it out in his mind and by four o'clock the plot had taken shape.

In Shanghai he contracted 'flu and, recovering slowly, spent his convalescence sitting up in bed writing. He completed *Private Lives* in four days and moved on to Hong Kong where he revised and typed it, cabled Gertrude Lawrence, asking her to keep herself free for the autumn, and sent her a copy of the play.

On his return to England, therefore, he was able to hand Cochran a new play. Cochran, Coward and Gertrude Lawrence each put up a thousand pounds of their own money. But Coward made a firm stipulation regarding his own appearance in *Private Lives.* He said he would play twelve weeks in London and twelve in New York. Cochran had no option but to agree, though he cherished the hope that, in the event of a smash hit, he could persuade the author to continue in the principal role for longer.

It was a smash hit. It opened at the then newly built Phoenix Theatre where it took roughly £3,200 every week from the beginning of its run to the end, with a little more on the last night owing to the crowds standing at the back of the stalls, and it was equally successful in New York.

But Coward was adamant and refused to continue in the play after the agreed period.

For the first time the press lauded his gifts as writer, actor and stage director and took the line that the play was only effective so long as he and Gertrude Lawrence played in it.

But Cochran proved them wrong by mounting it successfully with other artists in the provinces, America and Europe.

We are all, in varying degrees, human cash registers. Depress a certain key and a corresponding figure shoots up. Apply a particular stimulus, in other words, and the response will be roughly predictable, save for those freak occasions when people behave, as we say, out of character, either from perversity or because we do not know them as well as we think we do.

This principle showed itself again and again in Cochran's orientation to life and, to illustrate the point, we have to go back to 1927, the year of two of Noël Coward's most appalling flops. One was *Home Chat*, the other *Sirocco*, but the first night of *Sirocco* was no ordinary flop. It was an unmitigated catastrophe, with the audience booing and jeering and the less inhibited ones demonstrating outside the stage door and spitting at the author when he emerged. Critics and public alike bayed and protested and enjoyed the ugly glow of unifying emotion which – as history has so tragically demonstrated – the numerically superior mob feels towards its helpless victim. And, with the exception of St John Ervine, every critic predicted Coward's swift and ignominious disappearance from the theatrical scene.

Coward was so shattered by this exhibition, not merely of cool distaste, but of positive hostility, that he at once got in touch with Cochran and asked to be released from their latest contract. This referred to his undertaking to write a new revue. 'I won't hear of it,' Cochran answered. 'After these two failures, I know you will do your damnedest to please the critics and make them change their opinion. That will be my gain. I can't afford to have a failure. For your own sake as well as mine, I insist on holding you to your contract. We are going to have the biggest success of our lives.'

His magnanimity and courage rewarded him. The revue was *This Year of Grace,* a brilliant and immediate success.

This built-in reaction, signifying indomitable faith and tenacity, and a refusal to be discouraged by critical opinion, re-asserted itself a few years later.

The pattern was similar and, in reviewing the incident, it is necessary to backtrack a little once again in time and set the scene in the reception room of a London solicitor's office where an unmistakable figure in a morning coat, wearing a carnation and carrying a stick, walked in, and a woman stood up – clearly on impulse – and said, 'Mr Cochran . . . please forgive me. I just *had* to talk to you – I have a young son who writes music . . .'

The result of the lady's spontaneous action was that her seventeen-year-old son, Vivian Ellis, got an appointment with the great man at his Bond Street office. The walls were hung with old playbills and Toulouse Lautrec lithographs. Signed photographs of famous stars stood on the impresario's desk. The young composer was suitably awed. He nervously strummed a few of his songs on the piano. Cochran listened in his bland, impassive way, said a few kind and helpful things and promised to get in touch some time while giving the young musician no real hint of his opinion.

Several years passed before Cochran rang up and told him he would like to consider some of his songs for a new revue. One of Vivian Ellis's early songs he particularly admired: this was *The Wind in the Willows*, an ingeniously constructed melody which repeats the first eight bars a third higher, the whole composition evolving in logical progressions. In my opinion it is one of Vivian Ellis's best songs.

Beverley Nichols was writing the revue; sketches, lyrics and music.

'If I can have that song,' said Cochran, 'you and Beverley can finish off the show between you.'

André Charlot had been sitting on *The Wind in the Willows*, so Vivian Ellis promptly withdrew it and gave it to Cochran for his *1930 Revue*.

The show opened in Manchester. It was too long (three-and-a-half hours) and under-rehearsed.

In his room at the Midland Hotel next morning, Beverley Nichols became more and more depressed as he read bad notice after bad notice, sitting glumly on the edge of his bed, while great lumps of newsprint slipped to his feet. Only the *Manchester Guardian* had a modicum of praise for the production.

There was a tap at the door and in walked Cochran.

Disarmingly he said, 'Before you say anything, I'd just like you to read this announcement I've sent to the press.'

And he handed the author a slip of paper which read, 'Charles Cochran delighted with 1930 revue and is signing up his writers for another in 1931.'

It was in the same year that Cochran presented *Evergreen*.

This production came about through a chain of events that started when Archie Selwyn undertook to present *Wake Up and Dream* in New York. His choice of a leading man was Jack Buchanan whose popularity on Broadway was so enormous that his name on the billboards gave an almost infallible augury of success.

But the casting of Jack Buchanan for the New York version of the show presented personal problems that only the tact and diplomacy of Cochran could resolve. Sonnie Hale had acquitted himself so admirably in the show in London that it seemed grossly unfair to ask him to stand down in favour of Buchanan. His romantic involvement with Jessie Matthews, moreover, was at that particular time so deep that they were unwilling to be separated. But as neither of them was free from their respective marital entanglements, Cochran assumed his characteristic fatherly role and persuaded them that, until their legal positions were resolved, it would in fact be desirable and salutary for them to be four thousand miles apart for a few months.

They accepted his counsel of compromise. It was Jessie who went to America and Cochran starred Sonnie in the tour of the show.

He had a great affection for these two young artists and, as a reward for accommodating his wishes, he promised to star them in a London show when the two productions of *Wake Up and Dream* came to an end.

The question was: what was it to be?

He invoked the rare and exciting talents of Richard Rodgers and Lorenz Hart who had already written *My Heart Stood Still* and several other beautiful songs for *One Dam Thing After Another* and, at an early production conference, Larry Hart summarised the idea of a show built round a young business woman who, in order to promote the fortunes of her beauty salon, exchanges her birth certificate for her mother's and poses as a sixty-year-old rejuvenated by her own cosmetic preparations.

Cochran commissioned the book from playwright-politician Benn Levy who was at that time working on a Lilian Harvey film at the Ufa Studios in Neu Babelsberg. Taking Larry Hart with him, Cochran went to Germany and the three of them sat in various cafés and restaurants or Benn Levy's room at the Esplanade Hotel mulling over the plot and developing it according to the requirements of the theatre.

There were two things Cochran badly wanted to do on the musical comedy stage. One was to present a *Folies-Bergères* type of scene – spectacular, colourful, a dazzling eyeful of feathers and *diamanté*. The other was to reproduce the raucous, elemental gaiety of a fairground. And he seized the opportunity presented by *Evergreen* for doing both. He switched the action to Paris where, consequent on her successful deception of the public, the young woman became a star in revue.

During a performance of Max Reinhardt's *Fledermaus* in Berlin Cochran had been very impressed by the use of a revolving stage to give the appearance of guests in the party scene moving from one room to another. And when he was arranging to open the reconstructed Adelphi Theatre with *Evergreen,* he stipulated the incorporation of a revolving stage which in fact became the first in London.

He played happily with this fascinating new toy, using it to full advantage in the brilliant and exciting fair scene at Neuilly.

Just before the first night Cochran embarked on his routine tour of the dressing rooms to wish the artists luck.

To Jessie he said, 'Well, I have spent x pounds on the book, x on the music and x on the costumes. Now it's up to you!'

An example of Jessie's refusal to be intimidated by 'the old man' followed an acutely embarrassing incident during one performance when she and Joyce Barbour were doing a scene in a small enclosed set that contained nothing but a dressing table and chair and a wardrobe painted on the backcloth with a slit in the scenic material to represent the wardrobe door. At the point where Joyce Barbour had to exit she went to the real door at the side of the set, fiddled vainly with the handle and, to Jessie's astonishment, came back. She was trapped on stage! They ad libbed and tried to cover up as best they could; then Joyce Barbour suddenly disappeared through the only available opening – the flap of scenery representing the wardrobe door.

The next moment Sonnie Hale entered the same way.

When Jessie spoke her line, 'Who let you in?' the audience roared with glee. And every time she tried to say her next line, the attempt was drowned by a rippling chorus of spontaneous laughter. Then Jessie and Sonnie dried and laughed. It was impossible to do anything else.

Cochran was furious. How dare they wreck the show like that? They were the leading lady and gentleman and it was their duty to set an example to the rest of the cast.

When the tirade subsided, Jessie calmly said, 'Just a moment. If that door had opened, this wouldn't have happened, would it?'

He pondered for a second and replied, 'Well, no. You're quite right, it wouldn't.'

'Well, then, you can go and give your carpenter the telling off you've just given me!'

'Yes,' he agreed, 'you're right, absolutely right. I'm sorry. Forget everything I said.' And, although his admission indicated his fairness, he was human enough to exhibit a final splutter of self-vindication with a lame and sheepish rebuke: 'All the same, you should have controlled it, you should have controlled it.'

He repeated the pattern of his behaviour when Denys Blakelock committed a similar lapse six years later. In Blakelock's autobiography, *Round the Next Corner*,[1] you will find, 'My stage hysteria ran me into serious trouble for the first time in *The Black Eye*. At the end of the play one night I could hardly speak for laughter, when I had to call Stephen Haggard out to give him the black eye of the title. It was unfortunate that it was a packed Saturday audience and that the author's wife was in the front row. It was reported to Cochran, who wrote me a letter of reprimand and reproach.

'In my letter of apology I told him the simple truth: that

[1] *Round the Next Corner*, Denys Blakelock, Victor Gollancz, 1967

166

there had been no frivolity, that it was a breakout of a nervous symptom. I wrote a similar letter to the producer. How dissimilar were the replies! Ayliff's letter was a schoolmaster's, cold and unyielding. Cochran, the human, warm-hearted showman, wrote by return, assuring me of his complete sympathy and understanding.'

Conflict with Coward

DURING THE LONDON run of *Private Lives* a vague idea started buzzing round in Noël Coward's mind.

That niggling germ which activates the creative process set him thinking on this occasion in terms of a large-scale, spectacular production, a vivid, exciting pageant of colour, movement and visual appeal.

He considered the great events in history, including *The Decline and Fall of the Roman Empire,* as possible subjects but ruthlessly discarded them all.

Turning the pages of some bound copies of the *Illustrated London News* that he had bought at Foyles, where he often browsed while working at the Phoenix Theatre in Charing Cross Road, his attention was suddenly riveted by a picture of a troopship leaving for the Boer War. '. . . the moment I saw it,' he wrote afterwards, 'I knew that I had found what I wanted. I can't explain why it rang the bell so sharply. I only know that it did.'

The tunes of the time at once came to mind, *Dolly Gray, Soldiers of the Queen. . . .* This was the right starting point for recreating a phase in British history that would carry the audience from those not-too-distant events, poignantly remembered by many, to the drift and ennui of the contemporary world which ultimately found expression in a night club scene and Binnie Barnes singing *Twentieth Century Blues.*

He conceived a great panorama of major events strung together by the popular songs of the period. He excitedly played them over on the piano while waiting for G B Stern who was expected for afternoon tea. When she arrived he was in the middle of *Tipperary*. He outlined his idea to her and she supplied one or two notions: Mafeking Night and the Relief of Ladysmith . . . newsboys shouting the bulletins as the Queen lay dying. . . .

There was no hope of making a start on this vast project until he had finished the New York run of *Private Lives*. But he outlined the idea to Cochran, who liked it in principle. Then he let it simmer.

At the dress rehearsal of *Evergreen* he had been greatly impressed by the revolving stage and the means it provided for swift and elaborate changes of scene. But he felt the Adelphi stage was too small for the production he visualised and he told Cochran he would need the Coliseum.

He then sailed for America to play *Private Lives* in New York, leaving Cochran to open negotiations for the Coliseum.

Sir Oswald Stoll was presenting a season of variety there at the time. It was not going too well, and he next introduced a ballet programme under Balanchine's direction. This failed equally to attract large audiences and Cochran felt the prospect of getting the Coliseum looked hopeful until Stoll suddenly announced that he had engaged Erik Charell to produce *White Horse Inn* there.

He at once cabled Coward: NO CHANCE OF THE COLISEUM. DRURY LANE ONLY STAGE LARGE ENOUGH AND HOLDING ENOUGH MONEY. WILL NEGOTIATE IF YOU THINK STAGE POSSIBLE.

Coward sent Cochran the following reply:

PART ONE SMALL INTERIOR TWO DEPARTURE OF TROOP SHIP THREE SMALL INTERIOR FOUR MAFEKING NIGHT IN LONDON MUSIC HALL NECESSITATING PIVOT STAGE FIVE EXTERIOR FRONT SCENE BIRDCAGE WALK SIX EDWARDIAN RECEPTION SEVEN MILE END ROAD FULL STAGE BUT CAN BE OPENED UP GRADUALLY AND DONE MOSTLY WITH LIGHTING PART TWO ONE

WHITE CITY FULL SET TWO SMALL INTERIOR THREE EDWARDIAN
SEASIDE RESORT FULL SET BATHING MACHINES PIERROTS ETC
FOUR TITANIC SMALL FRONT SCENE FIVE OUTBREAK OF WAR
SMALL INTERIOR SIX VICTORIA STATION IN FOG FULL SET AND
LIGHTING EFFECTS SEVEN AIR RAID OVER LONDON PRINCIPALLY
LIGHTING AND SOUND EIGHT INTERIOR OPENING ON TO TRAFAL-
GAR SQUARE ARMISTICE NIGHT FULL STAGE AND CAST PART
THREE ONE GENERAL STRIKE FULL SET TWO SMALL INTERIOR
THREE FASHIONABLE NIGHT CLUB FULL SET FOUR SMALL IN-
TERIOR FIVE IMPRESSIONISTIC SUMMARY OF MODERN CIVILI-
SATION MOSTLY LIGHTS AND EFFECTS SIX COMPLETE BARE
STAGE WITH PANORAMA AND UNION JACK AND FULL CAST STOP
NECESSITATES ONE BEST MODERN LIGHTING EQUIPMENT OB-
TAINABLE TWO COMPANY OF GUARDS THREE ORCHESTRA FIFTY
FOUR FACILITIES FOR COMPLETE BLACKOUTS FIVE FULL WEEK
OF DRESS REHEARSALS SIX THEATRE FREE FOR ALL REHEAR-
SALS SEVEN ABOUT A DOZEN RELIABLE ACTORS THE REST
WALKONS A FEW STRONG SINGERS EIGHT FOG EFFECT INDIVID-
UALS NECESSARY ONE FRANK COLLINS STAGE SUPERVISION
TWO DAN O'NEIL STAGE MANAGEMENT THREE ELSIE APRIL
MUSIC SUPERVISION FOUR CISSIE SEWELL CROWD WORK FIVE
GLADYS SUPERVISION OF COSTUMES AND SCENERY AND YOUR
OWN GENERAL SUPERVISION STOP THIS SYNOPSIS IS MORE OR
LESS ACCURATE BUT LIABLE TO REVISION STOP PLEASE TAKE
CARE THAT NO DETAIL OF THIS SHOULD REACH PRIVATE OR
PARTICULARLY PRESS EARS REGARDS NOËL.

The size of the Drury Lane Theatre made it suitable for the
mammoth spectacle that Coward envisaged, and he aimed to
compensate for the lack of a revolving stage by using a series
of lifts that facilitated quick changes of scene but sorely taxed
the inventive resources of the stage carpenters.

Nineteen thirty-one was the year of the Great Depression and
a particularly hard one for the theatre. As soon as it was known
that Cochran was planning a big new Drury Lane production

to be called *Cavalcade* which would involve large crowd scenes, out-of-work actors and actresses besieged Drury Lane the moment auditioning began. Over a thousand applied for four hundred jobs and although it was only possible to engage this vast number of extras by restricting their salaries to thirty shillings a week, even this low rate was acceptable to the pathetic flotsam of the theatre, those grim, hungry, disappointed would-be stars for whom hope had almost vanished.

While, no doubt from mixed motives of genuine kindliness and vanity, a craving for admiration and an urgent need to be liked, Cochran would astonish an individual artist with the offer of some ridiculously inflated salary, he showed no such generosity towards the impersonal, defenceless crowd like the walkers-on and bit players in *Cavalcade*.

Although the British Actors' Equity Association had been formed in the previous year, it was still powerless to prevent the exploitation of a swollen labour market by those who offered a pitifully reduced 'take-it-or-leave-it' rate for the job. Girls who were lucky enough to get into *Cavalcade* disported themselves nightly in costly kid gloves and delicately hand-embroidered costumes made of the most expensive slipper satin, or perhaps specially woven French silk. . . . Then, after each performance, those stage door Cinderellas reverted to type. And on Friday night they would go home pathetically clutching their thirty pieces of silver.

'I lived with my parents,' one of them said to me recently, 'so it wasn't too bad for me. But it must have been terrible for the girls in digs. I don't know how they managed.'

Coward took the early auditions while Cochran was absent through illness, and that never-ending descent on the theatre by droves of workless actors had a saddening effect on him. He was deeply moved by the harsh necessity of selecting some applicants at the expense of others when the hairline differences forced him to make snap decisions that embodied the possibility of mistake. He also felt an irrational, if understandable, guilt in contrasting his own swift and brilliant success with the tragic position of impecunious actors twice his age.

The agonising responsibility entailed in deciding the fate of these desperate folk together with the mammoth task of auditioning itself had their inevitable effect on nerves and temper, and Coward and Cochran argued and bickered over a number of troublesome little points.

In one of his weak, melting, 'never-refuse-a-woman' moods, Cochran had promised walk-on parts to three vapid society girls who certainly did not need the cash. When these smart and bedizened young women arrived at the theatre, Coward told them they were not the type he was seeking. Cochran protested and insisted on engaging them. They both felt they were defending a principle and they argued long and bitterly over the point. Coward finally yielded on condition that, for each of the society girls, they engaged two more who really needed the work.

There was a further disagreement over the scene of Chaos which presented so many technical difficulties that Coward, directing rehearsals from the dress circle, wanted to cut it, together with the Night Club scene. Cochran inveighed strongly against this decision, arguing that fatigue, proximity and a desire to get on with the rest of the preparations had distorted Coward's judgment and that, with a little more patient effort, they would get those two scenes right; and that, moreover, they were essential components of the show.

'You thought the scene was good when you planned it,' said Cochran, 'and you've been quite happy about it up to now. Before we cut it out we will see it done perfectly even if we have to rehearse one, two, three or even more days. When it is mechanically perfect and you can judge it in the context of the scenes that precede and follow it, I am willing to cut it if you still think it is wrong.'

There had been a similar incident in an earlier production when Cochran had defended a piece of Coward's work against his own misgivings and been vindicated by the opinion of critics and audience. But Coward was more adamant on this occasion and less disposed to yield. It may have been because he was now better established and correspondingly more confident.

Eventually, however, he gave way. They called more rehearsals, made minor changes and deletions to overcome the difficulties and finally sculptured the scenes into their desired forms. Again Cochran was right. Audience reaction confirmed his judgment.

Contemporary witnesses declare that the inevitable battle of matched giants, the first signs of friction between Cochran and Coward, began during the early days of *Cavalcade.*

Owing to his long illness, Cochran had been absent not only from the auditions, but also from the early rehearsals, and when he presented himself one morning on the stage of Drury Lane, expecting perhaps to elicit a hushed and reverent welcome, he was aggrieved to find Coward so deeply engrossed in direction that he showed precious little awareness of his presence.

In the early thirties their letters to one another preserved the formal appearances of courtesy, the familiar affirmations of mutual respect expressed in that stagey effusiveness so general at the time.

But those letters were so much paper over the cracks of a slowly eroding professional relationship that finally dissolved after *Conversation Piece* in 1934.

In spite of one desperate mishap, when one of the downstage lifts stuck, the opening night of *Cavalcade* was a success. Its patriotic message had a tonic effect on a public that was jaded and depressed by the economic blizzard sweeping Europe as a result of the disasters on Wall Street.

And this was the first time since *The Better 'ole* that Cochran presented a show with a strong appeal to national feeling at just the right time.

Many felt some disappointment that Coward had written few original songs for this production, having made do with old favourites that reflected the mood of each episode in the play. But his instinct – and Cochran's too, of course – was right. Let any pianist at a party play the most engaging and tasteful new tunes and he will command little attention except from a small minority of guests who happen to be students of theatre music with a taste for the elegant and *recherché*. But let him rip off the punchy old favourites – *Lily of Laguna, My Old Man, Knocked 'em in the Old Kent Road* and so on – and he will at once electrify the assembled company. This simple, earthy response seems to appear as much, oddly enough, in the sophisticated echelons of the social order as the raw and bucolic, there being no apparent connection in this particular field between education and musical taste.

A Frightening Ordeal for Cole Porter

SAVE FOR HIS increasingly troublesome arthritic hip, Cochran now had every reason to be pleased with life. *Cavalcade* was a *tour de force.* Its great success had added considerable lustre to his personal reputation.

And in 1931 he once again became the happy puppeteer, manipulating as scintillating a group of artist-craftsmen as he had ever assembled for a new production. The show itself, moreover, gave him intense pleasure, for it was the Reinhardt version of Offenbach's *La Belle Hélène,* now simply renamed *Helen* for its new career at the Adelphi.

Cochran was thrilled and proud to be associated once more with the great Reinhardt. And, an incurable lily-painter, he recruited Massine to do the choreography and Oliver Messel the decor.

A P Herbert's adaptation of this gay, frolicsome operette was Cochran's special pride. He greatly admired his lyrics (which Churchill used to quote extensively from memory) and his skilful creation of an end to the story which Meilhac and Halévy had failed to provide in their original version. He also felt enormous satisfaction in having persuaded the great Max Reinhardt to come to this country and direct it, and he believed that it represented as near perfect a little gem of artistic unity as he had managed to achieve in his long association with the theatre.

His Helen had, of necessity, to be radiantly beautiful, and he achieved this challenging object by casting Evelyn Laye in the role. But he startled the purists by giving the part of King

Menelaus to George Robey, the Prime Minister of Mirth, as he used to be billed on the music halls. Once again, however, his instinct about this had been right.

Much of the preparation for *Helen* was specially pleasing to him and he enjoyed his trips to Salzburg with A P Herbert to see Reinhardt.

But he was deeply wounded when, despite a frenzied reception on the first night, a glowing press and capacity houses for about twelve weeks, the receipts started dwindling.

He noticed a slackness in the performances, a puzzling loss of freshness and grip. On more than one occasion he called the cast together and gingered them up with noticeable, but only temporary, effect.

One night he told George Robey to stay in his dressing room after the performance while every other member of the cast was ordered to report on the stage. Robey was extremely puzzled and consumed with anxiety. What was wrong? Why was he the one member of the cast instructed *not* to obey the mysterious summons? It seemed ominous. But Robey needn't have worried. Cochran had called everyone together to complain most bitterly of their indifferent, lack-lustre performances and demand an immediate improvement in the standard. All, that is, except Robey, whose personal effort was exemplary!

'It is hard enough to get success at any time', wrote Cochran, 'but it is doubly disheartening when, having achieved a measure of first-night success, the quality of the subsequent performances is dissipated by the players and the run of the play consequently shortened. It amazes me that so many actors and actresses receiving high salaries fail to realise the responsibility they carry on their shoulders. They are the controllers, not only of their own destinies, but of the manager's fortune and the livelihoods of all the people employed in the theatre. An actor or actress should never be tired. It is not unreasonable for a manager to expect his artists to adjust their lives in such a manner as to keep themselves fresh for the few hours they are compelled to give to their performances.'

He always cherished a hope of reviving *Helen*.

For *The Cat and The Fiddle* at the Palace Theatre, Cochran again starred Peggy Wood, and this production supplied yet another example of his acute perception of nascent talent which escaped the notice of others.

Sir Frederick Ashton has told me how, as a young man, when he was arranging dance routines for the Ballet Rambert at the Mercury Theatre, he happened to meet the Countess of Oxford and Asquith who asked him what he did, and when he told her, she gave him an introduction to Cochran.

Although Cochran knew little or nothing of Ashton and his work, he was so impressed by the young choreographer's personality that he at once hired him to do one of Delysia's scenes in this new musical play. It was a pure act of faith.

In his typical, rather casual way, Cochran had neglected to mention money, and Ashton was too diffident to do so until the first rehearsal when he steeled himself to broach this delicate subject.

Cochran asked him how much he wanted for the job. He had no idea what to ask. He only knew that his salary with the Ballet Rambert had been microscopic and he nervously said, 'Fifteen pounds.' Cochran showed no reaction, but walked back to his stall and murmured something, obviously reporting the conversation, to the writers of the show, Otto Harbach and Jerome Kern, who both collapsed with laughter.

Ashton was seized with terror.

'I've asked too much!' he thought, and only learned the truth when Cochran stomped back to him and, leaning heavily on his silver-knobbed cane, said, 'Never fifteen, young man. I'll pay you fifty.'

'That was so like him,' Sir Frederick told me. 'He would never exploit a greenhorn's ignorance of standard rates. If you did extra work, he would automatically put up your money. He would ask how much you wanted. You might say, "Three hundred pounds" and if he thought it was too much, he would say, "I was thinking of two hundred, but let's split the difference." Money matters were always settled very simply and quickly. That side of the business was a bit of a bore to him; he just wanted to get on with the show, so there was no long drawn out argument and haggling.

'No wonder his backers were sometimes a trifle apprehensive. If he learned to trust you, he would give you your head and respect your judgment. But if he didn't, you were out,' said Sir Frederick.

Cochran next engaged Frederick Ashton for his Coronation revue, *Home and Beauty,* which was directed by John Murray Anderson who, by universal agreement, was known to be one of the most difficult people in the theatre.

The trouble he created strained the limits of Ashton's endurance and the choreographer walked out of the Adelphi in the middle of rehearsals. Cochran hobbled after him as quickly as his arthritic leg would allow and seized his arm. 'I know the man's impossible,' he said, adding, with a look of abject supplication, 'but please stay for *my* sake.' Like everyone else, Ashton found him irresistible. He needed no further persuasion.

While *Cavalcade* was playing at Drury Lane, Coward took a long trip round the world and came back with a new revue. He was quite unequivocal about wanting Cochran to put it on exactly as he had conceived it. He prescribed the running order of the scenes and sketches, announced his own very definite ideas of production and even demanded the use of his own title, *Words and Music.* The cast was to be so and so and Gladys Calthrop was to do the settings and costumes.

Cochran felt a little chilled and dismayed by his new attitude. They had always collaborated, pooled and exchanged ideas, shared their enthusiasms and problems and enjoyed the lively interplay of their creative minds.

But Coward was adamant. *Words and Music* was to be a one-man revue and, in view of their long association, Cochran felt that he could hardly refuse to sponsor it, even if he did so merely in the unsatisfying role of theatre manager that demanded no personal contribution from him.

Much of the material was excellent. *Mad About The Boy* has been revived in recent months; *Children of the Ritz*, the 'poor little not-so-rich-girls' of the 1931 crash, was a crisp and biting satire, and Romney Brent's performance of *Mad Dogs and Englishmen* remains one of the most exciting memories of the musical theatre.

But the revue was no longer the light-hearted, whimsical satire of the Noël Coward who wrote *This Year of Grace*. It was a jaded, sulky piece of writing with overtones of bitterness that bruised Cochran's optimistic outlook.

Up to that time, Cochran had put on nineteen or twenty revues which had gradually acquired their individual stamp, the fingerprints, the recognisable hallmark of the man himself. Though indefinable, apart from its emphasis on spectacle, colour and an extrovert mood, its novel talent and the magic of a great showman's art, this special character was something that audiences grew to recognise and expect.

Of *Words and Music*, Cochran said sadly, 'It may have been an interesting Coward revue, but it was not a Cochran revue.'

During this same period he presented the Sacha Guitry company at the Cambridge Theatre and revived *The Miracle* with Tilly Losch at the Lyceum.

The following year, 1933, saw two outstanding Cochran productions: *Nymph Errant*, a musical show with Gertrude Lawrence and a Cole Porter score, and *Escape Me Never*, Margaret Kennedy's play in which Elisabeth Bergner gave such a monumental performance.

James Laver, poet, biographer, historian of costume and, for thirty-seven years, Assistant Keeper of the Print Room of the Victoria and Albert Museum, had been occupied in several abortive attempts to establish himself as a playwright. Discouraged, however, by the intrigues and egotisms of his theatrical associates, he turned to the more tranquil and independent pursuit of fiction.

He wrote a story about a girl returning from her finishing school in Switzerland and having so many adventures en route that the journey took her a year. He first called it *Finishing School,* but discarded this later in favour of the title of one of his satirical verses which seemed to fit the idea perfectly. This was *Nymph Errant.*

It is quite possible that this happy thought was largely responsible for its success. As against the flat, pedestrian character of the first title, his new one possessed an engaging element of whimsy, charm and the promise of an entertaining read.

The London publishing house of Heinemann at once paid the author a handsome advance and published it in Britain and the American house of Alfred Knopf brought it out in New York.

Its success was helped, no doubt, by *Time and Tide*'s description of it as 'the most unpleasant book of the year' and the fact that the Irish republic banned it as being 'prejudicial to public morals'.

While these ripples of controversy over *Nymph Errant* were agitating literary circles, a letter to its young author arrived for him at the Museum. It had been forwarded from his publisher and bore a German stamp. For a while he was unable to read the writer's signature, but received a little shock of delight on deciphering it as 'Charles B Cochran'. The very name in that era had a glamorous and electrifying quality.

By one of those fortunate turns of the wheel of chance that are capable of exerting a gratuitous influence on someone's life or career, Evelyn Cochran had given her husband *Nymph Errant* to occupy his mind and – an incredible piece of naivete! – 'keep it off the theatre' during a visit to Berlin.

Cochran's letter, written from the Adlon Hotel, expressed delight in *Nymph Errant* and suggested that Laver should call and see him at 49 Old Bond Street on his return.

The young writer contained his impatience as best he could and made an appointment at the first opportunity. Nervously he climbed the stairs to that breathless Olympian retreat, the private office of C B Cochran himself, where the master showman received him with his customary warmth and the manifestly genuine interest he always took in those who showed talent, drive and ambition.

Cochran then talked about *Nymph Errant*. He'd liked it. And it seemed to him to lend itself to theatrical treatment. A play, perhaps. Would young Laver accept a contract and a hundred pounds on account? He would indeed!

As Laver left the office in a radiant glow of excitement, Cochran called after him, 'I'd like to see some more of your work. Have you written anything since *Nymph Errant*?'

'Yes,' replied Laver, 'I've just finished a life of John Wesley.'

It seemed a rather comic and incongruous thing to say to Cochran. Yet – who knows? – there may have been a play in it. One only has to consider the latterday success of John Osborne's *Luther* and Robert Bolt's *A Man for all Seasons* to realise the dramatic potential of this type of subject.

Cochran's initial idea was to adapt *Nymph Errant* as a straight play, but he later changed his mind and came to regard the subject as an excellent vehicle for musical comedy. He asked Romney Brent to do the book and commissioned the music and lyrics from Cole Porter.

This incomparable wizard of urbane, tight-knit, sophisticated theatre music was then living in Paris where Cochran sent James Laver and Romney Brent to work with him.

Describing this episode in his recent autobiography, *Museum Piece*,[1] James Laver reports that when Cochran asked Cole Porter for his address in Paris, he replied, 'Ritz Bar'. 'Yes,' said

[1] *Museum Piece,* James Laver, André Deutsch, 1963

Cochran, 'but if I want to send you a letter or telegram or some money . . .' 'Ritz Bar,' repeated Cole Porter.

Laver discovered that Cole Porter had no banking account in Paris. The celebrated composer of *Let's Do It, Night and Day* and *What is This Thing Called Love?* deposited large sums of money with Harry, the Ritz bartender, and drew on them whenever he needed some.

When not in the Ritz Bar, Cole Porter worked in a studio in the beautiful seventeenth-century house in the Rue Monsieur on the South Bank which his wife had acquired, and it was there that James Laver listened rapt for the first time to *It's Bad For Me, The Physician, Experiment, Solomon* and the many other numbers in that excellent score.

During this period the Cochrans were living in a beautiful cottage in Winkfield Green, Berkshire, which they had rented from Lady Houston Boswell. Romney Brent stayed there with them and Cole Porter came over from Paris and lived nearby so that they could all work together on *Nymph Errant* in pleasant country surroundings. There seemed to be no need for Cochran to scurry along to his Bond Street office every day while the sun shone and his writers were so close at hand.

Dorothy Dickson recalls a dinner party there one hot summer night when Cochran brought the prospective backer home to hear a demonstration of the new show.

The cottage had no piano, so a mini-piano was temporarily installed for Cole Porter who sat down, looking curiously out of place, at this squat, graceless little instrument in the centre of the room.

For my personal taste, Cole Porter was a writer with a near-infallible gift, whose songs rarely fell below the masterly standards he had established by his early compositions, yet – and perhaps this is *why* – he said, as he sat down, 'Cockie, I am frightened to death!' which was obviously true, and no affectation of modesty.

He began to play the *Nymph Errant* numbers under the glare

of a lamp that had been roughly adjusted to cast its light on the scraps of manuscript on the music stand.

Between the numbers Cochran supplied a vivid outline of the story for the benefit of the visiting 'angel', a description that could not have been more inept for someone who was in fact a large, gross, cigar-puffing businessman, clearly out of sympathy with the delicate spirit of the sophisticated theatre.

The prospective backer remained impassive throughout, giving no hint whatsoever of his impressions or feelings. Everyone sensed this. Cole Porter battled nervously on with his own accompaniments while globules of sweat rolled slowly down his forehead.

And while he was singing *The Physician,* with its phrases like '. . . he said my epiglottis was darling' and '. . . he thought an awful lotta, My medulla oblongata . . .', the visitor began to look more and more baffled and obtuse.

When the presentation ended, everyone grimly awaited the verdict with the pessimistic feeling that the charm of Cole Porter's smart and brittle talent had failed to communicate itself to this dreary man.

But he had been so well victualled and lavishly plied with cocktails, wine and brandy that, to everyone's surprise, relief and delight, he suddenly roused himself from a momentary stupor and quietly said, 'Right, I'll put up the money!'

Cochran's particular joy was that *Nymph Errant* renewed his association with the rare and inimitable personality of Gertrude Lawrence of whom he once wrote, 'Not then and not since has any other actress had her quality of dramatic radiance; there is none so sparkling, none with such perfection of poise. Gertrude Lawrence has an infinite variety of mood and expression, beauty, a never-failing sense of fun, and astounding touches of exquisite tenderness in the right places.'

It is true that audiences adored her. If her voice satisfied no academic requirements, its meandering, evocative quality was strangely heightened by its rocky sense of pitch; and such was the power of her presence that this fault which, in others, would have offended the sensitive ear, was one of the very things that endeared her to theatre goers. For this was the era of those whose charm and personality compensated for the lack of a genuine voice, the era of Beatrice Lillie, Jack Buchanan, Bobby Howes and Noël Coward.

When I first saw Gertrude Lawrence on the stage she wasn't acting. It was during the early thirties when artists used to give their services for charity on Sunday afternoons at the London Palladium, and, introducing one of these shows in front of the curtain, she appealed for money to give poor children a day's outing.

In the course of this little talk she described her own childhood, her parents' lack of money and what it had meant to her to have a day in the country with a crowd of youngsters. And she did this with such simple warmth and sincerity that, in subsequent years, I cherished an impression of her as someone richly endowed with deep compassion and human feeling.

I didn't meet her until the late forties when she appeared in *September Tide* with Michael Gough at the Aldwych Theatre.

She was staying at the Savoy. We met to discuss a small business matter in the Grill bar, and I have most regretfully to report a feeling of shock at her bitter denigration of this country.

Perhaps my raw and tender nerves, mercilessly exposed like those of every other Londoner after five years of war, were a little over-sensitive, but I remember wincing when she complained, 'Why, it's *terrible* here. In France you can buy whatever you like, but here you can't — *even if you have the money.*' Precisely! She complained of the *one* aspect of British life of which we were justly proud, namely that while in countries like France and Belgium money itself quickly became once again a golden passport to unlimited goods and services, we as a nation refused to countenance this brutal return to the economics of the jungle. Instead, we instituted a system of genuine priorities.

(Left) Cochran poses with Jessie Matthews at the London Pavilion in December.1928, just twenty-three years before the picture *(below)* was taken which shows Jessie Matthews with the wrestler, Hackenschmidt, at the unveiling ceremony of a bust of Cochran shortly after his death.

(Right) Cochran congratulates Elizabeth Henderson after the first night of his 1950 show, *The Ivory Tower*. *(Keystone). (Below)* The author, Sam Heppner, with Noël Coward who has written the foreword to this book *(London Press Photos)*

At the Cochran memorial ceremony were many of the Cochran Young Ladies who worked for him over a period of twenty years. Among those shown in this photograph are *(standing front row)* Jessie Matthews, Anna Neagle and Florence Desmond.

(*Right*) A last curtain call (*Radio Times Hulton Picture Library*). (*Below*) Anna Neagle and A P Herbert, now Sir Alan, admire the bust of Sir Charles Cochran at the memorial ceremony at London's Adelphi Theatre in 1951.

The supporters of all the political parties gave assent to the principle that, in a time of universal scarcity, the possession of money was not of itself a warrant to more than one's fair share of basic necessities; that, until there was enough of everything for everyone, greed should be tamed by the ration book.

But, possibly through having lived in America where, even in wartime, the production of general commodities remained at such a high level that purchasing power was dictated solely by the purse, this was something she failed to understand.

The Autocratic Bergner

IN HIS HEYDAY, Cochran averaged four productions a year. And, in 1933, the year of *Nymph Errant*, he also staged another musical, *Music In The Air* – again with Jerome Kern's engaging and attractive songs – A P Herbert's *Mother of Pearl* with music by Oscar Straus, and two straight plays, *Wild Decembers* and *Escape Me Never*. By casting Mary Ellis in *Music In The Air*, he took a mischievous pleasure in revealing her magnificent voice to a surprised and delighted first night audience. For London had only seen her in Eugene O'Neill's *Strange Interlude* and knew nothing of her four years at the Met and the fact that Rudolf Friml had written *Rose Marie* for her. In *Escape Me Never* Cochran introduced the superb Elisabeth Bergner whose performance sent audiences dazed and dumbfounded from the theatre at curtain-fall every night.

Wild Decembers, a play about the Brontës, by Clemence Dane, was directed by Benn Levy and, despite a cast which included Emlyn Williams, Ralph Richardson, Austin Trevor, Beatrix Lehmann and Diana Wynyard, it made little stir at the time and is remembered by few today.

The career of every theatre manager is a vast speculation, an uneasy progress from peak to valley and, with good judgment and equally good luck, an eventual return to the peak. For most, the peak is signified by a roaring trade at the box office, bundles of crisp notes being carefully checked and duly put in the safe when the last seat has gone.

But Cochran was unlike the average theatre manager. Of course he liked financial success. But he was so quixotic, generous and muddle-headed about money that this consideration took second place to the joy of artistic fulfilment or the thrill of launching an exciting discovery.

And it was chiefly in this context that his career in 1933 touched a new peak of glory when he brought Elisabeth Bergner to England.

Finding he had a few hours to spare before catching a late train in Germany, he went to see *Saint Joan*. Friends in Berlin had urged him not to miss this production in which the principal role was played by a new Austrian artist, Elisabeth Bergner, whose name was unfamiliar to him.

Her acting impressed him so much that, whenever he was in central Europe, he made inquiries as to her whereabouts. He managed to see her several times – in *The Constant Nymph, Strange Interlude, The Last of Mrs Cheyney* and a good deal of Shakespeare; gradually learning more about her, he discovered that, in a few short years, she had also played the heroines of Ibsen, Strindberg, Schiller and Euripides.

Conscious of his limited German, he made no attempt to meet her. In an odd, rather schoolboyish way he sent her some flowers. Anonymously.

The morning after the first night of *Mother of Pearl* he happened to meet Incze Sandor, editor of a Hungarian stage journal.

The conversation went something like this:

'Yes, I was at the Gaiety Theatre last night. I took Elizabeth Bergner.'

'Bergner! What an artist! I didn't know she was in England. Tell me, Sandor; there's one thing I'd like to know. Does she speak English?'

'Oh yes; she does.'

'Then would you please tell me where she is staying?'

Armed with the address, Cochran at once sent her a note inviting her to lunch the next day. She declined, pleading a prior engagement, but said that she would be delighted to join him the day after.

Next day her 'prior engagement' was all over the evening papers. It was her marriage – to the ace film maker, Dr Paul Czinner!

On the following day Cochran called for her and drove her to his home in Montagu Street where he was giving a small luncheon party, Cole Porter and Viola Tree being among the guests.

Over the coffee and liqueurs, Cochran cautiously sounded her out on the question of appearing in London and, finding her agreeable in principle, set about looking for a play that would suit an artist who enjoyed a formidable reputation on the Continent, but was completely unknown here. She had already triumphed in a German stage version of Margaret Kennedy's famous book, *The Constant Nymph,* and was attracted by the idea of doing something else by the same author; perhaps a sequel.

After a lapse of some weeks, she and Margaret Kennedy drove out to Winkfield Green with the first draft of *Escape Me Never* which was in fact a sequel. Cochran's reaction was so favourable, his enthusiasm so infectious, that the two women returned to London in a bubbling, euphoric mood.

In making his arrangements for the opening of *Escape Me Never* at the Opera House, Manchester, Cochran was shrewd enough to recognise that, because Bergner was unknown in this country, it would be far better to surprise first night audiences with her sensational performance than prepare them for it with a publicity build-up.

He therefore gave her equal billing with the rest of the cast and instructed his publicity department to introduce her to the press in cold, simple, biographical terms, containing no rosy adjectives or descriptions of her exceptional qualities as an artist.

Cochran afterwards described that opening night as one of the most thrilling moments of his life.

In the charged and pregnant atmosphere of the final curtain, the audience were absolutely thunderstruck and temporarily muted by what they had just seen and heard. Then the silence broke as a hurricane of applause swept the auditorium.

On the subject of that memorable night, Cochran wrote in his book, *Cock-a-doodle-do*,[1] 'One hears and reads of the house "rising" to a performance. It is a rare phenomenon. In the old days the house would "rise" to Irving and Ellen Terry when they were at the height of their fame. At Covent Garden the house would "rise" to Caruso and to Melba. But one may be a theatre goer for years without experiencing the curious thrill which follows that silent descent of a curtain – that gasp of amazement, a realisation which heralds the frenzied acclamation of a great artist in a great moment of triumph.'

The morning after *Escape Me Never* opened at the Apollo Theatre, London, Cochran spent two hours trying to telephone the box office. But the lines were blocked. He eventually got through to the stage door keeper and asked him to tell the box office manager that he would like to hear from him as soon as possible.

Later that day the box office manager rang Cochran to say that the onslaught on the theatre was little short of a stampede. In his long experience, he had never seen anything like it. Disappointed applicants who had the slightest acquaintance with Cochran transferred their despairing appeals to him. Mounds of mail, from the modest and the mighty, landed on his desk every morning. H G Wells wrote: 'Can you tell somebody to do something about it, so that I can get two seats or a loge either Friday or Saturday evening or matinee? Don't let it bother you; but if a wave of your hand can do it, please wave your hand.'

Highly strung, and not too richly endowed with stamina, Bergner began to wilt under the strain of her demanding role and when she finally collapsed during a matinee, Cochran withdrew the play.

Poor Cochran. It happened so often that he was forced to close

---

[1] *Cock-a-doodle-do*, C B Cochran, J M Dent, 1941

a successful production because of some contingency beyond his control.

Although they had not met, Maurice Baring, whose biographies of Bernhardt and Duse were being widely read by lovers of the theatre, at once offered Bergner his house in Rottingdean where she might recuperate. This she readily accepted, staying down by the sea for a month.

When she returned, Cochran reopened the play and once again the public flocked in vast crowds to see her. But her recovery was not complete. She was still tired and weak, and when the hot weather began, she declared that she could not go on.

The curtain descended for the last time on a packed and excited house. And Cochran was certain that, but for Bergner's health, *Escape Me Never* would have filled the theatre for at least another year.

Peter Scott brought his godfather, Sir James Barrie, round to the back of the house one night to meet her. Barrie invited her to tea at his flat. She enjoyed her visit which afterwards became a weekly routine.

Bergner told Cochran that, on one of these occasions, Barrie, standing by the big fireplace in his flat in the Adelphi, said to her, 'What character would you most like to play?'

She didn't have to think. She at once replied, 'David . . . the young David who slew Goliath.'

The subject made an immediate impact on the Scots writer. His mouth fell open, his beloved pipe dropped with a clatter to the brick hearth.

'This is a historic moment,' he said.

A few weeks later Barrie read the first act of *The Boy David* to her. This development introduced a difficulty in Cochran's relations with la Bergner. They had agreed that she should next appear under his management in *Amphitryon 38* in which she had made a successful appearance on the Continent, and he at once secured the rights from Giradoux, the author.

This agreement was of limited duration and, now that Elisabeth Bergner insisted on doing *The Boy David* next, Cochran found himself obliged to buy an extended option or squander his original investment. He renewed his rights several times until, having paid the author something in the region of eight hundred pounds, he was next required to guarantee that Elisabeth Bergner would play the leading role. But now that she had privately opted to star in *The Boy David* he could clearly give no such undertaking.

This setback marked only the beginning of the dismal catalogue of obstructions which, thanks to the wayward and autocratic Miss Bergner, were to attend the production of *The Boy David*.

Three or four months later, when Cochran, left in the lurch and bereft of his rights in *Amphitryon*, was living in Cox's Green, Maidenhead, where he had rented the cottage of Priscilla, Countess of Annesley, he received a telephone call from Elisabeth Bergner who said she had the completed script of *The Boy David* and would arrive with it the next day.

She duly turned up and, so as not to prejudice his judgment, gave him no inkling of her own opinion, but merely bade him take it away and read it.

He did so and came back into the room with a broad grin of pleasure on his face. A fine play, he thought; a very fine play. And if, at that moment, someone had offered him £50,000 for the rights, he would not have accepted it.

Alas, he did not know what lay ahead. His zeal was boundless. He greatly admired the work and felt a deep sense of honour and privilege in being entrusted by the great Sir James Barrie to stage his latest play.

With Bergner in the lead, he was certain that *The Boy David* would repeat the infallible success pattern of *Escape Me Never*.

Not long after the press announced his plans for Barrie's new play, Elisabeth Bergner said she proposed to make the film version of *Escape Me Never* at Elstree, and that *The Boy David* would have to await its completion.

The trend of public taste in the theatre is so capricious that the right psychological moment has to be judged with exquisite subtlety. Delay, as every experienced impresario knows, may mean death. Worse, however, was to come.

While patiently awaiting the conclusion of the film, Dr Czinner told Cochran that his wife next planned to make a screen version of *Saint Joan*.

In desperation, Cochran appealed to Barrie who said he had had no option but to accept the postponement of *The Boy David* because he had written it for her and only she could appear in it.

Cochran, who was now beginning to feel like the victim of some vast conspiracy, went along with Czinner and Bergner to see Shaw.

Shaw was charming, but not very sympathetic. He wished to be left alone to get on with his writing and he treated the arrangements as a *fait accompli*. But he threw Cochran a scrap of compensatory comfort by asking him to handle the negotiations. 'I have so much literary work on hand,' he explained, 'that I have little time for business. You know what I want and what Miss Bergner wants, but you must not assume that these film people understand *Saint Joan* as well as you do!'

It looked, on this occasion, as if there would be no further hitches.

Shaw pointed out that, as the play took three hours to perform, cuts would have to be made for the film version and, a few days later, he wrote to Cochran, 'As no producer would venture to cut the play about as drastically as I, nor could write the new connective tissue in my style, I shall have to go through the play with a big blue pencil, and make a rough draft, indicating the material that must be discarded, and the nature of the scenes needed to replace it. The scenario will therefore be very different from the published play, shorter and more rapid and tragic in its action and character. This must be fully understood between the parties, or we may have them complaining that the article we shall supply is not what they bargained for. It will be much better for their purpose; but it will not be the same. So make the point clear at the start.'

It was now the summer of 1934. Cochran had made little progress in his affairs which, as never before, were subject to endless frustration, confusion and delay.

Shaw wrote in the following November to say that he had finished his screen version of *Saint Joan,* having introduced several new scenes and made the production as expensive as possible, because, he explained, '. . . the film people would not believe in anything that did not cost over a hundred thousand.'

Although he wanted to discuss the scenario with the Czinners, Shaw suggested that they had better wait until Elisabeth had finished screening *Escape Me Never.*

This meant a further delay. Meanwhile Shaw, who was then seventy-eight, had a spell in bed through overwork and presently went to Africa to recuperate.

In the autumn of 1935 Shaw wrote to Cochran from Malvern complaining that, in spite of the trouble he had taken to turn *Saint Joan* into a film, Paul Czinner had appointed James Bridie to work on the script with him. 'I was not surprised,' he said in this letter. 'These film people all think they know their business better than I know mine.'

But worse was to come. With an eye to the American film market, Czinner opened negotiations with the Roman Catholic Church in the United States, but Shaw protested that he would not have his plays subjected to Catholic censorship.

The Hollywood distributors claimed that, if the ecclesiastical authorities put a ban on the film, all American Catholics would be forbidden to see it.

Shaw then made the point that as there were only sixty million Catholics in the USA, this would still leave a potential audience of a hundred million for the film. This may have been a typical piece of tortuous Shavian logic, but the eminent buffoon raised considerable mirth by pertinently adding that the Church had also forbidden those sixty millions to drink, gamble, lend money at interest or have sexual relations outside wedlock, and that he had no reason to suppose that a prohibition on a film would be any more effective.

On 26th September Shaw wrote to Cochran: 'Paul has cut Elisabeth's best bits out of the scenario with a marvellous instinct for doing the wrong thing. However, I like him, and will not, if I can help it, shunt him completely into a siding.'

But this affirmation of continued support on the part of Shaw was purely academic because negotiations broke down over the question of religious censorship, neither side being prepared to give way.

This might have augured well for an early resumption of the plans for staging *The Boy David*, but Bergner released a further bombshell by announcing that, if her film of *Saint Joan* couldn't be shown in America, she would make a screen version of *As You Like It* instead.

Mysteriously, Sir James Barrie not only failed to object to these wilful procrastinations, he seemed to give them his blessing by visiting Elstree on several occasions to watch the filming.

Cochran was now in a 'willy nilly' frame of mind and, assuming that *As You Like It* would be finished in time, he announced that Elisabeth Bergner would open come what may in *The Boy David* at the King's Theatre, Edinburgh, on 15th February 1936, for a preliminary two weeks' run.

But, by mid-January, it was clear that the picture would not be finished in time and Cochran was again compelled to announce the postponement of Barrie's play, the new dates being 14th March for Edinburgh and 4th April for His Majesty's Theatre, London.

Rehearsals were scrappy and rather unsatisfactory at first. Confined to his rooms with a bad cold, Barrie could not be present to help a director handicapped by unfamiliarity with a new and strangely unusual play.

Twelve days before the opening, Bergner's maid went down into the stalls where Cochran sat watching the rehearsals, hunched over his cane. She told him that Miss Bergner was feeling very ill in her dressing room. Would he please go and see her?

He followed the maid through the pass door and limped along to the airy and spacious star dressing room where he found his leading lady obviously far from well. He at once escorted her to her car, saw that she was warmly tucked into a blanket, and sent the maid back with her to her home.

That night her doctor examined her and called in Lord Horder who confirmed his diagnosis of acute appendicitis and declared that she must have an operation at once. By the time Cochran received the news, she was already in the London Clinic; and when he called there the operation was over. According to the surgeon, the case was a bad one, the operation had been performed just in time and, for forty-eight hours, the patient's condition had been dangerous.

The announcement of yet another postponement in the press gave rise to the wildest speculation and rumour, much of it malicious.

Cochran and Barrie had quarrelled, it was said; the director couldn't agree with the author and – before the news of her serious illness disposed of this one – Bergner was being a *prima donna* once more; she didn't like her part and was throwing another temperament. . . .

There seemed, indeed, to be a curse on the play.

It was some days before Cochran was allowed to visit Bergner, but he did receive a card from her with the following message: 'My stitches are out, and I am really much better and having far less pain. Only sleeping badly, and feeling drowsy all day long. The whole thing seems a mad nightmare, and I do not know what to make of it. . . .'

With this new setback, it was manifestly impossible to think of putting *The Boy David* into production before December.

Bergner and her husband took a cottage in Sussex. And, on her recovery, she elected to make yet another film, thus vindicating the report of a particular newspaper which had suggested as much and found itself bombarded with passionate denials from Cochran, now a thoroughly crestfallen and exasperated man.

But plans for *The Boy David* still went ahead. It was to open at the King's Theatre, Edinburgh, on Saturday, 21st November, and again at His Majesty's Theatre, London, on 14th December.

In terms of the creative people concerned with this play, it had all the impressive trappings of a Cochran production. Stage direction by Komisarjevsky. Decor by Augustus John. Incidental music by William Walton.

But there were more early difficulties. Taking into account the many postponements, the production costs were now enormous.

Barrie was suffering from low blood pressure and violent pains in the back. This prevented him from attending rehearsals which, since no theatre was available, took place in a disused chapel in the Walworth Road.

On the opening night in Edinburgh, there were various little delays and technical troubles backstage. The front stalls had been put up to the extortionate price of thirty shillings which, for Edinburgh, was unheard of. Barrie was still too ill to attend and the audience was disappointed to find that their great literary compatriot was not among them.

Cochran had a gnawing anxiety that all was not well. It was already nearly half an hour after the scheduled opening time. The audience was becoming restless and impatient. And Cochran, usually so adept at wresting some advantage from an adverse situation, did something that was strangely out of character. For a man of such finesse, it was startlingly clumsy and ill-conceived.

He went in front of the curtain, welcomed the audience and ended his short speech with the words, '. . . and I am pleased to tell you, ladies and gentlemen, that what you have come to see is not the first performance of *The Boy David*. That will be given tomorrow night. But this evening, you are to have the rare privilege of attending *a dress rehearsal*!'

This saucy tactic was a dangerous gamble. Would the audience accept it? Or would they resent such a transparent insult to their credulity?

Luckily for Cochran the old magic worked. Everyone beamed and cooed, flattered at the thought of being privy to so exclusive an event, of seeing the mysterious mechanics of theatrical production, concealed by long tradition from the public eye, worked out in their favoured presence.

But their conciliatory mood gradually evaporated in the course of three-and-a-half long, dreary hours of dramatic invention that was indifferently written and clumsily mounted, and which ended – to the obvious chagrin of all – after the pubs had closed.

On my desk lies a cutting from the *Daily Mail* dated 21st May 1937. In it, Clive MacManus, the paper's dramatic critic, wrote: 'When we are old, and watch our plays from the chimney corner on television sets, we shall tell our children of the thrills of a Cochran first night. And they will listen sceptically, for such thrills will certainly never be theirs. . . .'

A Cochran first night was certainly an institution, a red letter event on the London calendar. It was a night of the stars and the richly plumed leaders of the social set, effulgent with jewellery and furs, tiaras and tailcoats.

The occasion itself – combined in a curiously subtle way with the pervasive ambience of the man behind it – attracted the stars, the principal theatre managers and agents, and the big personalities of every department of theatrical life. The crowded, bright-lit, scent-laden theatre foyer became a shop window for actors and actresses, a discreet and decorous market place where it was both self-flattering and professionally advantageous to 'be seen'.

It also attracted the business magnates and the aristocracy. Regular patrons of a Cochran first night included people like Winston Churchill, Gordon Selfridge, Charles and Margaret Sweeney, Noël Coward, Lady Asquith, Anthony Asquith, the Duff Coopers, Lord and Lady Kinross, Lord and Lady Shrewsbury, Sir Louis and Lady Sterling. . . .

And, although these ostentatious and bitchily competitive displays, which grossly emphasised the gulf between rich and poor, would perhaps seem less than admirable in our more egalitarian times, one can still look back and relive the bubbling excitement of those occasions, much as one may admire the architecture of St Petersburg or the beauty of the court of Louis XVI without condoning the inhumanities that made them possible.

Whether, as a compensatory reaction to his lower middle class beginnings, Cochran cultivated the duchesses and noble lords in order to persuade himself and the world at large that he was now acceptable in these privileged and guarded circles . . . whether, in other words, he was what we should now have no hesitation in calling a snob; or whether he believed that the presence of the leading and most controversial debs and social-ites whose names filled the gossip columns was a good thing for the box office, we shall never know. His motives may, of course, have been compounded of both considerations.

But the obvious pleasures he took in sprinkling his auto-biographical books with lists of titled first-nighters does sug-gest in fact that he was something of a tuft hunter. The reverse side of the coin of this interesting personality, however, must not be forgotten. We have seen that he could show a very warm and genuine human concern for the welfare of the most insignificant little walker-on, applying himself single-mindedly and as an adored father-substitute to her personal problems, adjuring her, for example, not to marry if he thought she was making a mistake; or giving her the gravest warning not to allow Mr X, the noted agent, to see her home in a taxi!

The crowds that assembled in the foyer of His Majesty's Theatre for the London opening of *The Boy David* three weeks after its trial run in Edinburgh were typical enough but, in a curious way, the glittering and gorgeous exterior of that merry trinket we used to call A Cochran First Night concealed a boomerang within. For it presented a real danger that the stars would outshine the show.

Looking supremely beautiful in magnificent raiment, Marlene Dietrich in particular proved such a cynosure that she distracted attention from the main business of the evening!

Cochran knew that Dietrich was expected at the first night of *The Boy David* and, fearing this effect, arranged for Constance Collier to smuggle her in by a special door where he was to meet and escort them to their seats when the house lights dimmed and the curtain was about to rise.

'I shall never forget that first performance at His Majesty's,' wrote Cochran. 'There was a chill about it which sometimes returns to me in the form of a nightmare. Before the curtain had been up half an hour I knew the play was doomed. It was only a minor irritation that the night was wet; there was a jam of cars, and Constance Collier and Marlene could not find the door where I was to meet them. We had drawn a so-called sophisticated audience, with their thumbs turned down, before the curtain rose.'

Three and a half years of misfortune and postponement had robbed the play of its lustre; the keen edge of the public's initial interest had been blunted by the continual delays, evasions and excuses.

Cochran had first announced that *The Boy David* would open

in July 1934 when Bergner's name was a magic talisman. But the curtain did not rise on it until December 1937.

The press gave the play a trouncing and the West End ticket libraries, merciless barometers of playgoing trends, could not sell the tickets they had taken for the first six weeks.

So they sold some at reduced prices and gave the remainder away, 'papering' the house to provide a satisfactory atmosphere for the benefit both of the paying seat holders and the artists, and also, of course, to create the illusion of prosperity. There was no alternative but to withdraw the play within a very short time.

Among the many hazards of theatrical management is the haunting problem of accommodation. Theatres are often leased for a limited period, and a manager with a short lease and a successful production is obliged to transfer to another theatre. If he can. Thus a game of leap-frog-cum-peggotty is constantly in progress among the West End play handlers.

When Cochran announced the withdrawal of *The Boy David* the people behind *Balalaika*, the Eric Maschwitz-George Posford musical show at the Adelphi, arranged to make room for another production at that theatre by transferring *Balalaika* to His Majesty's.

Then something else happened. In the maddeningly perverse way so familiar to theatrical entrepreneurs, the announcement of Cochran's intention to withdraw *The Boy David* sparked off a tremendous rush for seats. Every available seat for all the remaining performances was quickly seized. And on the final Saturday the crowds being turned away collided with those going in, and there was such confusion in the Haymarket that the police had to be called. If only Cochran could have transferred. But no London theatre was available.

This again was typical of the bad luck that haunted him throughout so many of his enterprises, particularly in connection with *The Boy David* itself.

On 19th June 1937, Sir James Barrie died. The news reached

Cochran when he was in New York. He was deeply grieved, not only by the loss of a friend and a writer for whose works he had unbounded admiration, but principally by the thought that he had been concerned with all the troubles and disasters that attended his last play which Cochran regarded as his best.

Barrie left two thousand pounds to Elisabeth Bergner – 'the actress who gave the best performance in any of my plays'.

Mr Adler from America

Nineteen thirty-four was a fateful year. It marked the end of the Cochran-Coward association.

Shortly before leaving for America to appear with Alfred Lunt and Lynn Fontanne in *Design for Living*, which he had written specially for this outstanding couple and himself, Coward was dining in Paris one night with Cochran who suddenly said to him, 'I've been thinking, Noël, about Yvonne Printemps – and a new play for her that I'd like you to write.'

Typically, Cochran had visited the most expensive flower shop in Paris, called on Yvonne Printemps, disarmed her with six dozen orchids and said, 'I am going to present you in London.' This was not a request. It was a bold statement of intention. And Yvonne Printemps succumbed.

There was now some discussion between Cochran and Coward about the adequacy of her English.

'She has very little,' said Cochran. 'You'll have to make her a French-speaking girl in English surroundings; then she can speak some English and fall back into French sometimes. I trust your ingenuity to find a situation that gives her the excuse.'

Coward said he would try to think of an idea, but promised no more than that. On his return from New York, he gave a cocktail party. Through mistaking the time it was due to start, Cochran arrived an hour too early so, until the guests began to arrive, they sat and talked. Coward said that he'd still not been able to find a vehicle for Yvonne Printemps, but they continued to talk and, within minutes of the first guest's arrival, something clicked in Coward's mind.

During the party, he sidled up to Cochran and whispered, 'I believe I've got the idea.'

He rang Cochran a few days later and told him he had worked out the story line – '. . . but don't say anything to Yvonne yet. There may be snags.'

A week or so later he rang again. 'It's all right,' he said, 'you can tell her.'

At Goldenhurst, his country house, Coward read his first draft to Cochran and played some of the music.

They offered Romney Brent the leading part, but he declined it on the grounds that he was a comic actor rather than a romantic hero, so Coward played the part himself. Cochran considered this a mistake. 'I felt that it would take his attention from the direction of the play . . . he lacked the romantic quality the part needed, and his French accent was very English against Yvonne's.'

In celebration of a Coward first night, Cochran always presented him with a little gift. He searched the antique shops for a Georgian snuff box which would be large enough to serve as a cigarette case.

When he gave it to Noël Coward after the opening of *Conversation Piece* it bore the inscription, 'In memory of a not altogether unsuccessful association'. Consciously or otherwise, he had chosen a valedictory form of wording. It seemed to hark back to the past and contain a hint of impending separation.

A couple of weeks later Cochran strolled into Coward's dressing room. Coward seemed awkward and ill at ease.

'Did you get my letter?' he eventually asked.

Cochran shook his head.

'Funny. I wrote to you. You should have had it. I wanted you to get it before you saw me.'

A day or two later the letter came to light. It was customary for Rosling, Cochran's manservant, to bring his master the mail every morning. Coward's letter had slipped on to the floor where the dog had seized it and manœuvred it under the bed where it was subsequently retrieved, crumpled and toothmarked.

Cochran sat down and straightened out the creases. And this is what he read:

My dear Cockie,

If you were a less understanding or generous person this letter would be very difficult to write; as it is, however, I feel you will appreciate my motives completely and without prejudice.

I have decided, after mature consideration, to present my own and other people's plays in the future in partnership with Jack.[1] This actually has been brewing up in my mind over a period of years, and I am writing to you first, in confidence, because I want you to understand that there would be no question of forsaking you or breaking our tremendously happy and successful association for any other reason except that I feel this is an inevitable development in my career in the theatre.

Particularly I want you to realise how deeply grateful I am for all the generosity and courage and friendship you have shown me over everything we have done together, and I would like you to know that in any of our future enterprises, where it is at all possible, you will be welcome to a share whenever it is at all feasible, and whenever you personally consider that the idea or the script shows a good chance of profit.

This is actually the result of our increasing activities in New York in recent years where, with considerable profit, we have bought interests in several productions of other managements and, as you know, have controlled and virtually presented several of them.

But above all, dear Cockie, I want to insist upon one important fact which, sentimental as it may seem, is on my part deeply sincere, and that is that without your encouragement and faith in me and my work it is unlikely that I should have ever reached the position I now hold in the theatre, and that whatever may

---

[1] Jack Wilson, a young American stockbroker who so admired Coward's performance in *The Vortex,* at the Little Theatre in the mid-twenties, that he sought an introduction. Within a short while of their meeting he became Coward's business manager and remained with him for many years.

happen in the future, I feel that there is a personal bond between us which has nothing to do with business or finance or production.

Please understand about all this, and continue to give me the benefit of your invaluable friendship.

Yours affectionately,
Noël

Cochran wrote back:

My dear Noël,

Many thanks for your letter of the 9th inst, which was found this morning under my bed, very much chewed up by my dachshund.

As you say, the development you refer to was inevitable, and I wish you and your associates the best of good fortune.

Meanwhile, believe me,

Yours as ever,
CBC

Coward was hurt. The reply seemed curt and formal. It lacked the writer's usual warmth, and Coward took the bit about the dog to be another of Cochran's curiously flat and inept jokes. But he was highly amused when he discovered that the dog had really been the culprit.

Cochran believed that '. . . *Conversation Piece* was a very clever piece of work, containing many charming things in writing and production. As a play it did not find high favour at the hands of the critics, but both press and public capitulated to the charms of Yvonne Printemps. It did big and profitable business at His Majesty's.'

In my opinion, the evocative quality of the rarely played verse to *I'll follow my secret heart*, with its ingenious key changes and extended intervals, is the closest approach that Noël Coward has ever made to the near-operatic *genre* and that, had the composer's musical education gone beyond his three lessons with Orlando Morgan at the Guildhall School of Music, he might well have written something of a less ephemeral nature.

Soon after the opening of *Streamline*, his revue at the Palace Theatre, with Florence Desmond, Naunton Wayne, Holland and Hart and Norah Howard, Cochran revisited America. While lunching in a Hollywood restaurant, the waiter handed him a note and five ten-dollar bills. The note read, 'Dear Mr Cochran, May I take this opportunity to repay in material value only, because I could never, I fear, repay you for the thought behind your kind action, a loan you made to me some six years ago in London. Very sincerely, Paul Draper.'

Cochran was touched. Turning his gaze to a neighbouring table he saw the gifted young dancer who had sent him the note, and who, he recalled, had visited him in his Bond Street office. At the time Cochran had no plans for a production in which he could offer young Draper anything, much as he admired his skill, and observing the look of stark disappointment on his face, divined his desperate pecuniary position and handed him ten pounds to help him over his difficulties.

Not long after this incident Cochran sailed for Britain. Whenever he returned from America, it was an established custom for the press men to besiege him on the quay at Southampton. And when he disembarked and they received him with the inevitable, 'Who have you brought back this time, Mr Cochran?' he blandly replied, 'A mouth organ player!'

'No, no, but *really*, Mr Cochran.'

'Yes, a mouth organ player – really!'

Treating his statement as a joke, a frivolous attempt to sidetrack questions about some exciting and mysterious importation whose identity he was trying to conceal, they felt cheated, until Cochran duly summoned to his side a thin, dark, kinky-haired young American with an intense and nervous look. 'Come along, Larry,' he said. 'Come and meet the gentlemen of the press. Gentlemen, this is Larry Adler. He plays the mouth organ.'

'Where will he be playing it . . . which theatre?'

'I don't know at the moment. Perhaps not in a theatre at all. I expect I shall take the Albert Hall!'

Trust Cochran, wizard of showmanship, to conceive the idea of presenting this raw, wiry, diminutive mouth organ player in the vast Royal Albert Hall.

Multum in parvo in reverse.

In fact when Cochran brought Larry Adler over, he had no plans for him at all. The mouth organ virtuoso, then nineteen, had been playing in a small theatre in New York, and the real 'impresario' in this particular case was ten-year-old Peter, son of Elsie April. The three of them called on Larry Adler after the show.

'I know nothing about mouth organ playing,' Cochran confessed, 'and don't know whether you are any good. But Peter says you are, and, as you're the first mouth organ player I've ever seen in a dinner jacket, I thought we'd better come round and see you. I'd like to invite you back to England, but I must tell you quite honestly that I have no job for you there at this moment, and if you did come over, you'd have to pay your own expenses. But I feel sure that if C B Cochran went back to England with a mouth organ player, something would open up.'

Once again, the combined influence of the irresistible Cochran charm, the persuasiveness and the reputation worked their magic. Larry had just received the highest offer he had ever had: a twelve-week contract for three hundred and fifty dollars a week at the Hollywood Restaurant, New York.

'I turned it down,' Larry told me, 'and sailed to England with Mr Cochran for no money and no guarantee and, looking back, I think the reason I did it was that Charles B Cochran was the first gentleman – and I *mean* gentleman – I had ever met in show business.'

Young Larry had heard of the Albert Hall and felt that he was certainly not experienced or confident enough to give a recital there.

The Times had evidently never heard of a mouth organ; so it called him a trombone player.

'I only knew,' he explained, 'that I wanted to be with Mr Cochran. I'd never met anybody like him. He was so kind. He treated me with respect. In the New York world of show business in those days, a nineteen-year-old boy didn't get much respect; and none at all from people older than himself.'

Despite *The Times'* ignorance of the mouth organ as a musical instrument, the other newspapers exploited the novelty appeal of Larry Adler's arrival so massively that Cochran took advantage of this valuable publicity by putting him into *Streamline*. This was approaching the end of its run, but it continued for an extra fifteen weeks, largely through public curiosity in this astonishingly gifted youth who was able to extract genuinely musical effects, with the correct phrasing, harmonies, artistic little figures and glissandos from an instrument that – so far as anybody understood – was capable only of a clumsy, inharmonious, suck-and-blow treatment by nasty children and office boys.

This had the unfortunate, if understandable, effect of inflating Master Adler's head which was the cause of a rather painful incident.

In those pre-television days, the most coveted assignment on radio was a spot in the Saturday evening programme, *Henry Hall's Guest Night*.

Cochran was cock-a-hoop at having arranged for Larry to appear on this programme, but rather hurt and deflated by his young protégé's reaction.

In a glow of excitement and pleasure, Cochran brought the glad tidings to Larry.

'. . . and I've got you,' he added with a broad grin, 'a fee of a hundred pounds!'

On hearing this, he thought, Larry would jump for joy; and he was so brimful of goodwill and warm-heartedness that he always took a positive delight in the good fortune of others. Hence his smiling eagerness to impart the news.

Larry had never received anything like a hundred pounds for a broadcast, but he thought it politic to appear sophisticated, tough and hard-headed.

'Not enough,' he retorted, giving no appearance of satisfaction or gratitude.

The great Santa Claus, eternally struggling to escape from the outward Cochran *persona*, meekly slunk back, chilled and deflated. The smile left Cochran's face. Obviously he was deeply hurt but, instead of remonstrating against the lad for his boorish ingratitude, as many another man in his position would certainly have done, he responded with characteristic dignity and instinctive psychological insight.

'Very well, Larry,' he said quietly. 'I think it would be a good idea for you to accept it, but it's entirely your own decision.'

This had a much more salutary effect than if Cochran had responded in tones of bitter and noisy reproach. Larry's artificial front collapsed. He at once felt chastened and guilty.

He apologised and agreed.

It was arranged that Cochran should introduce him on the programme. Larry finished his first number and although the next announcement was due, Cochran had stuffed his glasses into his pocket and couldn't read the script so, instead of giving the title of the number, he ad libbed.

'Larry uses a new mouth organ every time he plays,' he told listeners, 'don't you, Larry?'

This was a piece of sheer impromptu whimsy, of course, but it encouraged hundreds of listeners to send Larry various sums of money with requests for the discarded instruments.

That sudden, imaginative ploy for filling the gap, so typical of Cochran's quick brain and presence of mind, created a legend that has haunted Larry ever since.

The Cochrans 'adopted' Larry, and when they went to America, they gave him the free run of their house.

'Use it as your own,' said Cochran. Fascinated by anything that produced musical sounds the young mouth organ player naturally loved the piano on which – as Mrs Cochran told him – composers like George Gershwin, Cole Porter and Richard Rodgers had written some of their music.

'Cochran didn't have any of the phoney veneer of the other theatre managers,' says Larry. 'You never felt you had to get beneath that outer layer. What you saw was what he was – a direct, simple, extraordinarily kind man.'

Streamline contained one or two other interesting novelties. Sherkot was particularly memorable for his white-faced, clown-like impression of a nonchalant, gum-chewing goal keeper. Tom Webster, the famous sporting cartoonist, had spotted him working in restaurant cabaret. 'You must see him,' said Tom, so Cochran slipped into Romano's one night, decided that Sherkot would be excellent in revue and booked him for *Streamline* in which he displayed his drollery against a Tom Webster backcloth of spectators convulsed with laughter.

Apart from this one scene, the decor was provided by Doris Zinkeisen and Rex Whistler whose death, during the 1939–45 war in which he served with the Welsh Guards, robbed the art world of a highly original talent.

In his own biography of C B Cochran,[1] which appeared not long after the impresario's death, Charles Graves describes a conversation with Cochran that took place while they were crossing Piccadilly Circus. Plans for the new revue were already in hand, but there was as yet no title for it.

'I am looking for a name that somehow reflects the idea of those smart, new, streamlined American motor cars,' he said. 'Can you think of anything?'

Mr Graves responded at once with, 'What about *Stream-line?*'

He thought it an excellent suggestion and agreed to it at once, but Mr Graves privately suspects that Cochran had already

[1] *The Cochran Story*, Charles Graves, W H Allen, 1951

decided on the title and had merely used this crafty little charade to test his reaction.

Following the success of Louis Golding's novel, *Magnolia Street,* a warm, richly peopled story of Jewish life in Manchester, Cochran decided to present a dramatised version of the book and engaged Golding and A R Rawlinson to write the stage adaptation which was directed by Komisarjevsky.

Although in 1934 Hitler's anti-semitic campaign was fairly restrained in comparison with the fiendish policy of annihilation that he was to adopt in the ensuing years, it made a cruel mockery of this gentle family story with its homespun dialogue, its essentially Jewish humour. Even those who had enjoyed the book now felt robbed by the tragic events in Germany of their capacity to enjoy the subject again in play form. The Jews were too distressed; and sympathetic non-Jews did not wish to be tortured by feelings of helpless anguish. As Golding himself wrote in *The World I Knew,*[1] . . . . After the Reichstag fire, the Jewish thing could not be funny any more. It was not even tolerable any more. To the Jews, it was dismay; to the Gentile it was a reproach or an incitement and ultimately, excepting to fanatics on this side or that, a bore . . . a nerve-racking bore.'

Consequently *Magnolia Street* lasted just over four weeks.

In 1934 they pulled down the old London Pavilion. Despite the fact that Cochran had produced nothing there for two or three years and that, since relinquishing his connection with it, the old Pav had gone over to non-stop variety of a rather cheap and tasteless kind, its disappearance marked a milestone in theatrical history and gave Cochran that slightly desolating end-of-an-era feeling. Not only because of his long and spectacular association with it in the palmy days, but because it was at this theatre that he first saw Mary Lloyd, Vesta Tilley, Chirgwin, T E Dunville and G H McDermott in times when the idea that he might ultimately become its leading spirit would have seemed a ludicrous impossibility.

[1] *The World I Knew*, Louis Golding, Hutchinson, 1940

The Star from Hungary

IN THE FOLLOWING year Cochran ran into trouble with Equity. On the grounds that he paid his artists more than the minimum salaries this body had laid down, he felt under no obligation to respect its edict. His attitude to Equity, moreover, was distinctly hostile.

It could not be said that he was anti-unionist as a matter of political conviction because, so far as his friends and acquaintances could judge, he was simply not a political animal. His life was the theatre. All his thoughts and feelings were centred on it, and he evidently believed, like many others (mistakenly in my opinion), that it is possible to isolate oneself from the stream of political events and eschew all practical and emotional involvement in them.

It may be assumed, therefore, that he was a traditionalist, conservative in his general outlook, uncritical of the establishment and instinctively resistant to change. But he was undoubtedly liberal by nature and eminently free from bitterness towards those normally subjected to public opprobrium for standing outside the pale of political orthodoxy. He valued people for themselves and the contribution they made to his trade. The fact that Sean O'Casey, for example, was a communist was completely immaterial to him. It made not the slightest difference to his affection for him as a man or his reverence for him as a writer.

But Cochran grew up and matured, we must remember, in an atmosphere where 'individualism' and the 'rugged free enterprise' of William Randolph Hearst were the operative catch-

words of the conventional political outlook; and where union-
ism, or any attempt by employees to band together for purposes
of collective bargaining, were anathema at a time when similar
rights in this country had been largely won. Having, moreover,
been a free-lance go-getter of the most self-reliant and independent kind, it is perhaps not surprising that he became something of an autocrat in the theatre. How – in the light of
Cochran's outlook – could the impersonal machinery of a semi-
political body ever replace the warm and tender human links,
the free-and-easy salary agreements which formed the basis of
his casting policy?

He acknowledged that actors were entitled to reasonable pro-
tection from exploitation by some of the smaller and less open-
handed employers. But he regarded the blanket regulations of
British Equity as an implied criticism of his own methods of
bargaining, an unflattering attempt to identify him with the
disreputable managements whose questionable business ethics
had called it into being. He refused, for one thing, to pay his
Young Ladies a standard rate, varying their rewards according
to their individual qualities and length of service. He felt that,
in so creative and artistic a sphere as the theatre, it was wrong
to equate an actor earning several hundred pounds a week with
an industrial operative on the mass production bench.

The dispute came to a head when Cochran was warned that
any artists working for him in defiance of Equity rules might
afterwards be refused employment by other managements. He
thereupon announced that he would give up the theatre altogether, a mad, sensational bombshell of a threat that to him,
would have been comparable with slicing open an artery and
releasing his life's blood. He was, in any case, already in the
midst of preparations for his new musical comedy, *Anything
Goes*.

From the present time it is faintly amusing to look back on
earlier periods and observe the rebelliousness of the iconoclastic
young; to see how they asserted their independence, surprising

their parents and deeply shocking their grandparents with 'daring' ideas and the spirit of change.

Anything Goes, which starred Jeanne Aubert, yet another Cochran protégé, at the Palace Theatre in 1935, was by its very title – and its title song – a defiant allusion to what we should now call 'the permissive society' but which, by contemporary standards, was a very milk-and-water revolution in social attitudes and customs.

Cole Porter, who did the words and music, wrote:

> *In olden days a glimpse of stocking*
> > *Was looked on as something shocking*
> *Now goodness knows*
> > *Anything goes.*
> *Good authors, too, who once knew better words*
> > *Now only use four-letter words*
> *Writing prose,*
> > *Anything goes. . . .*

It should be pointed out that the expression 'four-letter words' did not have the meaning it has today. It merely referred to the revolt against polysyllabic writing on the part of contemporary authors like Hemingway and Saroyan.

After *Anything Goes* came yet another revue, *Follow The Sun,* at the Adelphi. Consistent with the policy he had adopted for earlier entertainments of this type, Cochran set about recruiting talent from more serious artistic sources than those normally tapped for revue. One of the items in *Follow The Sun* was a ballet with a theme by Sir Osbert Sitwell, music by William Walton and decor by Cecil Beaton. And it was in this revue that Sarah Churchill made her stage debut – as a Cochran Young Lady.

She gave her audition first of all to Frank Collins whose customary task was to filter away the dross and preserve the gold for his master. Passing this preliminary examination, she was next seen by Cochran himself who claimed that he engaged her purely on grounds of her looks and her merit as a singer and dancer and without the least regard to her family name. Indeed, her piquant looks proclaimed themselves to all with eyes to see, but knowing Cochran's sense of publicity and his astute and opportunist turn of mind, it is no denigration of Miss Churchill's talent to say that, while he might have been equally impressed had she been Lizzie Smith, her name must have ranked with him as a fortuitous bonus. Consciously or otherwise, this may have tinted his judgment. But he allowed protocol to govern his enthusiasm and, in his meticulous way, he sought her father's consent before confirming the agreement.

While casting *Follow The Sun,* he once again showed his remarkable flair for seeking out new talent in the most improbable places. He found a trim little Irish-American dancer named Eileen O'Connor, not in New York, but at the *Bal Tabarin* in Paris; and it was in Holland, of all unlikely countries, that he first saw Ciro Rimac and his band of Cuban singers, instrumentalists and dancers who introduced their new and exciting Caribbean rhythms with tremendous bravura.

Fog is a meteorological hazard that few Cubans normally encounter, and when the revue was preparing to open in a real Manchester pea-souper, the Ciro Rimac contingent were thoroughly miserable. They could find no decent lodgings with heating and hot water and were afraid that, even if they had succeeded in doing so, they would have had great difficulty in finding their way to the theatre in the fogs that descended with such grim regularity every night. So they begged Cochran to let them sleep in the theatre during that first try-out week and he at once gave permission.

Not being used to the worst rigours of the European climate, a number of the musicians fell ill. One of the girls who had never seen snow before wanted to bottle some and send it to her mother in Cuba.

Follow The Sun had its pre-London run during the last week of 1935. Press and audience had received it well; confidence was high and spirits so ebullient that, on New Year's Eve, Rimac and his band invaded Cochran's suite at the Midland Hotel, seeking to serenade him by way of tribute and celebration. Rimac's exotic and fiery daughter, Carito, wriggled her midriff enticingly and advanced on Cochran with arms outstretched in a manifest solicitation to dance.

Despite his arthritic leg, which had then been troubling him acutely, and feeling that to decline so dashing an invitation would show lack of chivalry and dampen the convivial atmosphere, he allowed himself to be propelled willy nilly out onto the landing and down three flights of stairs to make an electrifying appearance in the hotel's Parisian room where the assembled diners, already aglow with their revels, greeted the surprising visitation with thunderous applause.

In this innocent and genial frolic, alas, valour overcame discretion. It proved more than his arthritis could support. He retired to bed, weary and in pain, and slept little. Next morning it was worse. And he didn't – indeed, he couldn't – stir from his bed for a couple of days. Moreover, the episode had a lasting effect. He always walked with difficulty after that.

Follow The Sun played to over £16,000 in four weeks in Manchester and was poised for what promised to be a smash hit opening in London, but the death of King George V on 20th January forced Cochran to postpone it. This created new and costly overheads and the zealous anticipation of theatregoers wilted a little under the stress of delay.

It was in *Follow The Sun,* too, that Vic Oliver made his first appearance in the West End. Until that time, this Austrian comedian with his amusing Continental accent and distinctive brand of humour had merely toured the music halls, and it was on seeing him at the old Holborn Empire that, investing speculatively in his own judgment, as he had done so often before, Cochran decided to present him to West End audiences.

Two important events flowed from this decision. Vic Oliver became a West End star . . . and he married Sarah Churchill.

Once again in 1936 the spectre of trouble and failure was beginning to haunt Cochran. For this was the year of the exasperating affair of *The Boy David* which the public showed such a sudden and perverse craving to see only after the notices had gone up.

Two other ventures proved a waste of time and money. One was *Laughter in Court* with Yvonne Arnaud and Ronald Squire at the old Shaftesbury Theatre which stood adjacent to the fire station in Shaftesbury Avenue, and was destroyed in the blitz. (It may be imagined how readily Cochran would have welcomed the new theatre, The Yvonne Arnaud at Guildford, built as a memorial to that most entrancing and lovable actress.) the other was *Blackbirds of 1936*, an attempt to revive the dash and excitement of Cochran's original Blackbirds revue a decade before when the late Florence Mills raised such a furore in London's theatreland.

The Nicholas Brothers, starring in this new version of the famous revue, gave an excellent account of themselves.

The public was treated to a mild sensation when one of these gifted young men disappeared from the show, and press and public occupied themselves with baffled speculations as to his whereabouts.

He reappeared a couple of days later when it was revealed that he had taken himself up to Edinburgh to see Elisabeth Bergner in *The Boy David*; and since this episode succeeded in focusing attention on two Cochran shows, and stimulating considerable publicity for both, the identity of the person who engineered this crafty piece of publicity-mongering will not elude the sophisticated reader.

Following the abdication of Edward VIII on 11th December and the accession by his brother Albert, Duke of York, plans were made for the Coronation to take place on 12th May 1937.

In the early months of that year, Cochran began to plan his Adelphi revue, *Home and Beauty*. With a mind like a well-ordered filing cabinet from which he could extract a particular memory or experience to suit the needs of a current production he referred back to a visit he had paid some years earlier to Covent Garden.

He had then seen *Rosenkavalier* with a hitherto unknown Hungarian soprano named Gitta Alpar. She appeared only in this one performance, having been released by special dispensation from the Royal Opera, Berlin. The magnificence of her singing raised such a tempest of enthusiasm in Cochran that, when he was next in Berlin, he saw her again with Richard Tauber in some rather dreadful operetta about Catherine the Great, now mercifully forgotten. But this rubbishy affair did not affect the quality of Gitta Alpar's glorious singing which cast its spell on Cochran once again.

He saw her for the third time in Budapest which he visited specially for the purpose, taking John Murray Anderson with him.

One can feel only astonishment at Cochran's meticulous nature, his strict professionalism and artistic integrity on reflecting that here was this ageing impresario who, despite the handicap of an arthritic hip that gave him severe and constant pain, would visit the capitals of Europe, perhaps to see one artist, at a time when travel was not a simple matter of boarding an aircraft, as it is today, but an irksome and tedious upheaval of Channel crossings and long journeys by rail.

In Budapest too Gitta Alpar was given the sort of reception she had enjoyed in Berlin where the audience recalled her again and again after the final curtain and would not leave the theatre until she had given several encores of her solo numbers. How strange and ingenuous this practice of throwing in a song bonus for good measure must seem to the theatre goer of today.

Cochran began putting *Home and Beauty* together under some difficulty. Owing to the expectation of a prosperous season in Coronation year, all the theatres had been snapped up, and rehearsal facilities were at such a premium that he was forced to rehearse the revue once again in the disused Congregational chapel in the Walworth Road.

But it had the advantage of containing several rooms which meant that all the rehearsals could take place under one roof, thus sparing Cochran the customary inconvenience of having to do the rounds of three or four theatres to supervise the separate elements of a new show. Frederick Ashton would be directing the choreography in one room, let us say, while Frank Collins and A P Herbert rehearsed the artists in their dialogue in another. The sound of Elsie April taking the principals through their songs at an ancient and battered upright piano would issue faintly from a neighbouring room. Cissie Sewell, Cochran's ballet mistress, was probably rehearsing Sepha Treble in a dance routine at the same time.

When *The Boy David* opened at His Majesty's on 14th December, Cochran was completing his preparations for the first performance of *Home and Beauty* ten days later, Christmas Eve to be precise, in Canchester. Early press reports had referred to this production as *The Coronation Revue,* no doubt because it was conceived as a London attraction during the Coronation festivities, but Cochran knew better than to use a title based on a transient event.

The Manchester opening fulfilled his highest expectations. The audience went wild with delight over Gitta Alpar's captivating voice. It looked as if nothing could mar the success of the show since it was taken for granted that London audiences would react with the same enthusiasm when *Home and Beauty* opened at the Adelphi.

Christmas Day called for a double celebration: Christmas itself, of course, and a brilliantly successful first night. They had a gay and amusing Christmas dinner in the Midland Hotel but, as they were due to give two performances on Boxing Day, Gitta Alpar, who already looked a little tired, went to bed early.

As Cochran was about to leave the hotel for the matinee performance next day, the receptionist detained him with the news that Miss Alpar had been taken ill in the night and would he please go to her room.

He looked at his watch. It was 1.30. And curtain time was 2.15. He went at once to her room to find his Hungarian nightingale looking very pinched and poorly. She had been violently sick in the night and was clearly far from well. The hotel doctor was there, but unable to do very much for her.

As the rehearsals had been so long and arduous, Gitta Alpar's understudy had not been given sufficient time to prepare herself fully for just such an emergency and Cochran had no alternative but to go on stage, announce the disappointing news to a packed house and say there would be no performance.

Though still far from well, Miss Alpar made a valiant effort to appear that night and struggled on as best she could while a nurse and doctor stood by in her dressing room. But her performance lacked its usual vitality and lustre.

Although no one realised it at the time, her indisposition was a symptom of a more deep-seated complaint that demanded surgery after the London run of *Home and Beauty*.

While *Home and Beauty* was playing at the Adelphi, London theatregoers who had heard about the fantastic first night in Manchester were naturally disappointed in Gitta Alpar's indifferent performance. Cochran was baffled and perplexed. What in the world had happened to her?

He didn't know – how could he? Even she didn't know – that she had been working all those months under the burden of some obscure, debilitating malaise.

'Actually', wrote Cochran, 'that first performance in Manchester was the last time I heard Gitta sing as she had done in Berlin and Budapest. There were performances when she sang well, but never again sensationally.'

Sanctuary in California

THOSE WHO FISH in the tantalising and imponderable waters of the theatrical profession seem to learn little from experience and observation. They are repeatedly surprised by the uncomfortable discovery that, in this particular sphere of activity, reason and commonsense can be the most treacherous guides. Herbert Spencer's telling dictum about '. . . a beautiful theory demolished by an ugly little fact' applies very much indeed to the theatre.

It seemed axiomatic – and even the seasoned and experienced Cochran was deceived – that Coronation year in London would automatically spell prosperity for the theatre. The West End would open its doors to a public that, having been oppressed for so long by the aftermath of economic disorder and the demoralising canker of mass unemployment, now craved some escape into the distractions of flags, bunting and pageantry.

On the international scene things were as bad or worse. Spain, torn by civil war, was sinking into a vortex of unbridled savagery that was to crucify it for two more agonising years. A rearmed Germany had occupied the Rhineland and was manifestly in the power of a ruthless and dangerous psychopath with ambitions of world conquest. Italy had already used the most barbarous methods to subdue the Abyssinians and put their proud Emperor to flight. In the Far East, Japan was striving to solve her population problem by the annexation of Manchuria, as it was then called. The whole fabric of international morality was in a state of collapse and the air was full of menace.

The glitter and colour of the Coronation festivities did offer a brief, if illusory, respite to the people, so acutely depressed by these overshadowing events. Caught up in the gay atmosphere of a city decked out with the trappings of Royal celebration, everybody, it was thought, would besiege the theatres.

But the event betrayed the expectation. For some mysterious reason the theatres failed to attract. Was the public already surfeited with vivid spectacle and decoration, the free shows in the streets, the gorgeous 'production' of the Coronation itself?

The period immediately following the Coronation on 12th May was marked by a widespread feeling of emptiness and anti-climax. The festive spirit had spent itself. London's visitors went home, and the usual summer visitors did not arrive.

The box office at the Adelphi took £4,000 in the first week, not too disappointing perhaps, but less than Cochran had expected, and, despite the excellent cast that, besides Gitta Alpar, included Binnie Hale, Nelson Keys, Sepha Treble and Rawicz and Landauer, making their first appearance on the London stage, *Home and Beauty* ended after a short run. On the night it closed five other London productions were withdrawn.

The effect of yet another failure was beginning to erode even Cochran's celebrated buoyancy and confidence. He became depressed, fearful that his magic touch was deserting him. 'No one,' he said, as he contemplated his next production, 'can stand three flops in a row.'

And his next production was a strangely ill-conceived hodge-podge, doomed by a monumental piece of wrong-headed casting. This surprising error of judgment in one so fastidious was probably due to the adoption of a sort of cart-before-the-horse policy. Instead of seeking the right artist for a play, Cochran reversed the procedure. Now, it is quite legitimate, of course, to seek a suitable vehicle for an artist of special calibre, but having, in this case, secured a big name under contract, Cochran hastily pressed him into a production that was fundamentally unsuitable and, in the process, blindly rationalised his thinking to justify a bad decision.

Cochran had two great stars on his hands, Gracie Fields and Richard Tauber. He had signed them both up on the same day with the idea of profiting so handsomely from their talent and drawing power as to offset his recent losses.

His plan was to put them together in something at the Lyceum. This was a perfect gem of an idea, and like so many good ideas that are simple and obvious enough, it had eluded everyone except this master showman who, in conceiving it, had once again demonstrated his imagination and flair.

But Gracie Fields was then becoming romantically involved with Monty Banks, the film director, whom she subsequently married and Cochran decided to release her from the arrangement.

Mindful of Tauber's capacity to fill the Albert Hall, and the fantastic sales of his gramophone records, Cochran contemplated a new operetta for him that would draw the public much as Franz Lehar's Drury Lane success, *Land of Smiles*, had done a few years earlier. He secured the rights of *Paganini* by the same composer, reckoning that, given Tauber's magnificent voice, the mixture as before would magnetise and enthral the public.

A P Herbert and Reginald Arkell adapted the book and Evelyn Laye, radiantly pretty as ever, and looking exquisite in her mid-nineteenth century dresses, was cast to play opposite the most popular tenor in Europe.

Indeed, this new musical play had much to recommend it. It was beautifully staged, with lovely decor and costumes. The critics praised it. Yet there seemed to be something basically false and unconvincing in the spectacle of this fleshy, rotund personality meandering dreamily about the stage, filling the air, to be sure, with glorious cadences, but carrying a violin which he never played. It seemed so grossly incongruous for Richard Tauber, of all people, to be impersonating this tall, spare virtuoso whose blazing eyes had suggested diabolical possession and made him such a fearful legend in his time.

The public found it unacceptable. The Lyceum may have been the wrong theatre for it, but the most lethal influence in those uneasy days was perhaps the post-Coronation apathy that, as we have already noted, dealt such a wicked blow to *Home and Beauty*.

Cochran was having bad nights at this period. His unsuccessful theatrical ventures, and the complex financial problems associated with them, were troubling his mind, while his osteo-arthritis, which nothing seemed to allay, gnawed mercilessly at his body. Thus he was inclined, in those days, to take insomnia remedies and sometimes fall into a very deep sleep.

Their intimate friends and people who knew them for long periods of time have told me that Cochran and Evelyn shared a double bed throughout their married lives; and that this symbolised the success of their marriage, their mutual devotion which so profoundly outweighed his peccadilloes. That double bed, it seemed, confirmed and sanctified a spiritual fidelity beside which its physical default seemed unimportant. 'Blondes may come and blondes may go,' he used to say, 'but Evelyn goes on forever.' His sporadic escapades wounded her deeply and, despite his desperate anxiety to please her, to spare her needless misery, he was quite incapable of foregoing the pursuit of pretty women which was the sole cause of these occasional rifts and upheavals.

After taking one of his pills, he fell into so heavy a sleep that he did not hear the telephone ringing in the early hours of the morning. Evelyn answered it. She decided not to disturb her husband, but told him next morning that Delysia had rung from New York with great news. A fortune awaited him in America and he was to pack and leave at once. Would he cable her immediately and take the next ship? Instead, he telephoned her, but waited until the late afternoon to allow for the five-hour discrepancy in time, thus showing more consideration for her than she had done for him.

She explained, in cryptic and guarded terms, that she had business friends in the States who needed his wise counsel and that, if he would go over immediately, there were contracts awaiting him worth £25,000 a year. This had nothing to do with the theatre. Yet, once the initial negotiations were completed, he would be called on to make no further effort and could while away his time enjoying the sun in the South of France or his beloved Seville, rest his poor leg and hip and perhaps enjoy some alleviation of the pain they were giving him.

It spoke oceans for his endearing naivete, this man with a massive accumulation of tough experience behind him, that he could begin to entertain such a vague, airy-fairy proposal, particularly since it emanated from this delightfully well-meaning but impetuous actress, not too well versed – and why should she be? – in the murky world of American big business. His immediate response was to go through the motions of protest, to plead that his latest production was not faring too well and that this was no time to desert it. But she would have none of these excuses. Go, he must. And soon.

He talked the matter over with Evelyn and also with Elisabeth Bergner and her husband for whose judgment he had a deep respect. They urged him to go, partly maybe because they sensed his inner desire to do so – he always enjoyed visiting America and generally extracted some professional benefit from the trip – and also because it was just conceivable that, in the capricious, unpredictable world of American business, Delysia's extravagant promises may have contained more than a grain of substance; and Evelyn and the Czinners would reproach themselves for ever if they persuaded him to forgo a deal that might consolidate his financial position for all time. But their motives were complex because he was obviously reaching a stage in his chequered career when it was important to humour him discreetly, to flatter his desires and bolster his flagging ego. Evelyn and his close friends were beginning to be guided by shrewd considerations of kindness and elementary psychology.

She finally persuaded him to go, and the belief that he should do so represented a tribute to her inner wisdom, the correct order of her priorities and her astute capacity to sacrifice the smaller principle to the larger. For despite her lingering awareness of her husband's former association with Delysia, she applied the whittling blade of reason to any reservations that may have been inspired by the normal emotional responses of the feminine mind and heart.

So they invited Evelyn Laye and Richard Tauber to supper and, over the meal, broke the news that he would be sailing for New York the next day.

Disappointment was once more to be his reward. He had not been in New York long before it became abundantly clear that his journey was a fruitless errand, that the golden prospect held out to him by the enthusiastic and well-meaning Delysia was totally groundless.

In his report of this incident in *Cock-a-doodle-do,* his third volume of reminiscences, he gave no details of the still-born enterprise. Perhaps they are of little interest.

Once in the United States, however, he decided to make the most of his stay. He saw the latest shows in New York, of course, and went to Newark to see the Ringling Brothers' circus which had evolved from the original Barnum show. He spent much time in the company of his old friend, Morris Gest, who had presented *The Miracle* in New York.

There he was, having travelled to New York on a business mission, but with no business to do. The only course was to treat the matter philosophically and resolve to have an enjoyable time; which he certainly did. When the theatre trade journals announced his arrival, the invitations poured in. The Dolly Sisters, both now married and living in Chicago, begged him to visit them. Louis B Lurie, a Californian tycoon, invited him to

stay with him in San Francisco, and Archie Selwyn wired him
with an offer of hospitality at his brother's house in Hollywood.

He took up all the invitations, spending some time in
Chicago where he saw the Joe Louis-Braddock fight and, at the
behest of a London newspaper, cabled a report of it to Fleet
Street. While he was there Jenny and Rosie Dolly fêted him
lavishly and gave him a tour of the night spots where, amazed
by so much splendid talent in the most obscure and insignificant
bars, he experienced great difficulty in restraining his natural
impulse to sign it up for exploitation at home.

From Chicago he flew to Los Angeles; quite an event for an
Englishman in those days, though less of a novelty to the Americans who, even then, were acquiring the habit of covering their
vast inland territories by air.

After a short stay in Hollywood, attended by all the proverbial elements of that legendary golden age – opulent homes,
swimming pools, beautiful girls and film stars – Cochran moved
on to San Francisco, now at length with some business in prospect. For plans were in progress for the big Exposition and
when Cochran outlined an idea for some kind of mammoth
attraction, the organisers were extremely impressed ('the best
idea we've yet been offered', they breathed with frenzied
excitement) but were prevented from completing any arrangements by one major impediment, namely, lack of money. Yet
these mad, capital-starved enthusiasts spent long hours in their
own private cloud-cuckoo-land discussing, not only the archi-
tectural layout of Cochran's show, but the house they were proposing to build for his personal accommodation!

Cochran was duly regaled with the traditional rigmarole of
big talk, excessive zeal, flattery and lavish promises so characteristic of the heady, unrealistic atmosphere that seeped right
through the American entertainment industry in those days and
still does no doubt today, though perhaps not quite in such
vulgar, irresponsible and hypertrophied forms.

'You'd make a fortune in Hollywood . . . you're just the man they want . . . with your ideas you couldn't miss . . .' These familiar blandishments, and others in similar vein, were heaped repeatedly on Cochran throughout the early thirties, not only by visiting Californians, but also by English theatre people infected by the bug. And there he was, in Hollywood, with the inflated talk still going on, and nothing to do.

Owing to a strike, the hotels were closed, so Cochran lived as the guest of various film tycoons which, considering his straitened financial circumstances, proved a fortunate contingency. The volume of so much optimistic and ambitious talk in these affluent surroundings gave him an illusory sense of hope and prospective riches. He seemed to be moving in a golden dream world of money and success, and being the essentially gullible man he was, a social chameleon, prone to optimism, however baseless, he was due to suffer disappointment and a measure of psychological damage as a result of the inevitable let-down. Even when he returned to Beverly Hills and attended a party in Edgar Selwyn's home one Sunday morning, he was buttonholed by one of the guests who talked quite blandly of raising millions for his latest venture. This ebullient prophet then helped himself to excessive quantities of whisky and collapsed. And typically, that was the last that Cochran saw or heard of him.

Cochran was getting disturbing reports from home. *Paganini* was doing badly. Better to cut his losses and whip it off. He cabled his London office with this instruction. The response was a telephone call from Diana Napier (Mrs Richard Tauber). Her husband, she said, believed in the show and was prepared to underwrite it, paying all expenses and making good any loss it might incur.

Cochran was touched. He expressed his appreciation. But he declined the offer in the belief that *Paganini* had slipped below the Plimsoll line of possible recovery. Diana proved very persuasive, however, and he eventually accepted the offer providing there were to be no cuts in salaries and no publicity about Richard Tauber's intervention. Any such drastic measure to save a show always has an adverse effect on public opinion.

But the story leaked. A national newspaper published it. Cochran was furious. He bitterly accused Diana of breaking her promise. She protested her innocence. Harsh feelings were generated and harsh words exchanged. But he calmed down and apologised when she ultimately convinced him that neither she nor Richard had defaulted on their solemn undertaking. To this day she does not know who passed the secret to the newspaper.

Once the facts were known, Tauber was cheered by the cast for saving the show, but Cochran took a rather jaded and cynical view of his apparent magnanimity on the grounds that he would only be out of pocket should the receipts show a loss of more than the £600 a week that Tauber was getting as salary. It had not yet done so, and showed no sign of dropping to the figure below the break-even. As Cochran bitterly saw it, Tauber was only gambling on his salary which he would have forfeited anyway if *Paganini* ended. He didn't begrudge Tauber's large salary. He admired him greatly as an artist and believed he was worth every penny of it but, as a theatrical businessman, he showed a spiky and irritable resentment at the idea of performers meddling in management and the esoteric backwaters of stage finance.

Many years later, when Tauber adopted a similar course with the New York production of *Land of Smiles*, Cochran sniffed rather testily and said, 'Hm, history repeating itself! Why do actors always think they're financiers?'

Despite its shot in the arm, *Paganini* did not fully recover. It limped along for a further two months and was withdrawn on 17th July.

While these events were taking place, Cochran stayed in Hollywood. The beautiful sunshine, which he thought would help his arthritis, made him feel curiously relaxed and tranquil, though his financial position at that time was again far from secure. The ghost of Mr Micawber soothed his bruised spirit. Immersed as he was in the heyday of the American film industry by the ambrosial scent of opulence and success, how could he possibly miss the opportunity that lay just round the corner?

Under the persuasion of his friends, he decided to stay and cabled Evelyn to join him, instructing her to sell some of their books and pictures to obtain the money. She parted with their Sickerts, Loutrecs, the odd Degas and the Nevinsons.

There were times when his investment in pictures proved his salvation. The precarious ownership of his Tintorettos and Renoirs gave him intense pleasure. The sale of stocks and shares leaves no sad, empty spaces on the walls. It merely changes the figures on a bank statement. Equally, the possession of them affords no intellectual delight.

It is an inexorable law of life that you pay for what you get. When circumstances forced Cochran to sacrifice his beloved art treasures, he accepted the deprivation philosophically. Edward G Robinson once relieved him of a few cherished works. And there was an occasion when he desperately needed £10,000 and invited an art dealer to the house with instructions to help himself to paintings to the value of that amount.

It was gradually borne on him that Hollywood had nothing to offer. All the talk, the promises, the back slappings and the enthusiasm quietly died away. By now he was reconciled and philosophical. He had made money, dealt in astronomical sums, frequently spurned the help of backers and invested £600,000 in stage productions. Half a million of this was his own money. He had suffered catastrophic reverses, consecutive failures that whittled away his dwindling reserves. There were times when the greatest showman of our time, the man with a resounding, all-conquering name that rang like a magic tocsin in the ears of Mrs Worthington's numerous and passionately dedicated daughters, was stranded in New York, unable to raise the fare for the journey home. He wasn't a gambler and his drinking habits were moderate. Yet while his lesser contemporaries and

younger confrères – Laddie Cliff, Jack Waller, Tom Arnold –
were quietly amassing their fortunes, investing them sensibly
in non-theatrical business and property enterprises and salting
them away for the future, Cochran oscillated uncertainly between setback and recovery.

Shortly after Evelyn reached Hollywood, Winfield Sheehan
invited them to stay at his luxurious ranch. Besides launching
such artists as Shirley Temple, Janet Gaynor and Alice Faye,
Sheehan had made the film of *Cavalcade* for Fox.

The Cochrans received such lavish hospitality from Sheehan
and his beautiful wife, Jeritza, of operatic fame, that they afterwards treated this interlude as one of the most blissful periods
of their lives. It sliced them out of the frame of time; it isolated
them from the stresses of the real, material world and enabled
them to suppress and ignore their underlying anxieties. With
advancing age they were becoming shock-proof. Hard and
repetitious experience had given them an encrustment of
armour that the customary slings and arrows failed to penetrate.

Yet, when the protective and cosseting magic faded, Cochran
would fall victim to sadness and an overwhelming sense of
failure and despair. He would be plagued by regrets . . . for his
lack of foresight, his little vanities and, above all, his incom-
petence in the management of money.

It was possible, in the Californian sun and the artificial atmosphere of Hollywood, to enjoy some temporary refuge from the
black and menacing events in Europe. Although not politically
conscious, he was aware, like everyone else, of the growing
threat to peace in the late thirties; and he felt a decent compassion for the victims of persecution and war. The rebellion
in his beloved Spain was entering an implacable phase of
cruelty and bitterness. The Japanese were penetrating deeper
into China and the turmoil and unrest in Europe that flowed
from the propaganda, mass hysteria, sabre-rattling and violent
oppression of the Hitler regime filled the sensitive imagination
with anguish and horror. And although Cochran was forced in-

to a reluctant awareness of these events, if largely through their effect on the box office, he felt little personal or political involvement. His obsession with the theatre, his love of books, pictures and the company of friends left little room in his mind and little inclination to ponder and observe the headlong descent of civilisation.

It was during this period that he asked Milton Rosmer to call and see him in his Bond Street office. He asked Rosmer if he would be interested in producing a play for him.

'Interested?' Rosmer echoed. 'Yes, indeed. I should be honoured. It is something I have always wanted to do.'

'Why?' asked Cochran, roused by this manifest fillip to his vanity and egotism.

'Because,' Rosmer replied, 'there is a great deal of prestige in producing a play for C B Cochran.'

Cochran smiled sadly.

'Once,' he said, 'but not now . . . not now.'

Constant Pain

TRAPPED BY ADVERSE circumstances, Cochran thrust about in feverish attitudes of defiance. His extravagance and recklessness were now proving a bitter source of reproach and he struck sad postures of self-justification, turning his faults into virtues with revealing little aphorisms like, 'Any fool can save money. It takes a wise man to know how to spend it.'

He could no longer afford to keep Rosling, his manservant, who had joined him soon after the First World War when he was living in Aldford Street, Park Lane, and stayed with him for eighteen years.

Rosling went in 1937. During the Second War he worked for Princess Arthur of Connaught and is now in an old folks' home in Oxford.

'He was a good employer,' he told me, 'but he kept me on the go, and if anything went wrong – at his home or in business – I'd get it. If he got a message or a telegram from the office with bad news, he'd fly into one of his rages and there would be a gloomy atmosphere in the house for quite a long time.'

Cochran began thinking about a new show. While in New York, he had seen Beatrice Lillie with Bert Lahr in *The Show Goes On.* Casting this brittle, sophisticated artist with so broad and earthy a comedian had been a daring experiment. But it was abundantly successful. Cochran had been much impressed by this and he decided to repeat the formula in London by engaging Bee – improbably enough – with Flanagan and Allen for *Happy Returns,* another revue at the Adelphi. One has only to

recall the schoolboy, rumbustious comedy of The Crazy Gang
in the postwar years and the pleasure it gave, not only to music
hall addicts, but also to the intelligentsia, to realise that,
theoretically at least, Cochran's outwardly anomalous thinking
made good sense.

But in 1938 the public could not accept this quaint juxtaposition of talent. Cochran was right. It was the time that was
wrong and he merely suffered the familiar enough penalty of
being ahead of it.

Happy Returns opened cold, without the customary pre-
London tour. But it was good. Cochran liked it. So did the press
and the first night audience which, then as now – and perhaps
more so then – were not truly representative of the theatregoing
public.

But, after the opening, the box office remained quiet. This
was depressing enough, but Cochran also felt guilty at having
persuaded Bee to return from America where she had been
enjoying such an unbroken run of success.

At that time we lived from one international crisis to another
while the seeds of these political collisions multiplied and grew
in the intervening weeks and months.

It might be assumed that the times, with their constant uncertainly, did not provide a very healthy atmosphere for the
theatre, and managements looking for excuses may have been
forgiven for attributing the lukewarm acceptance of their offer-
ings to the instability of world conditions. An impresario can
always find excuse for failure, the weather as a rule being
Number One Scapegoat. It is either so hot that potential audiences are disporting themselves on the river, the tennis courts
or the green fields; or so cold, wet and blustery that they daren't
venture forth into Shaftesbury Avenue or the Strand. But it is a
proven fact that, whatever the handicaps and distractions, a
show will carry on for months, and possibly years, if enough
people want to see it. Thus Gerald Savory's *George and Margaret*
was doing well at Wyndhams, the young Emlyn Williams had

scored a considerable success with *The Corn is Green* and Dodie Smith's *Dear Octopus* was attracting large audiences. Terence Rattigan's early play, *French Without Tears,* which had opened in 1936, was still at the Criterion where it notched up a thousand performances.

Throughout these turbulent years the success of Ivor Novello's musical plays at Drury Lane proved completely impervious to the fluctuations of the international climate. *Glamorous Night* in 1935 was followed by *Careless Rapture* and *Crest of the Wave. The Dancing Years* was still running when war broke out. After the notices for *Me and My Girl* had gone up at Victoria Palace, its fortunes were suddenly and dramatically reversed by a BBC relay from the theatre in which Lupino Lane endeared the whole of Britain to his breezy costermongers doing *The Lambeth Walk.*

Besides his nightly cabaret at the Trocadero, the man who at one time had six or seven productions and various other entertainments going simultaneously now had nothing on in the West End at all. Being chairman of the Palace Theatre, he used a short period between productions to present *Flashbacks, a Cavalcade of Moving Pictures,* which was calculated to excite the nostalgic feelings of the public. But, even at popular prices, it proved rather a damp squib.

In the preceding months and years, Cochran's financial mainstay had been his suppertime shows at the Troc. At a time when the standard rate of income tax hovered between 4s 6d and 5s, his revenue from this source was substantial, though he had frittered most of it away in futile ventures.

But with the outbreak of war on Sunday, 3rd September, and its unpredictable consequences, all theatres and places of entertainment were closed. Cochran and Evelyn listened to Neville Chamberlain's historic broadcast at eleven o'clock that morning in their flat in Westminster Gardens and, almost as the first air raid warning sounded that same day (a false alarm, as it turned out) there was a ring at the front door and the Cochrans admitted their flat-neighbours, Sarah Churchill and Vic Oliver, who had called to help Cochran, now severely disabled by his leg, to reach the shelter down in the courtyard.

In those early, confused and bewildering days the expected mass attack from the air did not come. Everything was strangely and unnaturally quiet. In case of air raids it was the practice to stop the lifts in apartment buildings and Cochran had great difficulty in getting to and from his flat by the stairs.

On the Monday morning he went to his office in Old Bond Street and wrote individually to all his Young Ladies. The letter read:

4th September 1939

I want to thank you and all the girls for your loyalty and cheerfulness on Friday night. The performance was as good as any you have given.

Of the many shattering blows inflicted upon this old impresario by this terrible war tragedy none touches my heart more deeply than the separation from my Young Ladies, and the break in the continuity (over fifteen years) of Trocadero shows. My fondest hope is that we may work together again before too long.

With affectionate regards,
Yours sincerely,
Charles B Cochran

There being no immediate upheaval in the routine of life – indeed, we were embarking on the six-month period of eerie inactivity, the Phoney War, as the Americans called it – everyone strove to follow their normal behaviour patterns so far as the general conditions of the emergency would allow.

In the upheaval, the swift annihilation of personal interests, ambition and business plans, however distressing to the people concerned, were insignificant compared with the overriding call to preserve civilisation, freedom and life itself. We had a duty to prevent the total eclipse of our planet. Nothing else mattered.

But the new situation demanded, not the sacrifice of talent and specialist organising ability, merely its reorientation.

Compared with 1914, the authorities in 1939 showed a deeper awareness of psychological needs and the importance of providing something that was broadly called 'welfare', not only to the services, but to the civilian population as well.

This had much to do with the bolstering and preservation of morale and, in this important sphere, those with experience of the entertainment world had an important role to play.

J L Garvin asked Cochran to write an article for *The Observer* on the subject of entertainment for the troops, and it was surely only a matter of time before the long experience and rich gifts of Britain's master showman were to be recruited for their special place in the national crisis.

Shortly after this article appeared, Sir Seymour Hicks telephoned and asked him if he would join a committee to examine the problem of entertaining the services at home and abroad. Basil Dean and Lord Tyrell had already agreed to serve on it. He seized the invitation with alacrity and fervour. To feel wanted is one of the deepest needs of human nature, and nothing would have given him greater satisfaction than the knowledge that he was putting his mature and expert knowledge at the disposal of his country at war.

Mysteriously, however, he heard nothing. The creation of ENSA with Basil Dean at its head was presently announced and, for all that government officialdom seemed to know or care, Charles B Cochran might never have been born.

He stayed in the flat in the early days of the war, seeing few people – most of his friends were abroad, out of London or busy about their war-time avocations. This enforced inactivity combined with his abrupt loss of income from the Trocadero, which was then his only source, made him bored and restless. To the spirit of the man of action, idleness is slow poison.

The danger of his becoming neglected and lonely, and suffering the enforced seclusion which would have been unbearable to so dynamic a man, was averted by the loyalty of old friends like Vic and Sarah Oliver, Betty Shale (Mrs Eliot Makeham) and Ann Codrington.

An hour or two after dinner, Evelyn would rise and say, 'Good night. I'm going to bed,' adding with a covert, supplicatory look at these kindly stalwarts, 'Stay and talk to him for a while . . .' And, in the soft glow of the standard lamp behind his armchair, he would chat and reminisce, reliving the great days with enormous savour and zest.

'He'd been everywhere and he knew everyone,' Ann Codrington recalled, 'and the wonderful stories simply poured out of him in that quiet voice.'

With the continuing absence of any large-scale military activity, the order under which theatres were closed was presently lifted and some of the more adventurous theatre managers began to mount new productions.

This encouraged Cochran to plan another revue.

He wrote this letter to the Young Ladies he was still able to trace:

17th October, 1939

I propose to put into rehearsal a new revue next week, but probably the girls will not be wanted until the following Monday.

If conditions allow, we shall play Manchester a month, Glasgow a month, and perhaps a few more weeks in the provinces before coming to London.

Your salary will be £5 per week for eight or nine performances as the case may be. That is to say, if we play eight and not nine performances your salary will be the same.

I am holding an audition at the Palace Theatre on Friday afternoon next, 20th instant, at 4 pm and should like you to attend with your practice clothes for photographs if you care to be in the revue. If you cannot, please be good enough to let me know.

Yours sincerely,
Charles B Cochran

Under the title of *Lights Up,* the show did a month with Evelyn Laye, Phyllis Stanley, Clifford Mollison, Doris and Betty Hare and James Hayter at the Opera House, Manchester. It was a makeshift production, thrown together with odd costumes and bits of hired scenery and material, but the booking office took £5,000 before it opened, and it played to capacity houses during its Manchester run. It also did well over Christmas in Glasgow and opened in the new year with equally good results in Edinburgh.

The man who spent the earth, who would discard a complete wardrobe and order new dresses if he wasn't perfectly satisfied with the first lot, was now having to make do, to collect and salvage bits and pieces from every available source.

Lacking a piano in his flat at that time, he borrowed a little one from Ian Grant, one of his *Lights Up* lyric writers.

To his utter astonishment, Ian next saw his piano on the stage on the first night of the show. Moreover, it was painted white!

Having received no warning that Cochran was proposing to use and transform his piano in this manner, Ian quietly remonstrated with him.

Obliged to invent some defence for his action, Cochran quickly said, 'I thought you'd *like* it white. I always knew you had a soft spot for Edythe Baker!'

Cochran ploughed his profits back into the production in order to refurbish it for London where, as in the First World War, the theatre seemed to be in a relatively prosperous condition, and promoters of theatrical entertainment were confronted by formidable competition from George Black's well-attended revues at the London Hippodrome where *Black Velvet* was running very successfully at that time.

Valerie Frazer had impressed him with her rather unusual talent; he took her out of the chorus line in *Lights Up* and gave her some nice little parts and, on 13th February 1940, he wrote to her:

Dear Valerie,

I am delighted that I have been the means of giving you
a start as a principal, and I feel pretty certain you will go much
further.

The best advice I can give you is to be your own most severe
critic; never leave off working on your singing or dancing, and
your acting. Already you have one considerable asset in your
diction, but it can still be improved upon. When an artist ceases
going forward he or she always goes backward.

Don't take too seriously praise you get from your friends, but
give the greatest attention to adverse criticism.

You have always been a good worker, and I have believed in
you from the time I saw you doing *The Big Apple* upon my
return from America. I promised you then I would give you an
opportunity of advancement in good time, and I was happy that
the opportunity came in Edinburgh.

Upon my return from the North I will have a new contract
for you. Meanwhile I have instructed Mr Reeve to double your
salary.

With affectionate regards,
Yours very sincerely,
Charles B Cochran

In order to tour with *Lights Up,* Cochran and Evelyn let their
Westminster flat and, on their return to London where it opened
at the Savoy Theatre, they accepted an invitation to occupy a
suite at the adjoining Hotel as guests of the management during
its run.

Lights Up did moderately well at the Savoy, although, apart
from one or two of Noel Gay's songs which he rather liked,
Cochran didn't care greatly for it.

The Cochrans moved out of the Savoy when *Lights Up*
closed and, as their Westminster flat was still occupied by
tenants, they lived for a while with friends in a flat in Carring-
ton House, Mayfair, and moved thereafter to that delightful
and tranquil backwater – a welcome enough refuge in those

troubled times – the Hind's Head at Bray, where the proprietor, the late Barry Neame, deemed it an honour to accommodate the Cochrans at his own expense.

Dr Plesch, who looked after Evelyn and Cochran and treated Cochran's hip, used to say to his daughter, Honoria, dress designer for some of the Cochran productions, 'You can have no possible conception of the pain that man is suffering.'

Yet Cochran seldom referred to his disability and never complained of it. Honoria would visit him at Bray and take him out in the fine evenings of that beautiful but terrible summer, and push him along the towpath in an invalid chair. She too had arthritis and, indeed, is still troubled with it. This distressing complaint seldom afflicts the young, but it established a sympathetic bond between herself and Cochran and, during those walks, she would ask him about his plans.

'No more theatre for me,' he would say wearily. 'Never again. I'm past it.' And even while he said this, he undoubtedly cherished secret ambitions of a comeback. This is revealed in another letter to Valerie on 17th May 1940.

My dear Valerie,

Yes it is unfortunate, but world events are too strong to combat.

Don't worry but get very strong and I hope to be in the ring again if and when things become more settled. For the moment I am compelled to abandon all production plans.

You may rest assured I shall be more than happy to have you with me again when the right chance occurs. Meanwhile, don't wait for me if other opportunities present themselves. I say this with regret, but it would be unfair to you not to do so, as there may be others more venturesome than I am, or with greater facilities.

With affectionate regards,
Yours very sincerely,
Charles B Cochran

In the ensuing summer months the aerial power of Germany directed its fury on London and several other British towns and cities and were finally driven from the autumn skies by the heroism of 'the Few'.

Under aerial bombardment, London was no place for the elderly and the infirm and although many were obliged by circumstances to remain there, those who could leave it did so, thus providing a small measure of relief to the overburdened hospital, medical and civil defence services.

Only the unreasonable, the bitter and the jealous might have begrudged Charles and Evelyn Cochran their relative seclusion in the Thames-side retreat of the Hind's Head where the long and tedious summer was enlivened now and then by welcome visits from friends. Lady Diana Cooper lunched with them occasionally, bringing with her a breath of the past and the great days of *The Miracle* . . . Charles Morgan, A G Macdonnell, James Agate, Robert Gibbings, who would travel down from Reading University, Aneurin Bevan and Jennie Lee, and Rex Whistler who drew enchanting little sketches on the menus.

Many of the provincial theatres were open and plans were already in hand for the post-Christmas pantomime season. Valerie Frazer, having missed an opportunity in some production, received a warm and sympathetic handwritten letter from Cochran :

30th October 1940

My dear Valerie,

  It was nice to hear from you; I always like to know what you're up to. Your case is tough – even in these days when everybody is up against it – as you were just about to get your chance.

I should have thought you would be snapped up for pantomime. Have you tried?

I have a plan to do something soon but am not sure whether I shall bring it off.

I want to see your bandy legs dancing again; they are very sweet.

Be careful of your ARP work – we don't want anything bad to happen to you.

Keep in touch with me – 49 Old Bond Street will reach me although I am not often there.

If I am in town next week I will let you know and you must tell me if there's anything I can do for you – introductions or what not. It would make me very happy if I could get you a nice job.

I haven't seen Babs B since she left the hospital and am glad she's looking well, poor darling.

I am going to Cambridge tomorrow for a few days.

Love and a Kiss,

Yours,
CBC

Mercifully, however, Cochran was not now completely idle. Broadcasting in war-time had secured a very important place in the lives of the people, and programmes like Tommy Handley's *ITMA, Garrison Theatre* with Jack Warner and *Happidrome* did much to maintain the spirits of the urban populations, huddled together in their air raid shelters, and the families trying to escape the bombs by dossing down night after night in the relative safety of the underground stations.

The BBC invited Cochran to present a series of programmes at eight o'clock every Saturday night. As a tribute to his stature he was virtually given a free hand to select his artists and produce the programme as he chose. Alan Herbert supplied the title: *Cock-a-Doodle-Do.*

Radio was not only a new medium to Cochran. To the man whose conception of entertainment lay mainly in spectacle and the presentation of visual beauty, the blind, aural dimension of radio created unfamiliar and limiting problems. Added to these was the difficulty in recruiting artists who were either touring the provinces, serving in the Forces or staying out of London.

The first programme included John McCormack, Vic Oliver, Sarah Churchill, Fred Emney, George Jackley, Arthur Fear,

Florence Desmond, Pat Kirkwood, Phyllis Stanley, Dorothy Carless and Jack and Daphne Barker.

In the ensuing programmes Leslie Howard and Sarah Churchill played a scene from *Romeo and Juliet* and among others who took part were Benno Moiseiwitsch, Vera Lynn, Jack Buchanan, Gabrielle Brune, Judy Campbell, Bebe Daniels and Ben Lyon, Valerie Frazer and Carroll Gibbons.

Cochran had been struggling along on nothing but his small income from the BBC, but he now applied himself to his third book of reminiscences, *Cock-a-doodle-do,* which came out in October 1941, and, despite his avowed intention of turning his back on the theatre for good, he began planning another revue with the substantial advance paid to him by his publisher. The result was *Big Top,* starring Beatrice Lillie, Fred Emney, Cyril Ritchard, Madge Elliott and Patricia Burke, at His Majesty's Theatre.

His faithful old associates flocked back to him. For the pleasure of working with Cochran again Elsie April forfeited a much more lucrative assignment on the Noël Coward picture, *In Which We Serve* – to say nothing of the alluring prospect of getting established in films.

Big Top played not only against a world background of disaster and military reverses; the theatre itself carried its own overtones of tragedy. While she was playing in *Big Top,* Beatrice Lillie's son was killed in action; and a backcloth of a French boulevard scene proved to be one of Rex Whistler's last pieces of work for the stage.

It was in *Big Top* that Beatrice Lillie sang *Wind Round My Heart,* a show-stopper with which many theatregoers still identify this comedienne; and Patricia Burke sang Duke Ellington's version of *Flamingo,* after Cochran, finding it very much to his taste, cabled New York for the rights.

Big Top was Cochran's last war-time show. It was also the last revue he ever produced. It contained several attractive and amusing things and some fine sets by Oliver Messel. But much of it was dull and pedestrian.

The knockers, in their unkindly way, had lost no time in re-naming it *Big Flop*, a *mot* that was not very *bon* and scarcely calculated to improve the temper of a spent, elderly man, well past his heyday, and striving pathetically to rehabilitate his fortune, his reputation and his self-esteem.

His hip was deteriorating and he was now in constant pain. One leg was visibly shorter than the other and his rubber-tipped stick, from which he was now quite inseparable, helped to mitigate his limp. It affected his usual equanimity. He became crotchety and ill-tempered and was now inclined to express himself in cruel and bitter ways. During the rehearsals of *Big Top* he conceived an intense dislike for one of the artists he had been reluctantly compelled to employ because of factors arising in his negotiations with certain other players. He sat in the auditorium, hunched over his stick, growling and muttering and, when this actress appeared for rehearsal in a very tight and scanty leotard, he was heard to murmur, 'I know every wrinkle of that famous old arse intimately!'

Marking Time

ADMITTEDLY IT WAS a hurtful disappointment to Cochran that he had not been invited to contribute his large reservoir of expert knowledge to one or other of the troop entertainment schemes.

But it did not discourage him from organising troop shows independently – for British and American forces and the Free French at home. A lover of Yugoslavia, where he and his wife had spent many an enjoyable holiday, Cochran felt an urge to do what he could to aid that unhappy country and, in the summer of 1942, he organised a circus and fair on Hampstead Heath for the Yugoslav Relief Fund.

In the following year his ego blossomed once more when the Earl of Clarendon, treasurer of Toc H War Relief Fund, asked him to arrange a large scale entertainment at the Albert Hall in support of this cause.

Rather than assemble a miscellaneous collection of artists who would merely appear consecutively in the conventional style, Cochran cast round in his mind for a good subject, a theme, a unifying idea.

For several days nothing clicked. Then he suddenly conceived the notion of a broad survey of popular music covering the last half century.

He seemed well away with *Fifty Years of Song,* which was to have been the title of the show, but when he began to build the programme, he came across so many excellent ditties of a pre-1893 vintage that, in order to accommodate them, he increased the period of his survey by twenty years and changed the title to *Seventy Years of Song* which, besides being more euphonious and slightly alliterative, exactly represented his own age.

It was certainly to his credit that, although he needed money badly, he refused the fee he was offered on the grounds that he had never accepted payment for a charity concert or fund-raising effort and was not prepared to do so now.

The enterprise was perhaps best described by *The Times* as '. . . an entertainment, a cavalcade, a jamboree, an orgy of musical reminiscence – the precise word is lost in the array of performers from the operatic, concert, musical comedy, and music hall stages. . . .'

There were problems galore, and this made Cochran happy because it plunged him back into his familiar challenging element. Since the artists were giving their services, they could not be expected to attend early and often enough for adequate rehearsal. Many, furthermore, were scattered in different parts of the country. And the absurd limitation on artists wearing fancy costumes on a Sunday robbed Cochran of his *forte* – the creation of entertainment with a visual appeal.

Nevertheless, with the splendid co-operation of everyone, not least Geraldo with his seventy-piece orchestra, the show delighted the Albert Hall audience which seemed scarcely conscious of the many faults and hitches due to the lack of rehearsal.

Right up to starting time, Cochran had slashed this and shortened that, switched and rejigged, working tirelessly. Order was somehow extracted from muddle and, even though artists kept losing themselves in the labyrinth of passages behind the organ and Honoria Plesch slept for two nights on a great pile of costumes; even though there had been just enough time to rehearse the first half only, *Seventy Years of Song* went with a swing.

It began in a darkened hall to the strains of *In The Gloamin'* played on a penny whistle. Then the evocation of the London streets in past decades was achieved by contemporary figures: butcher's boy, baker's boy, knife-grinder, one-man band. An old street organ played *Grandfather's Clock, Pop Goes The Weasel* and *Champagne Charlie.*

And so the pageant unfolded, a pageant of the mind, reconstituted from the past by such songs as the *Tritsch-Tratsch* polka, *We don't want to fight, but by Jingo if we do* (the Charlie Dilke lampoon), *Take a pair of sparkling eyes, Little Annie Rooney, Two Lovely Black Eyes, The Man who broke the Bank, The Lost Chord, Dolly Gray, Tell Me, Pretty Maiden, Alexander's Rag Time Band* and *Tipperary* . . . melodies that continued right up to the song hits of 1943 and, carrying their own social comment, recalled events of the recent past more powerfully than any historical record.

Those who helped in this mammoth presentation included Reginald Foort, Janet Howe, Bill Stephens, Leslie Mitchell, George Baker, Heddle Nash, Stanley Holloway, Joan Young, John Rorke, Doris Hare, Tessie O'Shea, Adelaide Hall, Mary Ellis, Phyllis Stanley, Evelyn Laye, Edythe Baker, Hutch, Vera Lynn and Eva Turner. As production manager, Fred Wilby did a sensational job.

What particularly pleased Cochran was the social calibre of people in the audience like the Duke and Duchess of Gloucester, the Earl of Clarendon, Lord and Lady Louis Mountbatten, Mrs Churchill, Mrs Anthony Eden, Prince Bernhard of the Netherlands and important representatives of most of the allied governments.

This brief spurt of personal recovery was honey and balm to Cochran's spirit. Even in so strange and *outré* a context, he was again at the centre of things – organising, directing and, above all, receiving praise from his friends – how his spirit hungered for it – and the plaudits of the press, now perhaps a trifle patronising to the Grand Old Man of the theatre.

In addition, as one-time manager of the Royal Albert Hall, he enjoyed his renewed association with it. It was as long ago as 1927 that his appointment as manager resulted from a strange combination of circumstances.

Built in the late 1860s, this large auditorium was to have been called The Hall of Arts and Sciences. And only when she arrived to lay the foundation stone did Queen Victoria let it be known that she desired the words 'Royal Albert' to be added in memory of her husband who had died in 1861.

The money for building the hall was raised in a curious way. First of all the Royal Commissioners sold the site at a peppercorn rent of a shilling a year. This rent is still paid to them annually by cheque on 25th March. But the cost of the building, a sum of £200,000, was raised by selling the seats to members of the public for £100 each. This entitled them to the use of the seat and the right to occupy it for any performance for nine hundred and ninety-nine years. No one could have stopped a man (should he have chosen to do so) from taking up residence in a box providing he owned all the seats in it.

Over 1,300 seats, representing about a fifth of the hall's total capacity, were sold in this way. A Corporation was set up to administer the hall, each seat-holder having voting rights.

In the 1920s the seat-holders' corporation criticised the controlling council which, represented by Lord Howe, offered them a new manager to be chosen by the council and the Corporation from a single list. Both groups nominated C B Cochran and he was confirmed as manager for a term of five years. At the end of this period, the arrangement was renewed for another five, and although Cochran was offered a further extension in 1937, he declined it because he was so busy in the theatre.

When he converted the hall for dancing by superimposing a huge dance floor over the seats, he met with stern opposition from two of the seat-holders, the Misses Mirchhouse, who owned J 894 and J 895. The problem was solved by cutting out a square of dance floor over these seats and guaranteeing access to their owners who, it was said, could 'enjoy the strains of the orchestra and the patter of feet overhead'.

The gentle glow of illumination in which Cochran's personality waxed and quickened at the time of *Seventy Years of Song* presently sputtered out, and he occupied himself with little during the rest of the year.

It was in 1943, however, that a new spirit began to animate the musical theatre. London claimed to have 'discovered' that superb comedian, the late Sid Field, notwithstanding the fact that he had been known to provincial audiences for many years and, in George Black's scintillating revue, *Strike A New Note*, at the Prince of Wales Theatre, he caused what might be genuinely described as a furore. Nor was he the only attraction in this popular show. Pretty Zoë Gail's exuberant threat to get *Lit Up When the Lights Go On in London* had a tonic effect on war nerves and blackout blues, and Cochran was himself so captivated by the whole thing that he took the unprecedented – and, indeed, magnanimous – step of allowing his enthusiasm for something created by a rival management to bubble over in the correspondence columns of *The Times* which published the following letter to the editor :

28th March 1943

A few days ago, expecting little, I experienced my first war-time excitement in a theatre. On the same night, I laughed hilariously at a new comedian – and, wonder of wonders! – a clean comedian.

Were it now the custom for comedians to insert personal advertisements as they did formerly in the *Entracte,* the *Music Hall* and the *Encore,* Mr Sid Field might have borrowed, with great humility, the slogan of a famous comedienne, 'I hope I am clever but I know I am clean.' Rumour had reached me that Mr Black was bringing to London a new funny man, but, when I accepted his invitation to the opening of his new show, I was unprepared to find a comedian with charm, of great originality, who caused the greatest laughter I have heard in the theatre for many years without a questionable joke or gesture, and who stood comparison with all the great ones of my crowded memory.

Mr Field and Miss Gail, the girl who brought back memories

250

of Nellie Farren, are both unknown to me, except on the other side of the 'floats'. They are real finds.

I am, Sir, your obedient servant,
Charles B Cochran

Nineteen-forty-four was probably the most unproductive year of Cochran's busy life. Not that he was bereft of ideas, projects and plans or the will to carry them out. But he was sensible enough to realise that, at seventy-one, it would no longer be wise to remain on his own, a solitary impresario, still no less a great name, but now in need of a partner to share the burdens of a profession that was becoming increasingly arduous. Besides the obvious war-time difficulties, a new breed of tough, younger, opportunist impresarios like the former band leader, Jack Hylton, were now in commanding positions, monopolising the theatres and narrowing the field of ownership by making special arrangements with one another.

There was an acute theatre shortage. All building had stopped with the outbreak of war. A number of theatres had been damaged or destroyed in the blitz and, although London had, and still has, more theatres than many other cities, New York included, this parvenu coterie succeeded in attracting most of them into their orbit.

Cochran turned to his old friend, Bill O'Bryen, now Major O'Bryen of 'A' Branch, HQ Eastern Command, and formerly of the famous theatrical agency partnership, O'Bryen, Linnit and Dunfee Ltd.

I am indebted to Bill O'Bryen for allowing me to reproduce a letter which Cochran wrote to him on 6th April 1944, and which, more than anything I could possibly elaborate from impersonal research data, gives a most penetrating insight into Cochran's position, thoughts, anxieties and hopes at that time:

My dear Bill,

Thanks for your very helpful letter, although I am disappointed that I shall not be seeing you over the weekend.

I had not thought of your joining me *only* for the presentation of Herbert's play, I was hoping that we might have a permanent alliance.

For over thirty years I have stood all alone in the business and in my most prosperous days did not even have the help of outside finance. Since the death of Hal Lewis I have not had a manager, and in the first year of the war I lost my personal accountant Ted Reeves. I am in fact without an organisation, but have no intention of going out of the business unless Divine Providence ordains it. Apart from my hip trouble I am in the best of health, and I proved to my own satisfaction, when I did *Seventy Years of Song* at the Albert Hall, that my powers of organisation and ability to work for hours on end are not impaired.

What I want is for an active, experienced, clever man like yourself to join me. I have offices which, owing to sub-lets, stand me rent free.

The number of years I can last must of course be limited, but while I am as I am I should like to see an organisation built up which can be carried on with a firm name of 'blank and Cochran' or 'Cochran and blank'.

For the production of musical plays, which I would not very much care to embark upon until after the war, there would, I think, be commercial value in the label 'Cochran's production'. For straight plays I would suggest the firm name.

The value of the Cochran label to a musical show was proved as recently as with my last show *Big Top*, which was not a very good show because I just simply could not get the elements I wanted, and I was jockeyed into a position through my author and one of my stars of making engagements which I did not like.

Despite this, I beat my own and the house's record in Manchester; at the Royal Court Theatre, Liverpool, the record of the house (Ivor Novello held it previously with *Dancing Years,* I had never played there before) and I created a record at the Grand, Leeds, where I had never played before. Although a big cast, the names were not provincial draws. This was in the period before every show did well. For instance, the present Hulbert and Courtneidge show at the Palace played at Liverpool on their best week to £1,200 less than on my best week, and in Manchester to over £1,500 less. In each case two weeks before *Big Top*.

Of course in London no name carries a show in normal times unless the show clicks, it only gives it a big send off which I had at His Majesty's.

For the compilation of musical shows, young blood is necessary, after the war it should be possible to create new teams. I should expect to become less and less active, but my taste and experience should be of value for some time. I can command considerable capital for musical shows.

Now as to *No Quarrel* or *The Dolphin* and the *Swan* (the latter is perhaps the better title).

Your own reservations were in the main mine also, and A P Herbert has already dealt with them, except that we have left the long speech. When he wrote it Herbert himself felt that it might be far too long, and was not surprised when I said that it was. He read it to Newton and me however the other night, and now I do not feel at all sure that it will not keep an audience in roars of laughter as it did me. At any rate I should like to get the feeling of it at rehearsal, and then it can be cut or split up as one feels. One thing is sure. Herbert should have a lot to do with the production, his reading of the play was a revelation to me. He is steeped in the atmosphere of the river life, and the success of this play depends largely on atmospheric touches and quaint characterisations.

To a certain extent this answers your criticisms on the lack of humour. As APH read the play there were many laughs, even in the original version. As he has revised it the humour is full and warm, moreover the author intends to inject more.

I am arranging for APH to give a reading of the play shortly, and I should be glad if you can make it convenient to be present, even if you do not join me in the presentation of the play.

I should not have thought of Liz[1] for this play because it is essentially for a man star. Nothing would give me greater pleasure than to find a play for Liz.

I understand your fear of BN. I must confess to tremors myself at first, but the play was written for him, he adores it and

[1] Elizabeth Allan, now Mrs Bill O'Bryen

I have a hunch that he will be all right. I have dealt with him before, but I do not rely on that so much as his great love of the play.

Johnny Mills is of course ideal for the stoker, and we are trying to get him.

With him in mind APH has already built up the part, and the reading I refer to is being given especially for him.

Morland Graham will not go out of town even for one week; if we can open in town he would like to play the part.

I should not have thought of Trevor, but I did not see him in the play you refer to.

As to the amount of money to be set aside for the production and to cover all contingencies I have allowed for £3,000, but wanted your guidance. There is no difficulty about this money being available, and I wanted your co-operation far more than your money.

Being uncertain of a date for a London theatre I have pencilled in our own tour (Howard and Wyndham) the first sequence of good dates available as follows:

July 31	New Theatre, Oxford
Aug 7	Court, Liverpool
„ 14	Opera House, Manchester
„ 21	Lyceum, Edinburgh
„ 28	Royal, Glasgow
Sept 4	Royal, Newcastle
„ 11	Grand, Leeds

I have made the reservation that if I can get into a West End theatre beforehand I can cancel them.

I have had the Lyric in mind, and Arnold has told me that if I can wait there is a possibility of the Phoenix.

I do not think I will write to Jack about the Lyric until I know whether I can get Johnny Mills.

Has Liz read the play?

When you are in town again I should love to have a talk with you.

Yours as ever,
Charles B Cochran

Success from the Sick Bed

IN THE NATURE of things, Cochran's idea of bringing Bill O'Bryen into partnership with him could only have been tentative. The war was still on and, although D-Day was imminent, no one could predict when the fighting would end or the time it would take for people to leave the services and return to civilian life.

It was, for Cochran, still a matter of kicking his heels and waiting as patiently as he could.

He started writing again; another book of reminiscences. Like the previous ones, it was a symptom. It meant he was marking time.

Entitled *Showman Looks On*, it was dedicated to Liz and Bill O'Bryen and it appeared '. . . in conformity with the authorised economy standards', as the phrase went, in 1945.

And then suddenly . . . a windfall. His spasmodic attempts at authorship bore rich fruit when the J Arthur Rank company paid him £10,000 for the film rights of his autobiographies.

Cochran introduced two special conditions into the standard contract. The first was that he should choose the actor who would impersonate him. The second stipulated that the scriptwriter should treat the subject in such a way as to suggest that no one had ever heard of Charles B Cochran.

He started going to the cinema more and began studying the technique of film production, a hitherto unknown field, to equip himself with the knowledge he would require when he came to help in the direction of the film about his life.

Alas, the film was never made. But when a BBC television

version of Cochran's life was produced as a memorial programme by Michael Mills in 1953, two years after his death, the
part of C B Cochran was played by Frank Lawton whose wife,
Evelyn Laye, had had such a close association with the old man
over the years. Lawton used Cochran's famous walking stick in
this production.

Cochran was now in funds again and, with the war ending, he
began to think of making a comeback in the theatre. But he was
still resolutely wedded to the idea of reentering management
in partnership with somebody else.

His old retinue had gone and that 'somebody else' turned out
to be Lord Vivian who had worked for Cochran as his press
representative.

Tony Vivian had brought Cochran a play by Hugh Hastings,
one of his friends. Cochran read it and turned it down. Its title
was *Seagulls over Sorrento* and it was afterwards presented with
enormous success by George and Alfred Black, sons of the war-
time impresario who had presided so majestically over the
London Hippodrome and the Prince of Wales Theatre during
the war. And *it* was subsequently filmed with John Mills,
originally a Cochran protégé, in the lead.

Over lunch in the Savoy Grill one day, Cochran and Tony
Vivian discussed their proposed association.

'I think we could do well together,' said Cochran. 'But, of
course, it might not work. And if we are unlucky in the theatre
there must be something else we could do.'

He waved expansively about him. 'This, for example,' he
continued. 'A restaurant. We should need a first class chef. But
you know about wine, Tony. And I understand cigars . . .'

An interesting corollary to this conversation is that after
Cochran's death, Tony *did* open a restaurant – Vivian's in
Chelsea.

Shortly after the legal formalities of their partnership had
been completed, Cochran picked up his telephone and heard the
voice of a distinctly worried and anxious Tony Vivian.

'What is it, Tony?' he asked. 'You don't sound quite yourself. Is anything wrong?'

'Yes,' answered Tony mysteriously. 'I'm afraid there is, and
I've rung to ask you to release me from our partnership.'

'Why? Whatever for?'

'Have you seen the afternoon paper?'

'No, what's in it?'

Then Vivian explained. The night before he had been to a
dinner party at Noël Coward's house. This was in Gerald Road,
famous not only for its celebrated resident, but also for the
Police Station that serves the area of the Sloane, Eaton and
Chester Squares. Unhappily the juxtaposition proved something of an embarrassment to this convivial guest. For when he
left the place where he had been so lavishly wined and dined,
his uncertain steps took him no farther – and under escort at
that – than the neighbouring building which proved to be a
little more grim and austere. For one thing it didn't have two
pianos on a raised platform at the far end of the main room.

Tony was mortally ashamed of the ugly newspaper reports
next day and, feeling that they would react unfavourably on his
new partner, the correct, dignified Elder Statesman of the
theatre, he begged to be released from their contract.

But Cochran responded just as he had with Coward after the
Sirocco disaster. 'My dear Tony,' he protested warmly, 'you don't
want to bother about that. Forget it. It's nothing. It doesn't worry
me in the least. Why, I used to be a member of the Vine Street
Club myself in my younger days!'

He was harking back to the era when young roisterers in the
West End were charged so regularly at Vine Street that they jocu-
larly gave themselves the status of a club. This confession does
not accord too readily with Cochran's reputedly moderate drinking habits, and one wonders whether, in his kindly way, he was
indulging in a little fantasy as a sop to Tony's guilty feelings.
Whatever the truth may have been, Cochran's reaction was
typical.

Illness, failure and war-time frustration had taken their toll of Cochran's resilience and morale. When, in former times, would this dedicated man of the theatre have otherwise contemplated, let alone mentioned, the extraordinary idea of going into the restaurant business? It was all the more remarkable and gratifying therefore that, in his mid-seventies, and despite constant pain, he joined Tony Vivian and reappeared on the post-war entertainment scene with three big musical shows at the Adelphi, the second of which – *Bless The Bride* – proved to be one of his greatest successes. It was also perhaps his happiest and most young in spirit.

The three shows were the result of a felicitous and tested collaboration between A P Herbert and Vivian Ellis. AP wrote the book and lyrics and Vivian composed the music, as they had done together in *Streamline*. The first show was *Big Ben*, a gentle satire on the esoteric charades that take place in the Palace of Westminster. It was less successful than *Bless The Bride*. But I much enjoyed its witty and amiable mockery of parliamentary institutions, the economy of its astringent lyrics, Joan Young's memorable performance and the fine singing of the late Trefor Jones. I also liked *Bless The Bride,* but found its sentimentality and Panglossian optimism a little too cloying. I make these points in no spirit of objective criticism, but merely to express my own taste which in the commercial theatre does not necessarily correspond with that of the public and is often contradicted – as it certainly was in this case – by the evidence of the box office.

Big Ben started with a long provincial tour, longer than Cochran and Tony Vivian had intended and, because of the difficulty of getting into a theatre, its London opening was subject to infuriating delays.

The first night at the Adelphi on 17th July 1946, however, was a great occasion. Never before had members of the Royal family attended an opening. But that night the audience included Princess Elizabeth and Prince Philip, the Duchess of

Kent, Field Marshal Montgomery, the Prime Minister and members of his cabinet.

The frenzied clapping after the *finale* signified a complex reaction. Many undoubtedly liked the show. Some did not. But it was a very emotional few minutes. Whether people enjoyed *Big Ben* hugely, moderately or not at all, their passionate applause was mainly addressed to the real star of the show: Cochran. For 'Cockie' was back.

Back, yes, but not in the theatre. And in response to repeated calls of 'Cochran!' 'Cochran!' Alan Herbert went on to the stage and shocked the excited audience into a hushed silence with the news that Mr Cochran was at home and had been much too ill to attend the performance.

Skipping the conventional first-night supper party at the Savoy, Vivian Ellis ran along the Strand. All the cabs were full, so he took the underground to St James's Park Station and walked to the small flat in St James's Court where the Cochrans were living.

Evelyn had gone to bed. Cochran was alone, huddled in a dressing gown and looking dreadfully ill and pathetic, like a crumpled small boy.

Vivian told him about the night and reported the audience reaction. A minute later the telephone started ringing. Cochran must have found it a strain and a great effort to give a bulletin on himself to every friend and newspaperman who rang. But he insisted on speaking.

Two weeks later Cochran was having a major kidney operation at the London Clinic. And it was from his sick bed in the clinic that he commissioned yet another show from A P Herbert and Vivian Ellis.

This was *Bless the Bride* with Georges Geutary and Lizbeth Webb, transformed by Cochran from a relatively unknown dance-band singer to a big London star.

Anona Winn had created such interest by her conspicuous wit and skill in *Twenty Questions* that most people forgot –

and nowadays scarcely know – that she is primarily a singer with an excellent soprano voice. But not Cochran, who cast her in the part of Duckie, the maid. The late Brian Reece was another Cochran discovery whose 'silly ass' role delighted audiences in *Bless the Bride*.

When Cochran and Evelyn attended the Royal investiture, he to receive the King's well-earned, if belated, accolade in 1948 and arise Sir Charles, the Band of the Coldstream Guards played *Bless the Bride* in the forecourt of Buckingham Palace.

Two and a half years after the opening of *Bless the Bride,* when it was still playing to capacity, Cochran took it off. Better, he thought, to withdraw it in a blaze of success than to let it run down and peter out shabbily. Besides, he was aching to do something new, so he instructed the same team who were now, it seemed, assuming the habiliments of a latter-day Gilbert and Sullivan, to write yet another show. This was *Tough at the Top.*

In the context of those three consecutive Adelphi shows, its fate symbolised the anti-climactic pattern of Cochran's life.

It was a flop.

But Cochran was not too dismayed. He philosophically accepted this slump in his fortunes as a temporary setback, one of the expected toss-of-a-coin hazards of theatrical speculation.

The important thing was that he was back, really back, exploring this possibility and that, withdrawing his many irons from the fire of opportunity, to judge the temperature and condition of each in turn.

Ram Gopal was in the offing, a newcomer to the London theatre, full of lively production ideas and plans. There was a suggestion that Cochran might present this brilliant Indian dancer and he asked Tony Vivian to make the preliminary inquiries as he was leaving for Lisbon to have some treatment for his hip.

The question of finance loomed large. Cochran was disposed to present Ram Gopal if the dancer could find the necessary backing. No money was, in fact, available, but Gopal was willing to invest a number of valuable Indian carpets worth many thousands of pounds and representing a sum equal to three times the cost of production.

Tony sent a wire containing this somewhat bizarre suggestion to Lisbon. Next morning Cochran rang up.

'Tony,' he said, 'we are not in the carpet business!'

On his return from Lisbon Cochran said he was feeling better. The treatment had done him good and he began wondering whether he should go back fairly soon and have an operation that his Portuguese doctor had recommended as a means of giving him considerable and permanent relief.

Largely because of his great admiration for Jan Masaryk, Cochran agreed to present a first play by William Templeton called *The Ivory Tower*, based on the Czechoslovakian tragedy which was then so fresh in people's minds. It was not successful.

Then Vivian Ellis brought him his own musical adaptation of *The Importance of Being Earnest*. Cochran found the book and music entrancing but, when he mentioned his interest to one or two of the dramatic critics, they expressed the fear that, because this Oscar Wilde classic was such a charming vignette of its time, some of the critics might resent the gratuitous intrusion of a contemporary talent, however worthy.

So he gave a luncheon party to the critics, seeking their reaction to the idea in principle. And when the consensus tended to confirm earlier suspicions, Cochran decided not to do it.

He and Tony next became involved with plans to produce *The Lion and the Unicorn* by Clemence Dane. Sybil Thorndyke was to play Queen Elizabeth.

Fanny Holtzmann, a famous New York theatrical lawyer, called to see him one morning with a proposition for putting on a musical version of *Pygmalion*.

He was almost numbed with horror.

'I can think of nothing more frightful, Tony,' he cried irritably, 'than GBS to music!'

He had evidently overlooked *The Chocolate Soldier*.

The Cochran Enigma

IT IS THE custom in revue to yield the scene before the *finale* to a solo performance by the star of the show, and I propose to observe this custom now by casting the spotlight of scrutiny on Charles B Cochran the man.

I naturally hope that some rough intimations of his personality and character have already emerged, if only as illuminating by-products of this biographical exercise, but I also feel that a little filling in and touching up are necessary here and there to complete the portrait. If you say – as I have indeed said – to people who worked with Cochran, 'What sort of man was he?', you will get a fascinating assortment of replies including some that contradict each other. So much of the charm, warmth and benevolence that have cast their glow over these pages already belong to the legend, the recognised stereotype. The superlatives and praises are so numerous as to border on the fulsome. It would perhaps be more realistic, therefore, to try to recreate Cochran's personality largely from impressions that are more detached, objective and, in some cases, unequivocally hostile.

The man who goes through life giving offence to none is little more than a jellyfish. But Cochran had his statutory share of faults, weaknesses and vanities.

Agnes de Mille, the American choreographer, for example, differs sharply from most in her estimate of him.

'I had a four-month working relationship with Mr Cochran,' she wrote to me from New York, 'and got to know him very well. I do not share the general opinion that he was a great artist or that he was a gentleman. He was highly successful and lived with enormous style and zest. He was ruthless to failures, broke his word, and behaved with great cowardice whenever the pressures got hard. He treated me abominably and later, when I made a great success, wrote a letter of profound apology, but it was rather too late.

'I brought *Nymph Errant* into London with a very good press. Cochran promised me two recitals at his theatre, which he later reneged on after I had brought my mother to England and cancelled jobs in America. There was hankypanky at the box office and the expense accounts were padded so that I lost all my earnings. He himself did not trouble to come to see me. Mrs Cochran did, although she could only stay for the first half of the programme. She wrote me a pencilled note to the effect that she was astonished that I was so good. It's a disagreeable story.

'Cochran had very few opinions of his own but always took the advice of experts and followed the leads of other people. For instance, if you put five or six dancers or singers on the stage in audition, and asked him to tell which was a talented one, he would not be able to do so, but he was very prompt to pick up hints from his gifted friends, box office gossip or press reports, and moved in swiftly to acquire people who were attracting attention. All his productions were very elegant and he spared no money to make them so. He was also enchanting about sending flowers and giving little dinners and luncheons as long as one was succeeding, but at the first hint of trouble he disappeared, or denounced and disappeared, and when tragic decisions had to be made, such as firing people, he left town or even the country and the dirty work had to be performed by his stage managers. He had no patience with lack of success, was absolutely without pity, and I think he had no real imagination or any creative taste.'

Again from New York I have received this blissfully entertaining note from Peggy Wood: 'When Charles B Cochran (hereinafter called "Cockie", as he was known to everybody) engaged me to play the leading role in *Bitter Sweet* in London he did so on the assurance from Mr Coward that I had not grown fat in the ten years since he had last seen me play on Broadway. Noël was in New York, Cockie was in London, but Cockie took Noël's word for my singing and acting ability – his only question was that of my avoirdupois.

'Cockie was a new kind of impresario to me, for outside of Winthrop Ames, the New England Brahmin with a passion for the theatre and for whom I played Portia, none of my employers had added anything to my social and cultural enhancement. Sam Harris was a dear and clever showman; the Shuberts had no thoughts other than money and theatres; Archie Selwyn was a clown; Henry W Savage a patriarch of business management with a background of real estate and Grand Opera in English (in the latter he did rise to the realm of culture by producing the first *La Bohème* and the first *Parsifal* in America); George M Cohan was a brilliant Broadway product; I had never been engaged by either of the Frohmans, for they produced dramas while I was a musical comedy actress; and Belasco's embodiment of culture to me was to show me a small bronze of a naked young girl being played upon by a musician as if she were a cello. He made the symbolism quite clear to me. By those whom I really admired such as Arthur Hopkins I was never approached.

'Thus Cockie was a delight to me. He combined every quality of the showman with respect for the art of the theatre. He could manage a prizefight or produce Max Reinhardt's *The Miracle*, he could present Suzanne Lenglen as the greatest female tennis player or a season of Eleanora Duse; he could produce brilliant revues and encourage young composers like Sir William Walton, then "Willie" Walton to him. And above all he was a connoisseur of painting. He was buying the Post-Impressionists before anybody was much aware of them in England. Every wall in his London home was crowded with treasures – Gauguins, Utrillos, Degas, Toulouse-Lautrecs as well as Sickert, Aubrey Beardsley and Augustus John. Who but Cockie would have commissioned Augustus John to design the powerful second act of *The Silver Tassie* by Sean O'Casey?

'I was the more flattered then, indeed I was flabbergasted, when one whose taste I so admired sent a note to my home in London after the dress rehearsal of *Bitter Sweet* which said that in appreciation of my performance he was presenting me with two per cent of the rights of *Bitter Sweet*: I never knew impresarios did things like that.

'The note didn't say just what that two per cent represented. It was just two lines typed on his stationery. But no mention of the matter followed. Nor did I receive box office statements. But, thought I, it will show up on monthly statements to the partnership. Did it mean movie rights, touring rights, recording rights – what? But weeks, months went by with no statements or cheques.

'One day Cockie said he was sending his accountant to help me with my British income tax. To the accountant's question, "What other income have you in the UK?", I replied that I was supposed to have two per cent of *Bitter Sweet*. The accountant stared at me.

' "But," said he, "Mr Cochran has not the right to declare it to you in this company." I took this to mean there were others to consult, but evidently Cockie had not done so or the accountant would have known of it.

'I said nothing further to Cockie but the accountant must have done something, for eventually during the two-year run he made me two payments, one for £150 and one for £180. Bonuses, I expect. Nevertheless, I was still vastly flattered.

'We were close friends as long as he and Evelyn Cochran lived and I am the richer by many times two per cent for having known him.'

Although many people have said to me, 'I worked for Cochran for years and never had a word in writing; we merely had a gentleman's agreement which he always honoured,'

Ronald Jeans was badly let down by him during their initial
negotiations soon after the First World War. Cochran had been
very impressed by a burlesque revue of his at the Liverpool Play-
house, sought him out and, during a talk at the Adelphi Hotel,
asked him to write a revue for the Ambassadors Theatre. The
young writer, naturally very thrilled by this glamorous commission, set to work and, when the revue was nearly finished, he
was thoroughly shattered to receive a letter from Cochran saying
that he had had second thoughts which now prompted him to
question the wisdom of staging a complete West End show by
a newcomer, and withdrew his invitation.

It is true that Cochran eventually approached him again – but
not until 1926, five years later, by which time Jeans had established himself as a successful writer of revue material for
Charlot. And the result of this second approach was *One Dam
Thing After Another.*

Benn Levy described Cochran to me as '. . . a Texan at heart;
everything he did had to be gigantic, bigger and better. . . .'
And it is true that, for Cochran, size was a virtue in itself. His
artistic perception was therefore vitiated by an odd contradic-
tion: he displayed subtle taste and a shrewd eye for the spatial
relations of colours and objects. But he also cherished a vulgar
preoccupation with size for its own sake.

'He knew how to make everything look chic and fresh,' Levy
continued, 'and he had a flair for knowing what was fashionable and acceptable at any given time. But basically he was a
showman, a barker, with a simple love of spangles and glitter.
He was also a great egotist.'

He had no sense of humour. This point has been made again
and again, and I have found confirmation of it in some of the
allegedly humorous incidents, sayings and stage lines he
included in his books. As one example, I would cite the
approval he mysteriously conferred on a pun by Herman Finck,
theatre conductor and composer of *entr'acte* music (*In the
Shadows* was his most popular melody). Now Finck was indeed

a witty man and many of the things he said are enshrined in the traditions of the Savage Club. The example of Finck's humour that Cochran quotes so admiringly in *Showman Looks On* concerns the engagement of Mlle Regine Flory as the star of a new revue at the Palace Theatre, at which Finck commented that the theatre was now under a new 'regine'.

He could, and indeed did, do better than that, yet it said little for Cochran's sense of humour that he could be amused by so embarrassingly inept a pun. Finck himself no doubt would have been happier if this painful indiscretion had been allowed to slip into the limbo of forgotten sayings.

During the rehearsals of *Magnolia Street*, Cochran rushed into the theatre and shocked everyone into a dismayed and horrified silence by crying, 'Gertrude Lawrence is dead!' 'Gertrude Lawrence' was the name of one of his tropical fish, and this announcement was meant to be a joke.

While he loved to talk of the theatre or books and pictures, he took no pleasure in exchanging funny stories, clean or otherwise. The smutty ones were no doubt distasteful to him; yet even the most innocent of light-hearted tales failed to raise a flicker of interest. It may truly be said of Cochran that he was not amused. Most people tell jokes from a desire to communicate something that has pleased them, to observe the delighted response at the pay-off and the ensuing afterglow of shared appreciation. But Cochran felt no such desire. He never told a story and, if he listened to one, his motive was to avoid hurting a companion or appear priggish and stuck up.

His eyes would twinkle, and he would occasionally make a brittle or sententious remark and sometimes a rather cruel one, but he was never funny in the way that some of his contemporaries – Jack Waller, let us say, Alfred Zeitlin and Val Parnell – were funny. It is for this reason, many believe, that so many of his revues gave the emphasis to spectacle and song rather than comedy which tended on the whole to be a minor ingredient, and some of his artists complained that, owing to his limited appreciation of humour, he would fail to note the significance of a blackout line and, in scrubbing it, ruin the whole point of a sketch.

It was enough, he seemed to imply, to have one comedian in the family. For Evelyn was undoubtedly the jester. She was justly celebrated for her swift and witty response to situations. Her caustic aphorisms and *bon mots* were a source of great delight to him; he gazed at her admiringly and took enormous pride in her enviable facility for the slick, apposite comment or riposte. A gentle smile would play about his lips on these occasions. He was a fascinated spectator, extracting vicarious credit from her adroit performance.

Cochran was seen occasionally in the Savage and the Garrick clubs as the guest of members, but he would never have remotely qualified for the description – to quote the expression so familiar in the newspapers of his day – 'a London clubman', which readily suited so many of his confrères.

Although a member of the Beefsteak Club, he rarely visited it. He would lunch and dine in the Savoy and perhaps take an aperitif in the American bar. And he was often seen at tea in Stewart's Restaurant which adjoined his office at the corner of Bond Street and Piccadilly, and is now no more.

He would always answer a letter, it was said. He was a stickler for protocol both in his social and professional life and, as his Young Ladies certainly knew, he was a strict disciplinarian, unpunctuality being his particular *bête noire*.

If anyone was a minute late for rehearsal, he would be furious. When Florence Desmond arrived panting and breathless for one of the *Streamline* rehearsals on a Monday morning, she found Cochran pacing up and down outside the Palace Theatre stage door and studying his gold hunter with an angry expression.

'Dessie,' he remonstrated, 'this is unforgivable – an hour late for rehearsal!'

She apologised. 'I know it sounds like a tale,' she said, 'but, honestly, I was down at the cottage and my car wouldn't start.'

'Then if you have an eleven o'clock rehearsal on a Monday morning,' he said, 'you have no right to spend Sunday night in the country . . . and you of all people, Dessie; one of my Young Ladies, setting such a bad example.'

He imposed one-pound fines on the girls for petty misdemeanours and acts of indiscipline. He forbade drink in the theatre and would not allow his actresses to risk creasing their stage costumes by sitting in them.

Diana Morgan accidentally brushed the hem of her pink ball gown lightly against the stairs as she walked up to her dressing room and Cochran's form of punishment was to tell the wardrobe mistress to give her a blue dress with a black hemline and consign her to the back row of the chorus for six weeks.

In *Cavalcade* he sacked two girls for not wearing their corsets on stage. When one of his Young Ladies fainted during rehearsal, and he discovered that she had not been eating enough, he sent them all to neighbouring restaurants with strict instructions to order steaks. He then made the eating of steak compulsory – he also forbade hazardous sports and pastimes, horse riding, for instance – and exacted his one-pound fines for violating these conditions.

He was excessively generous with some people and inclined to be careful, even cheeseparing, with others.

When Esmond Knight started going into musicals at the beginning of the thirties, '. . . he asked me what salary I wanted. I asked exactly double what I'd been getting at Drury Lane and he instantly agreed. That was typical: if he thought you were worth it, he'd pay without trying to cut you down.'

Yet when he asked Richard Murdoch how much he had been getting in his last show, and Dickie replied, 'Twenty pounds a week,' Cochran said, 'I didn't know you were that well established; I'll give you fifteen!'

Douglas Byng says, 'If you asked him for a rise, you always got it, but he had petty meannesses. He once refused to allow me to do cabaret while I was in one of his shows. He afterwards relented, but took ten per cent of the fee.'

Cochran's habit of changing the running order of revue scenes became so regular that a last-minute reshuffle of the items was always expected. It caused frightful confusion among the stage management staff and the artists. Misunderstandings were frequent. In one of the shows Sonnie Hale, due on stage in white tie and tails for a light and frolicsome dance routine, clumped on in a suit of armour.

For all his long and mature experience and despite his quick-witted response to unexpected and difficult situations, Cochran sometimes acted, as we have already noted, in incredibly wrong-headed ways.

I am reminded in this connection of a strange episode that dates back to 1933 when Cochran was on holiday in Morocco. His French driver had stopped the car among the foothills of the Atlas mountains and recommended proceeding by mules through a narrow gorge to a place inhabited by Berbers, a people of rare and extraordinary beauty who are descended from the early inhabitants of Libya. Unexpectedly this particular group had fair hair, blue eyes and ivory skins.

Among these child-like, unsophisticated people, Cochran noticed a girl of fourteen who seemed to him to be the most beautiful creature he had ever seen and, true to type, he immediately tried to arrange for her to come to London and appear in *Streamline*, his next revue.

For once, however, the Cochran magic collapsed, for, although agreement had been virtually reached, the obstacles put in the way of the young girl's journey by her guardians and the Moroccan authorities proved insuperable.

Meanwhile, however, Cochran had advertised the projected appearance of 'Abdaga', as he called her, in a mammoth cabaret at Grosvenor House in aid of the Actors' Benevolent Fund.

It was a great occasion. There were three stages with decor by Oliver Messel, and Cochran withheld the news that the Ber-

ber child would not be appearing. Instead, at the appointed time, 'Abdaga' entered, accompanied by an escort of veiled women that included Evelyn Laye, Jessie Matthews, Gertrude Lawrence and Tilly Losch. 'Abdaga' discarded her veils and revealed herself as . . . Duggie Byng!

Cochran thought this silly and tasteless hoax uproariously funny. The audience didn't. And many of those present, including the Prince of Wales, made no attempt to conceal their displeasure.

Cochran maintained an extensive library, the contents of which were catalogued in a huge tome that bore his famous cockerel insignia on its tooled leather cover. It consisted mainly of books on ballet, the circus and the theatre. Quite a large section was devoted to these subjects in French. He also possessed a number of presentation volumes, most of them inscribed with personal messages from his playwright and novelist friends.

He enjoyed the look and feel of a beautiful book, its elegant typography, quality paper, good illustrations and handsome leather binding. His library gave him the sense of tranquillity and repose that booklovers feel in the midst of their treasured collection. It was so large that Winifred Myers, the Bond Street dealer, took a month to catalogue all the titles. It included few works of fiction – though Cochran professed a great attachment to the novels of Arnold Bennett – and little on subjects outside his own artistic field. That he took comparatively no interest in the problems of philosophy or the physical, mental, sociological and political sciences was abundantly clear from the absence of any works on these fundamental subjects.

As for music, Cochran certainly loved it, but could scarcely have been called a music lover in the full sense of the term. I say this not entirely because his tastes were simple, as they certainly were, but largely because his musical interests covered a relatively small and restricted area. He was deeply roused by the extravagances of Russian ballet music, the barbaric splendour of Borodin and Rimsky-Korsakov, the rich orchestral textures of Tchaikovsky with their driving percussion and cascading woodwind figures, the gentle cadences of Stravinsky's *Firebird* and the savage rhythms of *The Rite*. He could never hear Beethoven's Fifth Symphony often enough, though it is doubtful whether his mind and soul ever penetrated to the ineffable beauty of the late quartets. It would not have been in his restless and mercurial temperament to make the necessary investment of time and effort.

He adored Spanish music, though one suspects here again that, because of his consuming passion for Spain itself, this represented a sentimental indulgence rather than a genuine appreciation of the gifts of Albeniz, Granados, de Falla and the rest.

The records with which he chose in 1942 to be cast away on Roy Plomley's celebrated desert island included Chaliapine singing a short excerpt from *Boris,* an aria from *Thäis* by his friend Jeritza and Prokofiev's *Love of Three Oranges.*

Musicians who worked with him say that, although he was certainly no musician himself, he had a good ear for a tune and showed considerable taste for theatre music of quality; the music, that is, of people like Gershwin, Rodgers and Hart, Jerome Kern, Noël Coward and Cole Porter. But it is unlikely that he ever confronted the world of serious composition full square, trying to come to terms with the more *recherché* and adventurous experiments, let us say, of Schoenberg, Webern and Bartok, the innovators and the serialists. He would have shied away in horror and disgust from the incomprehensible dissonances of Boulez, Stockhausen and Henze and the bizarre musical languages that are emerging in our own day.

His liberal outlook and tolerant social attitudes were very much to his credit. Confronted with the delicate and explosive issue of racial differences, he always strove to isolate and pinpoint the virtues rather than the vices of other peoples. His estimate of the negro character expressed itself, for example, in generalisations from his great admiration for particular artists like Florence Mills and Buddy Bradley and, even though his views on racial characteristics may not have been logically supportable, they provided a refreshing counterweight to the bitterness, rancour and prejudice that all too often bedevil the emotional response to this subject.

The statement, '. . . Larry Hart, who, like ninety-eight per cent of the cleverest people in the theatre world, is a Jew . . .', written by Cochran at a time when the Hitler virus was beginning to corrupt feeble minds in Britain, says much for his liberal sentiments, if little for his devotion to statistical accuracy.

The End of a Great Showman

HIS DEATH WAS tragic, senseless and terrible. The osteo-arthritis killed him, though not directly.

In the first weeks of 1951 some work was being done on the plumbing in their Chesham Street flat, and Sir Charles and Lady Cochran moved into the Hyde Park Hotel.

They had been back in the flat only a few days and now, with the water system repaired, Cochran could again enjoy one of his minor pleasures: a warm bath which he found so soothing to his complaint. Although it was a daily commonplace, it never lost its feeling of luxury for him. He would lie there, nicely relaxed like a snug foetus in its amniotic medium. Evelyn generally ran the bath for him, carefully testing the temperature.

They were both taking pills for insomnia and because Evelyn had had a disturbed night, Cochran decided, on the fatal morning, to leave her sleeping. He tip-toed to the bathroom wondering, no doubt, how he was going to enjoy *Le Malade Imaginaire* which he had arranged to see that night with Bill O'Bryen and Dorothy Dickson. Evelyn had not been feeling too well. So it had been arranged that Cochran should take 'my understudy', as she called Dorothy Dickson.

He locked the bathroom door and ran his bath, mixing the water from the hot and cold taps to produce just the right temperature. It was on the tepid side when he was ready to get into it, so he shut off the cold.

What happened then nobody knows except that he was now already in his bath and – with all the horror of the most unspeakable and hideous nightmare – his arthritic hip fixed his body so immovably that he could not turn off the hot tap. Indeed, he could not move at all.

His frantic shouts might have been heard a few seconds earlier if the maid had not at that moment been doing the carpets with a vacuum cleaner.

Evelyn, now awake, fancied she heard muffled cries and went to the window to see if there was some disturbance in the street below. She saw nothing, of course, but, on a sudden and intuitive impulse, rushed to the bathroom, realised there had been some terrible accident and summoned the porter who, with the help of some of the other tenants, battered the door down.

Dr Armando Child, their own doctor, who lived two doors away, quickly arrived in the flat and administered drugs. The office was notified and, as Cochran was being moved into the ambulance, he murmured to Tony Vivian, 'Look after the show, Tony. Look after the show.'

They took him to Westminster Hospital.

Evelyn, of course, was completely shattered. His condition was serious. Between brief periods of delirium, he was conscious most of the time and suffering badly.

By the third day he was still very poorly. Evelyn said, 'I feel I couldn't bear to see him, but I will if he wants me to.'

The scalding had literally flayed his body. She saw him on the fourth day. It was a deeply harrowing experience. 'Can't you get them to give him a little more of something?' she pleaded with Tony. 'See the doctor, please. Make him do it. Tell him it has my blessing.' If he recovered at all, she was told, he would be a permanent invalid, confined to a chair, reduced to complete inactivity and incapable of doing anything in the theatre.

'Then they should let him go,' she whispered softly. 'They should let him go.'

The hospital doctor shook his head. 'It is our job to save life,' he said, 'not to take it.'

His condition deteriorated and all hope vanished.

To be with Evelyn, Tony moved into the flat. Friends rallied magnificently, but her anguish was worst at night, and the knowledge that Tony was in the next room was reassuring. They lived a kind of dissociated dream life, following the routine of living mechanically and without heart.

Evelyn, Tony and Dorothy Dickson were the only people Cochran saw.

Nine days after the accident the hospital sent for Evelyn. Cochran was sinking. But he would last, she was told, until the morning. Tony called at the flat for her in a Daimler hire car. Her appearance made his heart leap. She had made herself look wonderful for Cochran. 'She was almost like a Cochran Young Lady,' Tony has since said.

Just as she was going into Cochran's room, Evelyn paused and tugged at Tony's sleeve. 'I'm afraid, Tony,' she said. 'Please come with me.'

They went in. Evelyn crouched by Cochran's pillow. Tony stood at the foot of the bed.

'Cockie,' she murmured, 'do you know what happened to you?'

He shook his head and quietly answered, 'No.'

'Well, you must close your eyes. You've had that operation . . . you remember the doctor in Lisbon? . . . Now you are cured. Close your eyes and when you open them you will never feel any pain again.'

And she seized Tony's hand and walked silently from the room.

Whether her last words to him came to mind as something we call inspiration or whether they merely demonstrated the power of love and its capacity for mobilising true nobility from deep and mysterious sources . . . these are questions that cannot be answered. But there was the stuff of genius in them.

At a charity concert on the evening of 31st January 1951, the day he died, Lizbeth Webb sang – or, rather, tried, through

her sobs to sing – *This is my Lovely Day* from *Bless the Bride* –
because Cochran had asked her to.

The clock stopped in theatreland on Saturday, 3rd February,
the day he was cremated at Golders Green. A black Spanish
shawl embroidered with flowers lay on the coffin.

The news reached A P Herbert in the liner that was bringing
him back from Australia. He cabled these words:

> *Dear master, this blue sea is sad today,*
> *That Fate should finish you in such a way!*
> *But I will think of all the joy you made,*
> *Of gallant fighting in a fearful trade.*
>
> *I think how many famous folk there are*
> *You found and fostered – and behold a star!*
> *Of brilliant memories you leave behind,*
> *Of one courageous, courteous and kind.*
>
> *No more we'll put our harassed heads together,*
> *About the plot, the critics, or the weather.*
>
> *Unless in heaven there's an angel cast*
> *The Prince of Showmen is at rest at last;*
> *Though few of us will be surprised, I swear,*
> *If you devise new fun and beauty there.*
>
> *Farewell, dear friend and master, could we all,*
> *See with such pride the final curtain fall!*

.   .   .   .   .

A memorial tablet was dedicated to Cochran at 'the actors'
church', St Paul's, Covent Garden.

Sir Alan Herbert and John Clements attended the service as
mace-bearers. The procession included Dame Sybil Thorndike,

Vivian Ellis and Lord Vivian. Ernest Thesiger read the lesson. And when the simple ceremony was over, Lady Cochran slipped back into the empty church and silently contemplated these lines from *Coriolanus* engraved on the commemorative plaque:

> *I thank you for your voices,*
> *thank you*
> *Your most sweet voices.*

The Young Ladies saw to it that he was not forgotten. Whitie Neeson and Valerie Frazer collected subscriptions from the others and commissioned Peter Lambda to do a bust. The question was: where should it be placed? Everyone naturally thought first of the London Pavilion, but this theatre had now become a cinema and was therefore unsuitable.

It clearly had to be the Adelphi. Jack Hylton's permission was sought and given. So the Adelphi it was.

And still is.

The invitation list was prepared in consultation with Lady Cochran and at 11.30 am on Friday, 14th September 1951, in the presence of the Young Ladies, the bust was unveiled in the foyer by Anna Neagle who, as I write, is playing in *Charlie Girl* in the same theatre seventeen years later.

The effect was startling. The head was so lifelike that it sent a tremor of emotion through the muted assembly.

It was a deeply moving reunion. Besides the loyal and devoted Young Ladies, some of them now perhaps not so young, were other old friends like Agatha Christie, James Agate and Sir Norman Joseph who had gone along to register their tribute to a great showman – 'Cockie'.

Acknowledgments

A great number of people who worked with C B Cochran have shown tremendous kindness in helping me with this biography. I have no doubt that their enthusiastic interest is inspired largely by the affection and regard in which they hold his memory.

I should like in particular to thank: Larry Adler, Harold A Albert, Elizabeth Allan, Sir Frederick Ashton, Stephen Bagnall, Cecil Beaton, Denys Blakelock, Romney Brent, Edward Brooks, Gabrielle Brune, Marie Burke, Patricia Burke, Douglas Byng, Gladys Calthrop, John A Carlsen, Dr Armando Child, J A Cochran, Ann Codrington, Lady Diana Cooper, Peter Cotes, Peter Daubeny CBE, Agnes de Mille, Florence Desmond, Dorothy Dickson, Adele Dixon, Margaret Edgerton, Mary Ellis, Valerie Frazer, Vere French, Olive Hammerton, Phyllis Harding, Betty Hare, Doris Hare, Winifred Hare, Tommy Hayes, Daphne Henry, Sir Alan Herbert, Percy Hoskins, Inson Jackson, Ronald Jeans, Sir Norman Joseph, Max Kester, Esmond Knight, Evelyn Laye, James Laver, Benn Levy, Mollie Liggett, Emile Littler, Peter Lupino, Constance Luttrell, A N S Marshall, Jessie Matthews, Alan Melville, the late B A Meyer, Billy Milton, Diana Morgan, Phyllis Digby Morton, Richard Murdoch, Winifred Myers, Diana Napier, Margaret ('Whitie') Neeson, Beverley Nichols, Bill O'Bryen, Eileen O'Casey, Honoria Plesch, Roy Plomley, Charles Prentice, Lady Robey, Peregrine Rosling, Milton Rosmer, Ivy St Helier, Betty Shale, John Shaw, Geoffrey Spencer, Beatrix Thomson, Michael Thornton, Lord Vivian, Dorothy Ward, Arthur Webb, Lizbeth Webb,

Fred Wilby, Emlyn Williams, Eric Williams, Anona Winn, Peggy Wood, Joan Young, John Young.

I also wish to thank Noël Coward for his introduction and Fuan Nan Yoe, my delightful and hard-working secretary, who typed the manuscript, much of it in what might be laughingly called her own time.
You have to be Chinese to read my handwriting. Luckily, she is.

I am grateful to the following publishers for permission to quote extracts from copyright works: Wm Heinemann for *Secrets of a Showman*, 1926, by C B Cochran, and *Present Indicative*, 1937, by Noël Coward; Hutchinson Publishing Group for *I Had Almost Forgotten*, 1932, by C B Cochran; J M Dent for *Cock-a-doodle-do*, 1941, and *Showman Looks On*, 1945, by C B Cochran; Wm Collins for *More Escapers*, 1968, by Eric Williams; Victor Gollancz for *Round the Next Corner*, 1967, by Denys Blakelock; André Deutsch for *Museum Piece*, 1963, by James Laver; W H Allen for *The Cochran Story*, 1951, by Charles Graves; Hutchinson for *The World I Knew*, 1940, by Louis Golding.

For permission to quote from Cole Porter's *Anything Goes*, I am grateful to Chappell & Co Ltd.

Index

Bless the Bride, 258–60, 277
Bloomfield, Jack (Blumenfeld, Corpl J), 86
Blue Room, 138
Bohème, La, 264
Bon-Ton, 120
Boy David, The, 190–201, 217, 219
Boy Friend, The, 137
Breezy Time, A, 27, 30
Brent, Romney, 58, 139, 179, 181, 182, 203
Bridie, James, 193
Brighton Herald, 14
British Actors' Equity Association, 171, 212–13
British Empire Exhibition, 113
Brooklyn Daily Eagle, 91
Buchanan, Jack, 163–4, 184, 244
Buddies, 150
Butt, Sir Alfred, 76, 78, 110
Byng, Douglas, 137, 138, 269, 271

CALTHROP, GLADYS, 149, 178
Camille, 79
Canterbury Theatre, The, 43, 46
Caprice, 156
Careless Rapture, 235
Carlito, 98
Carlton, Billie, 77–8
Carminetta, 79
Carnival, 61
Carpentier, Georges, 86–92
Castle, Irene and Vernon, 75–7
Cat and The Fiddle, The, 177
Cavalcade, 18, 49, 171–5, 178, 231, 269
Chaliapin, 152, 272
Champagne Time, 120
Charlie Girl, 278
Charlot, André, 121, 135, 163, 266
Children of the Ritz, 179
Chirgwin, 211
Chris and Lena, 24
Christopher Columbus in A-merry-key, 14
Chuckles of 1922, 105
Churchill, Lady Randolph, 68
Churchill, Sarah, 214–15, 217, 236, 238, 243–4
Churchill, Sir Winston, 198
Clark, Scotston, 17, 19–20, 34, 38

Clements, Sir John, 277
Cliff, Laddie, 231
Cochran, Alec, 10, 55, 56
Cochran, Lady Evelyn, 52–4, 92, 98, 103–4, 116, 138, 140–1, 180, 224–6, 230–1, 235, 238, 240–2, 259–60, 263, 265, 268, 274–6, 278
Cochran, James Elphinston, 10
Cochran, Minnie, 35–8
Cochran Story, The, 210
Cochran Young Ladies, *see* Young Ladies
Cochran's 1929 Revue, 144
Cochran's 1930 Revue, 163
Cock-a-doodle-do (book), 189, 226, 244
Cock-a-Doodle-Do (radio show), 243
Codrington, Ann, 238
Cohan George M, 112, 264
Coliseum Theatre, The, 169
Collins, Frank, 80, 124, 145, 170, 214, 219
Comedy Theatre, The, 78, 138
Concert Hall, Lewes, 14
Constant Nymph, The, 187, 188
Conversation Piece, 173, 203–5
Coppelia, 119
Corn is Green, The, 235
Cornwallis, Lord, 73
Cornwallis West, Mrs, 68
Coronation Review, The, 219
Corri, Eugene, 87, 129
Coward, Noël, 121–5, 133, 134, 146, 147, 148–54, 160–2, 168–74, 178–9, 184, 198, 202–5, 244, 257, 264, 272
Crawford, C P, 57, 58
Crawford, Mimi, 127, 137
Crest of the Wave, 235
Criterion Theatre, The, 235
Critic, 39
Curtis Bennett, Sir Henry, 116
Cyrano de Bergerac, 39–40, 83–4
Czinner, Dr Paul, 188, 192, 193, 225

DADE, EVELYN, *see* Cochran, Lady Evelyn
Daily Express, 128, 152
Daily Mail, 43, 68, 101, 197
Dallas, Mervyn, 29, 30
Daly's Theatre, 151
Dance, Dance, Little Lady, 134